Understanding children
with special needs

resources 13, 14, 21, 52, 53, 250–1, 253, 255, 259
reviews and reassessments 11, 245
rhesus incompatibility 89
rubella 89, 106, 108, 121

school
  attendance problems 137, 159, 162, 165–72
  costs 229
  ethos 74–5, 145–8
  factors 62, 72–6, 143–52, 162, 168–9, 170–2, 181–2
  knowledge 81–2
  organization 149, 182, 222–3
  special 2, 36, 45, 229–30, 254–5
  streaming 74
  teacher expectations 73
  (*see also special educational needs* and *resources*)
school doctors 26, 127, 237
scoliosis 104
Scottish Education Department progress report 44
segregation (*see integration*)
Select Committee report (1987) 13–4, 249–51
self-concept 73, 140–2
self-fulfilling prophesy 73, 82
sensori-neural loss 106
sensory disabilities (*see visual* and *hearing difficulties*)
shared reading 202
short-sightedness 110
signing 212–13
single parent families 68
skeletal disorders 88
SNAP 200–1, 223
Snellen's chart 107–8
social class
  classification 65
  cultural and linguistic differences 70–2
  and health 68, 95
  and income 66, 68
  (*see also family* and *delinquency*)
social disadvantage 35–6, 61, 64–70, 137–8, 142, 164, 207, 209, 243
Social Services Department 238–42, 247
social workers 163, 241–2
solvent abuse 173–6
spasticity (*see cerebral palsy*)

special educational needs
  concept and definitions 7–11, 14–15, 17, 20–1, 52–3, 83–4, 182, 183, 184, 250–9
  meeting needs 181–2, 185, 194–5
  provisions 2, 36, 45–6, 51–2, 227–30, 250, 256, 259
  (*see also assessment statements* and *advice*)
speech difficulties 115–18 (*see also language difficulties*)
speech therapists 15, 236–7
spelling 38, 75, 201–2
spina bifida 94–7
spinal injury 104
squints 110
stammering and stuttering 115
statements 9–11, 15, 17, 52, 183–4, 229, 244, 252, 256
statutory agencies 15, 230
structured teaching materials 199–201, 208–9
Sturge-Weber syndrome 88
substance abuse 172–6
support teaching 52, 55–7, 132, 232, 259
Swann Report 66, 73
systems approaches 221–3
syphilis 89

task analysis 63, 189, 196–7
teacher
  expectations 19–20, 51, 73–4
  -pupil relationships 145
  stress 222–3
  support groups 224
teaching
  learning task 62
  effective 75
  methods and approaches 191–2
  styles 145
testing (*see assessment* and *intelligence*)
total communication 212
toxaemia 89
toxins 80–1, 135
truancy (*see school attendance problems*)
Turner's syndrome 86

unemployment 66, 68–9, 143, 245

visual impairment 94, 107–12, 214–15

Warnock Report
  concepts 4, 50–2, 132–5, 249, 251,
    259
  continuum of needs 17, 254
  major recommendations 4–7, 44–8,
    84, 248
  model of assessment 5–7, 12, 26,
    242
  surveys 37–8, 45, 51

Understanding children with special needs

LYNN STOW & LORNA SELFE

Series Editor: Peter Huxley

London
UNWIN HYMAN
Boston   Sydney   Wellington

Published by the Academic Division of
Unwin Hyman Ltd
15/17 Broadwick Street, London W1V 1FP, UK

Unwin Hyman Inc.,
8 Winchester Place, Winchester, Mass. 01890, USA

Allen & Unwin (Australia) Ltd,
8 Napier Street, North Sydney, NSW 2060, Australia

Allen & Unwin (New Zealand) Ltd in association with the
Port Nicholson Press Ltd,
Compusales Building, 75 Ghuznee Street, Wellington 1, New Zealand

First published in 1989

British Library Cataloguing in Publication Data

Stow, Lynn
Understanding children with special needs. –
(A handbook for the caring professions).
1. Great Britain. Schools. Students with special
educational needs. Education
I. Title II. Selfe, Lorna III. Series 371.9'0941

ISBN 0–04–445311–6
ISBN 0–04–445367–1 pbk

Library of Congress Cataloging in Publication Data
Stow, Lynn
Understanding children with special needs/by Lynn Stow
and Lorna Selfe.
p. cm.
Bibliography: p.
Includes index.
ISBN 0–04–445311–6. – ISBN 0–04–445367–1 (soft)
1. Handicapped children – Education – Great Britain.
2. Special education – Great Britain. I. Selfe, Lorna.
II. Title
LC4036.G7S75 1989
371.9'0941 – dc20   89–14741
                                                                CIP

Disc Conversion by Columns Typesetters of Reading in 10 on 12 point
Bembo and printed in Great Britain by Billing and Sons,
London and Worcester

For our children
Amy, Justine, Jessica and Jacob

Contents

Introduction   *Page* xiii

1   *The changing concept of special education*   1

The framework of legislation   1
Central issues in special education   16

2   *Learning difficulties*   30

Introduction   30
Early conceptualization and definitions   31
Prevalence   36
Reading and spelling difficulties   38
Remedial provision   41
The changing concept of remedial education   42
The Warnock Report's concept of learning difficulties   44
Learning difficulties and the 1981 Education Act   52
Developments since the 1981 Act   54
Parental involvement in learning   57

3   *Why do learning difficulties occur?*   59

Introduction   59
Theories to explain learning difficulties   61
Social and environmental factors   63
School factors   72
Organic and within-child factors   76
The nature of 'school knowledge'   81

4   *Physical and sensory disorders and disabilities*   83

Introduction   83

ix

Organic disorders which primarily affect intellectual
development   85
Disorders which primarily affect the child's physical
development and mobility   91
Sensory disabilities   104
Speech, language and communication disorders   112

5　Maladjustment, emotional and behavioural difficulties   123

Introduction   123
Early conceptualizations and definitions of
maladjustment   124
The frequency of adjustment difficulties   128
The growth of provision   129
The concept of maladjustment in the Warnock Report
and the 1981 Act   132
Factors influencing emotional and behavioural
difficulties   135

6　Some behaviour problems of social concern   154

Deviant behaviour and delinquency   154
School attendance problems   165
Substance abuse   172
Child sexual abuse   176

7　Meeting special educational needs   181

Introduction   181
Meeting the needs of children with learning difficulties   185
Meeting the needs of children with mobility problems   204
Meeting the needs of children with speech, language
and communication difficulties   206
Meeting the needs of the hearing impaired child   212
Meeting the needs of the visually impaired child   214
Meeting the needs of children with emotional and
behaviour difficulties   215

8 *Meeting special educational needs – the wider context* 227

Educational settings 227
The statutory agencies 230
Preschool provision 243
Post-school provision 244

9 *Conclusions: future trends* 248

Introduction 248
The 1988 Education Act and children with special
needs 257

Appendix 260

Bibliography 267

Index 284

Introduction

This book is designed to be an introduction to the field of special education for all those students and professionals; teachers, social workers, psychologists, medical officers, nurses, speech therapists, and others, who encounter children with special needs.

The book first discusses current legislation in its historical context and draws attention to some of the recurrent issues in special education. Next, a variety of learning difficulties; physical and sensory disabilities and emotional and behaviour problems are examined which may give rise to special educational needs. The book then describes how children's special needs may be met in terms of curriculum, resources and provisions. The book concludes with some prognostications and with a critical review of the present state of the art; five years after the implementation of the 1981 Act.

The whole of special education has been through upheaval in the last decade and many underlying assumptions and concepts have been questioned or abandoned. Following on the Warnock Report, the 1981 Act embodied many of these changes, and parents, teachers and other professionals in the field have undergone a period of reappraisal. The book introduces most of the main issues and concerns and undoubtedly reflects the controversies and confusions that inevitably follow in the wake of a major 'paradigm shift'. The last ten years have been challenging and exciting for developments in special education, but the process of change and reevaluation is ongoing and gathering momentum. We have had to spend many hours in questioning and wrestling with concepts basic to the Warnock Report such as 'needs' and why 'special' education? We have been forced to conclude that, despite the relative enlightenment of the Warnock Report and the 1981 Act, many inherent confusions still exist. We hope that the reader will profitably share our doubts and reservations and that we have achieved a measure of circumspection about current concepts and practices. Writing the book has had the effect of demolishing any complacency we may have had about our own practices as well as about the current structure and future of special education.

We were asked to produce an update of an earlier volume and we started out assuming that the task would be relatively straightforward. The whole conception of special education has changed so radically since we wrote the previous book, ten years ago, that we found we had to begin again and write a new one. Despite qualms about gender stereotyping and adverse labelling, we have adopted the convention of referring to the child as 'he' and the teacher as 'she'. We hope that our readers will bear with us.

July 1988   L. S. and L. S.

1

The changing concept of special education

OVERVIEW

In this chapter the central issues and concepts in special education will be introduced. The chapter will commence with an outline of legislation in special education from its origins to the present day. Some of the main themes and issues which dominate discussion in the field of special education will then be considered. The ideas introduced in this chapter are fundamental and will be returned to throughout the book.

1 THE FRAMEWORK OF LEGISLATION

Historical context

Two major themes have dominated the history of special education; first, the belief that children with certain disorders and disabilities require distinct schools to cater for their requirements: and secondly, that local education authorities (LEAs) have a legal duty to provide suitable education for these children.

1

In the last decade, the LEAs' duties have further extended, as we will see when the legislation of the 1981 Education Act is discussed. What has changed more radically however, is our conception of special children, and the provision we believe is most likely to meet their educational needs.

From the earliest days of organized education it was assumed that some children were 'special' in the sense that they could not benefit from ordinary schooling, so segregated educational establishments were gradually provided. Special schools for blind and deaf children were set up as early as the eighteenth century by charitable organizations, and by the end of the nineteenth century legislation was passed permitting provision to be established locally for blind, deaf, physically and 'mentally defective' children. Epilepsy was next acknowledged as a condition requiring specialist education, so that five categories of handicap were officially recognized by the 1921 Education Act. This was extended by the 1944 Education Act, and for the first time it became the legal duty of the LEA to provide education for children of varying age, ability and aptitude, and special educational treatment for children with a 'disability of mind or body' in 'special schools or otherwise'.

The regulations that followed distinguished eleven categories of handicap: blind, partially sighted, deaf, partially deaf, physically handicapped, delicate, diabetic, epileptic, maladjusted, educationally subnormal and speech defective. The categories 'delicate' and 'diabetic' were combined in 1953, and the term 'partially deaf' changed to 'partially hearing' in 1962. Finally, of more significance, the 1970 Education Act legislated for children with severe mental handicap, so that they became the responsibility of the local education authority for the first time. Prior to this, such children were regarded as ineducable, and so were given training and care by the local health authority.

Special education expanded gradually, with a variety of provision across the country. In all, about 1.5 per cent of the school population attended special schools.

Table 1.1 gives some idea about the proportions of children with various handicaps who were awaiting or receiving special school provision in 1977.

In the 1960s and 1970s there was increasing unease about the growth of special education and the allocation of scarce

Table 1.1 Categories of handicapped children

	%	
Blind	0.7	
Partially sighted	1.4	
Deaf	2.4	
Partially deaf	3.4	
Physically handicapped	9.1	
Delicate	3.5	
Maladjusted	11.9	
Educationally subnormal (moderate)	45.7	
Educationally subnormal (severe)	19.3	
Epileptic	0.8	
Speech defect	1.3	
Autistic	0.5	
Total	100.0	(177,117)

Source: adapted from *Statistics of Education* (1977), Vol. 1, *England & Wales* (London: HMSO).

resources. In particular the fundamental philosophy of establishing segregated provision for certain groups of children was questioned, and it was generally believed to be wrong as a matter of principle, to segregate children from their ordinary peers. The categories of handicap were also felt to be unhelpful in practice, since a medical condition does not of necessity have educational implications. Finally, the vast majority of children with learning difficulties – children with reading problems in ordinary schools, who were also receiving additional resources in the form of remedial help – were not acknowledged officially. All these issues remain of central current concern, and will be discussed in more detail in the next section.

The Warnock Report (1978)

It was in this climate of opinion that the Warnock Committee was set up in 1974 by the Minister of Education, in order to review the educational provision, 'for children and young people handicapped by disabilities of body or mind'. The committee's terms of reference were wide, enabling them to make far reaching suggestions, and all children between the ages of 2 and 19 were included. It was not the committee's brief to attempt to examine the factors leading to educational handicap, nor to establish the best methods to overcome such problems. Their prime task was to consider the organization of resources for this group of children.

In all, the committee made over 200 recommendations and their report, published in 1978, has been highly influential in restructuring thinking about children with special educational difficulties and the provision required. The following is a brief overview of some of the major recommendations. The ideas and concepts introduced here are returned to throughout the book.

MAJOR RECOMMENDATIONS

(a) *Categorization and the concept of special need*   The committee's most far reaching recommendation was to abolish the categorization of children in terms of their handicapping condition as was laid out in the 1944 Education Act, and instead to instate the concept of special educational needs. This term would take into account both the child's strengths and weaknesses, and the focus would be on his educational requirements. Specialist resources and facilities were highlighted, as well as any curricular needs, and all children requiring some form of additional help in school would be said to have special educational needs.

The committee acknowledged that some categories are required in order to refer to particular difficulties, and so proposed that the terms 'mild', 'moderate' and 'severe' learning difficulties should replace the old categorizations of remedial and educationally subnormal. It was also suggested that children experiencing difficulties in just one area of the curriculum should be referred to as having 'specific learning difficulties'. After due consideration it was felt that the term 'maladjustment' could usefully be retained.

(b) *Redefinition of special education*   The Warnock Committee defined special education more broadly than in the past.

Referring to various surveys and reports, they concluded that about one child in five is likely at some time to require some form of special educational provision. A more flexible system of provision would be required to meet the variety of individual needs, and special education was no longer synonymous with special schooling; the emphasis was changed from where education takes place to what form that education should be. Moreover, the focus was no longer on the 2 per cent attending special schools, but on the 20 per cent who need special educational resources at some time in their school careers.

(c) *Integration* The committee supported the notion of integration as a matter of major policy, thus reinforcing Section 10 of the 1976 Education Act which states that, subject to certain qualifications, handicapped pupils in England and Wales will be educated where possible in ordinary schools rather than in special schools. They proposed a flexible provision so that children with special needs would not necessarily be educated in the classroom with their ordinary peers. They could be taught in special units attached to ordinary schools, segregated from lessons, but socially integrated at break times. Alternatively, they could be taught with ordinary children on a part-time or full-time basis, according to need and available resources. Various degrees and forms of integration are possible – what Warnock terms locational, social and functional or academic integration. The committee recommended that special schools would still be required for some children where integration was impractical.

(d) *Partnership with parents* The committee recommended a greater partnership between parents and the school, since parents are acknowledged to be the prime educators of their children. They stressed that parents should be kept fully informed of available facilities and supporting services, and a 'person be named' who could advise parents about local services.

(e) *Assessment* The report stressed the early identification of children's special needs so that appropriate help could be provided, and suggested that parents should be able to request an assessment and local authorities be empowered to conduct one, if it was felt to be in the child's best interests.

A five-stage model of assessment was proposed, the first three stages being school-based, with the final two referring to specialist assessment from professionals outside the school:

STAGE 1   assessment should be conducted by the class teacher using observations and records of progress. Early consultation with the headteacher and parents is recommended.

If further assessment is required:

STAGE 2   the teacher can consult with specialist teachers on the staff or support teachers who visit the school.

If more specialist assessment is still required:

STAGE 3   experts such as educational psychologists or teachers from specialist services, such as teachers for hearing-impaired children, might be consulted.

If it is thought the child requires special forms of provision and resources, other than is normally available within the school:

STAGE 4   a formal multiprofessional assessment might be initiated.

If the problem is extremely complex or unusual and more specialist assessment is required:

STAGE 5   referral can sometimes be made to specialist regional centres which are frequently in hospital settings.

The stages of assessment were intended to describe a progressive sequence, each stage involving more refined procedures and expertise. However, it was not intended that the stages should always be passed through in this order. In many cases assessment would go no further than the first stage, but on occasion, stage 4 might be started immediately after stage 1, if the child's difficulties are clearly profound.

(f) *Under 5s and Over 16s* The Warnock Report paid special attention to the needs of preschool children and the early identification of special needs. Stress was also placed on the transition from school to adult life, and it was proposed that educational opportunities in higher and further education should be expanded for children with special needs.

(g) *In-service training* The report recommended that all teachers should receive initial training in special education, and in-service training should be available for practising teachers, with financial inducements for those taking one-year courses. Support service personnel would also require additional training.

(h) *Research* The need for continued research in various disciplines concerned with special education was emphasized. For example, it was felt that research was needed into the management of behavioural difficulties in secondary schools, the effectiveness of integration, the incidence of severe handicap, and the efficacy of working with parents.

The Education Act, 1981

The Warnock Committee's recommendations were published in 1978, and formed the basis of the Education Act, 1981. This is the legislation under which we are now working and is therefore of particular importance. The Act has changed the framework of special education and sets out the duties of the LEA to provide for children with special needs. The Act repealed previous acts relating to special educational provision, and established a new framework for the education of children requiring special provision within both special and ordinary schools.

DEFINITION OF TERMS
In abolishing the old categories of handicap, the Act established special educational needs as a central concept, and with it the

linked concepts of learning difficulties and special educational provision.

A child is said to have 'special educational needs', 'if he has a learning difficulty which calls for special educational provision to be made for him'.

A child has 'learning difficulties' if:

(a) he has significantly greater difficulties in learning than the majority of children of his age; or
(b) he has a disability which either prevents or hinders him making use of school facilities in the area for children of his age provided by the LEA concerned; or
(c) he is under 5 years old, but would be likely to fall under (a) or (b) above if special educational provision were not made for him.

The Act clearly excludes from this definition children whose learning difficulties arise solely because the language taught in school is different to that spoken at home.

Finally, for a child of 2 years or more, 'special educational provision' means educational provision which is 'additional to, or otherwise different from, the educational provision made generally for children of his age within schools in the local authority'. For a child under 2 years it means educational provision of any kind.

THE PRINCIPLE OF INTEGRATION
The Act supported the principle of integration set out in the Warnock Report. It is made clear that a child with special educational needs should be taught in the ordinary school whenever possible, providing:

(a) he can receive there the special educational provision he requires;
(b) it is compatible with the efficient education of the other children with whom he is educated;
(c) it makes efficient use of resources.

The local authority has a duty under the Act to make suitable provision for children with special educational needs, and keep the arrangements for this provision under review. All who teach the child are to be made aware of his special needs, and understand the importance of identifying and providing for such children. It is also the duty of all concerned to ensure that, as is reasonably practicable, the child with special needs should engage in activities with ordinary children.

FORMAL ASSESSMENT PROCEDURES UNDER SECTION 5 OF THE ACT (see Figure 1.1)

The Act sets out the formalities for making an assessment, once it has been established that the child's needs call for the LEA to determine the special provision required, or it is believed that he probably has such needs. Parents themselves may request an assessment, and the authority must comply with this, unless it is considered to be an unreasonable request.

If the LEA proposes to make a formal assessment of the child's educational needs it should 'serve notice' on the parents, informing them of this proposal and the procedures to be followed. Parents must be told of an officer who can give them further information, and the parents' rights to make representations and submit written evidence within twenty-nine days should also be pointed out. Once this time has expired, the authority can proceed to assess the child, but must inform the parents in writing of this decision.

Parents must also be informed of their right to appeal to the secretary of state if the LEA decides that no special provision is required. Local authorities must also inform parents in writing if at any stage they decide not to proceed with a formal assessment.

For children under 2 years old, LEAs may assess at parental request, or with parental agreement, when it is thought that the authority should ascertain if special provision should be made. After informing the parents, the health authority has a duty to inform the LEA if it feels that a child under 5 years has special educational needs.

Once the assessment is complete, if special provision is thought to be necessary, the local authority must make and maintain 'a statement' of the child's special educational needs and arrange the specified special educational provision.

Before the statement is issued, parents must be sent a copy of

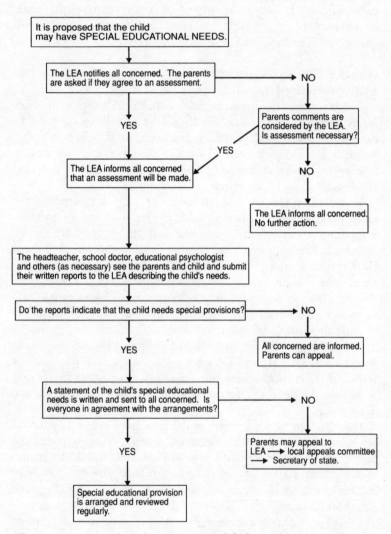

Figure 1.1 Formal assessment: a simplified step-by-step guide.

the proposed statement, along with an explanation of their rights should they wish to challenge the content. They may discuss with appropriate professionals disagreements over the submitted advice, as well as make further representations themselves at this stage, should they wish. The local authority may wish to modify or cancel the proposed statement following this, otherwise parents will next receive a copy of the final version of the statement.

The Act states that appeal procedures must be established locally, and parents ultimately have the right to appeal to the secretary of state, who will confirm, amend or cease to maintain the special educational provision specified in the statement.

REVIEWS AND REASSESSMENTS
The Act requires LEAs to review the arrangements made on the statement at least annually and this should also be part of the process of continuous assessment. Parents' views should be included where possible. Reassessments are required if there has been a 'significant change' in the child's circumstances, or when the child reaches 13 years of age, and previous assessments were made more than one year prior to this.

Circulars 8/81 and 1/83

These circulars, which were issued following the Act, explained the provisions more fully and offered advice to the LEA about interpreting the Act in practice.

Integration as a principle was emphasized, as far as this was a practical proposition. It was also made clear that children should be given a statement in all cases where the LEA had to provide additional resources in the ordinary school, and it was to be expected that a similar number of children would receive specialist resources as prior to the Act. Thus, approximately 2 per cent of children would receive a statement of their needs. Although the LEA is obliged to secure provision for all children with special needs, it need only maintain statements on the smaller group with more complex and severe difficulties.

The circulars also pointed out that 'a child's special educational needs are related to his abilities as well as his disabilities, and to the nature of his interaction with his environment'. It was emphasized that the purpose of an assessment is to arrive at a better understanding of the child's difficulties in order to provide a guide to the child's education and act as a basis against which to monitor progress. Assessment thus serves a practical purpose and is not intended to be an end in itself.

Warnock's notion of assessment as a continuous process, rather than a one-off event, was also stressed. In most cases it will be for the school, guided by the LEA, to decide how a child's needs should be assessed and met. Further investigation will be required only when the interventions made at school do not seem to be meeting the child's needs.

It was made clear that the decision to undertake formal assessment of children with unusually severe or complex problems may arise from school-based assessment, or from the local authority's psychological service, parents or other sources. Formal procedures should be initiated when *prima facie* grounds are established which suggest that the child's needs require provision additional to, or different from, the facilities and resources generally available in the ordinary school. This will vary between areas, but normally would include all children with severe or complex learning difficulties requiring extra resources in ordinary school, and all cases of children in special units attached to ordinary school. It would not usually be required when the pupil receives remedial provision nor when he attends a reading centre or unit for disruptive pupils if this is provided from the school's own resources. In addition it is not required if help is needed for a short duration only, or when the child is placed in a special school as part of the assessment process.

Assessment is to be seen as a partnership between teachers, other professionals and parents, in a joint endeavour to understand the nature of the child's difficulties and his needs. The LEA must seek educational, medical and psychological advice in every case, and also seek other advice necessary to make a satisfactory assessment. In turn, professionals are asked to consult with others having relevant information.

In an annex to the circular, a checklist was offered for professionals to use as an aide-memoire when preparing their advice; they are asked to select points from it which are relevant to their specialisms. Professionals are also asked to prepare their advice under three main headings to assure a common approach:

(i) relevant aspects of the child's functioning – including strengths and weaknesses, his relation with his environment at home and school – and other relevant aspects of his past history;

(ii) the aims to which provision for the child should be directed to enable him to develop educationally and increase his independence;

(iii) the facilities and resources required to promote the achievement of these aims.

It was noted that professional advice should not be influenced by considerations of eventual school placement since 'that is a matter to be determined by the local education authority at a later stage'. Professionals were warned not to pre-empt decisions about provision and school placement which would commit the local authority.

The multi-professional nature of a formal assessment was also emphasized: 'By bringing together the skills, perceptions and insights of professionals in different disciplines, it should be possible to arrive at a more complete understanding of a child's special educational needs . . . effective multiprofessional work is not easy to achieve, it requires co-operation, collaboration and mutual support'.

The government select committee report, 1987

As outlined, the last decade has been one of great change and innovation in special education, and professionals and parents have had to grapple not only with new legislation and procedures, but also with a fundamental change in orientation brought about by the 1981 Education Act. An evaluation of the working of the new legislation was therefore awaited with interest.

In 1987, a government select committee reported on the implementation of the 1981 Education Act (Acts of Parliament,

1987). The committee sat early in 1987 and visited three LEAs and invited witnesses from various professional bodies and organizations to give evidence. They concluded that a great deal had been accomplished since the 1981 Act, and that there had been little call for radical revision. However, three major areas of concern were highlighted, and some specific recommendations were made for modifying procedures.

(a) *The role of parents*   The committee felt that LEAs were failing to provide adequate information about the range of provision available, were giving insufficient help to parents when completing their contribution and were not taking sufficient account of parental views. It was also felt that some parents from ethnic minorities, where English was not the language of the home, were finding the procedures difficult to understand.

(b) *The principle of integration*   The committee concluded that the LEAs should prepare a clear policy statement on integration as part of its overall policy on special education. It was stressed that the principle of integration does not mean that all children should be educated in ordinary schools, and that special schools still have an important function. The quality and appropriateness of educational provision should be taken into account in any moves towards integrated forms of provision.

(c) *Resources*   The committee concluded that a lack of resources had restricted the implementation of the 1981 Act, so that a commitment to extra resources was needed if significant progress was to be made. The question of resources was raised most consistently by those submitting evidence.

Apart from these three main areas of concern, the committee reported on other aspects of the Act. They were concerned with the relativity of the concept of special educational need and the fact that a 'significant difficulty in learning' is interpreted narrowly as poor achievement in traditional academic subjects and is not seen as an appropritate description of emotional and behavioural difficulties. It was also acknowledged that 'special needs' and 'special educational needs' are used in a variety of ways. There was a suggestion that the wider range of special needs which require additional or different provision (such as giftedness or English as a second language and social disadvantage) should be included in the Act. There was also concern about the variation in the number of statements produced between LEAs and the percentage of children who had their needs met in ordinary schools. The committee urged that there should be more guidance about when a statement might be required and about what constitutes 'special educational provision'.

The committee also considered that it was 'unacceptable' that there were no arrangements made for those children who had special educational needs but were not statemented. They pointed out that provisions within schools can become distorted if additional resources are allocated on an individual *ad hoc* basis. They therefore recommended that there should be a systematic allocation of resources, and concluded that every LEA should have a clear and coherent policy on special education.

Another area of concern addressed was the time taken for the completion of a statement, and allied to this was the committee's concern with the assessment of children under 5 whose needs change rapidly. It was recommended that the DES should examine ways of improving the procedures.

Finally, the committee considered the involvement of other statutory agencies, such as the social services, and noted several shortcomings in provision; in particular, the shortage of speech therapy time allocated to LEAs.

The committee concluded that difficulties were too wide ranging to be soluble by schools and too localized to be capable of close direction by central government. On balance 'it is the way these statutory procedures operate which is unsatisfactory, not their scope and purpose'. It was recommended that the department should examine ways of improving procedures, and disseminate examples of best administrative practice; but the 'successful implementation of the 1981 Act is very much dependent on the development by an LEA of a clear and coherent policy', which is supported by teachers, parents and voluntary organizations.

THE REVISION OF CIRCULAR 1/83 – 'ASSESSMENTS AND
STATEMENTS OF SPECIAL EDUCATIONAL NEEDS: PROCEDURES
WITHIN THE EDUCATION, HEALTH AND SOCIAL SERVICES'

The DES have recently published a draft circular which is
intended to revise Circular 1/83 in the light of the recommendations of the government select committee. It also takes
into account the provisions of the Education Reform Act, 1988,
relating to the new national curriculum. The draft circular
proposes that statements will still be required for all children
with severe or complex learning difficulties who require extra
resources in ordinary schools, and for all those who spend most
of the day in a special unit in an ordinary school or a special
school. In addition, in future, a statement may also be required
where any requirements of the national curriculum need to be
'modified' or 'disapplied' for an individual child. It is made
clear that all children, including those with special needs,
should benefit from the national curriculum, since the attainment
targets should be wide enough so that the vast majority of
children will be able to demonstrate progress. However, for
some children, it may be desirable to modify their attainment
targets, or programmes of study, or exclude a subject from
their programme for various reasons.

The new circular which will offer guidelines on the
implementation of the 1981 Education Act, is due to be
published in its final version in the summer of 1990.

2   CENTRAL ISSUES IN SPECIAL EDUCATION

In this section some of the major central issues in special
education will be introduced. Since they will recur in various
chapters throughout the book, it may be helpful to take some
account of them at this stage.

Why 'special education'?

A fundamental question is why do we need special education?
The basic concept of a distinct type of 'special' education,
which is different to the education other children receive, and is
undertaken in a separate establishment for different groups of

children, has come under close scrutiny in the last ten years. For some time it has been questioned whether we really help children by segregating them. Recent changes in legislation have made the distinctions between 'normal' and 'special' increasingly unclear. Questions are raised about who is special and who is normal; who should receive a statement, and who should receive additional special resources?

The notion of 'special needs'

In abolishing the various categories of handicap, the 1981 Act instated in its place the concept of 'special needs', but this notion is far from clear. The term is intended to embrace all the factors relating to the child's educational progress, his abilities and disabilities. The Act points out that the term is relative, and the needs of the child depend on many factors such as what is considered to be normal behaviour for the child's age; what resources are available; and whether the child's disabilities prevent him from making use of the educational provision normally provided. However, children will only have special educational needs if there are shortcomings in the educational system; if special resources are readily available in ordinary schools they will not have special needs.

In Booth's view (1983), 'the number of children with special needs within a school will vary with the extent to which the needs of the children are actually being met', and most children sent to special schools have special needs 'because ordinary schools have not adapted their curricula and forms of organisation to the diverse needs, interests, and talents of children'.

The Warnock Report highlighted the fact that there is no sharp distinction between children who have special needs and those who do not, and proposed the idea of a continuum of needs, matched by a range of flexible educational provision. This runs counter to the old notion of distinctly separate special schools to serve children with various types of disability. The last decade has been marked by increasing attempts to introduce a wider range of special educational provision to meet the diversity of special needs.

Integration

Another fundamental issue is integration. As noted earlier, the recommendations of the Warnock Report were enshrined in the 1981 Act, and as a matter of principle, with certain exceptions, children with special needs should now be educated with ordinary pupils.

Integration generally implies that a child with special needs is educated in the same class alongside his peers, rather than being segregated in a special school. However, the Warnock Report interpreted the concept far more flexibly, pointing out that many forms and degrees of integration are possible, so the dichotomy between integration and segregation is not clear-cut. Some children with special needs may attend a unit attached to an ordinary school but their curriculum and social activities may be separate (locational integration). Some may mix for social activities (social integration), and some may spend some time in ordinary classes for certain lessons. Some children are based in class but they may be withdrawn for individual specialist teaching, or they may be supported by a specialist teacher within the same classroom (functional integration). Various part-time arrangements between special and ordinary schools are also possible.

ARGUMENTS FOR AND AGAINST INTEGRATION

The Warnock Report's principal argument for integration was based on an appeal for social justice and for the rights of the individual, rather than on evidence of psychological or educational effectiveness. Like the comprehensive principle, integration is linked to the principle of equality of value. 'Ideally all children should be equally valued regardless of sex, background, colour, economic or class position, disability or attainment' (Booth, 1983).

The debate about integration has a long history, and the Warnock Report was echoing the experience of America and Scandinavia. In Scandinavia 'normalization' has been the educational philosophy for some time; and in the United States 'mainstreaming' is now embodied in legislation so that the education authorities must prove that the child with special needs would be better off in a segregated special school before he can be placed there. Since 1975, when an integration law was passed in the United States, all people with disabilities have a right to share in community life.

Disquiet about segregated provision arose in Britain for various reasons. Although 1–2 per cent of children were attending special schools, large numbers of children in ordinary schools were also receiving additional help, so that the decision to use segregated provision was somewhat arbitrary. Moreover, once a child's educational requirements were determined, many children remained in segregated provision for the rest of their school careers without any reassessment of its suitability.

It was regarded as wrong as a matter of principle to separate children from their peers, and stigmatizing to send them to separate educational establishments. Many people perceived special schooling negatively; the Spastic Society's factsheet on integration talks about 'barriers of fear, ignorance and prejudice', and goes on to say that unless these are broken down they lead to 'discrimination and a refusal to accept handicapped people as full members of society'.

Several other arguments can be advanced in favour of integration. Perhaps the most convincing is that if education is supposed to be a preparation for life and adulthood, children should learn to mix with one another. The Spastic Society notes, 'children with special needs, who are educated in the ordinary schools, cope with many little battles every day rather than one huge battle at 16 or 19 when they leave the protected environment of the special school'. Most children with severe difficulties will be expected to live in their local community as adults, albeit with support, and therefore the most realistic and educative experience should be within that ordinary community. Residential education, it is argued, fits the individual for institutional life and deprives him of vital experiences of family and community life. Furthermore, peers and people within the locality are likely to be more accepting and sympathetic if they have grown up with handicapped people. Again, to quote the Spastic Society, 'it has been shown that young people quickly overcome their inhibitions or lack of knowledge and relate to their handicapped peers as people first'.

As will be discussed in Chapter 3, it has also been shown that children can raise or depress their academic performance according to the expectations of teachers, parents and peers (see, for example, Pidgeon, 1970). Where expectations are based on normal behaviour and attainments, children with special needs can frequently 'rise to the occasion'. Contact with normal children tends to stimulate less able children, and this is particularly crucial with language development. The child exposed to normal conversation is likely to learn to talk, whereas the child placed with non-communicating peers has little need to speak.

Other arguments in support of integration revolve around the lack of evidence of the effectiveness of segregated provision. For example, despite the fact that residential maladjusted provision is an expensive resource, there is no evidence that it ameliorates or cures the child's problem, at least as measured by future adjustment and delinquency rates (Topping, 1983). In general, such schools seem to offer containment rather than therapy or behavioural change, and although containment may benefit society at large it is hardly a sufficient reason for segregated provision in terms of the child's needs.

Against these views, others argue that segregated special schools can offer specialist teachers, a fully appropriate curriculum and specialized facilities and resources, such as hydrotherapy pools, mini buses, etc. These resources are likely to be of a higher standard than can be provided in the ordinary school because of economies of scale. It is also argued that children with special needs require protecting and some feel isolated, lonely and vulnerable in ordinary schools. Finally, there are a group of children who will need constant supervision and support throughout their lives and segregated specialist educational provision can be regarded as a suitable preparation for life.

Many commentators have expressed concern that the policy of integration could lead to the dismantling of some excellent special schools whilst special needs' children are reintegrated into the classes of frequently ill-prepared, overworked staff in ordinary schools, with a minimum of additional resources. Bookbinder (1983), for example, states 'the concept of special educational need with its accompanying assumption that such needs can be adequately met in our present educational system, is thoroughly unrealistic and is likely to lead us astray'.

As noted earlier, the government select committee report on the implementation of the 1981 Act also revealed considerable anxiety over this point, and asked that the principle of integration should not override the individual child's best interests. There has been concern expressed in the press over this recommendation, as those who advocate a swift change to integration have seen it as a retrograde step, which appears to justify the status quo. They maintain that better resourcing will inevitably follow integration.

The response to recent legislation on integration has varied between LEAs, largely because of their pre-existing provision. The report of the Inner London Education Committee, chaired by John Fish (Fish Report, 1985), called for the closure of special schools and the reorganization of special provision in London. Oxfordshire has closed many of its special schools and redeployed teachers as support staff in ordinary schools. Other LEAs have been more cautious, but new initiatives have proliferated. Outreach arrangements between special and ordinary schools have been established in some areas, whereby there are exchanges of staff and pupils between the two schools. In addition, peripatetic support services have been expanded in most LEAs to meet the demand for extra help in ordinary schools.

However, educationalists fear that, if integration is to be a viable alternative to segregated provision, adequate resources must be provided and additional specialist teachers, ancillary helpers, an alternative curriculum and a wide range of special aids will have to be made available. All those involved will need adequate preparation for such children and a sense of genuine commitment must prevail. There is considerable anxiety that although integration is now an established principle by law, the conditions for its proper implementation are not available.

Normalization

The principle of normalization is another concept which originated in Scandinavia, was adopted in the United States in the 1970s and has been imported into Britain in the 1980s. As

yet the concept is not enshrined in British law, but the principle
has gained widespread acceptance across health, education and
the social services.

Nirje and Wolfensberger (1975, 1988a) have done most to
popularize the principle of normalization which can apply to all
groups of people who are devalued, or at risk of being
considered less valuable in society, such as the elderly, those
with physical disabilities or mental illness, and particularly those
with a mental handicap. Nirje pointed out that mentally
handicapped people have little social or economic power and
frequently are unable to develop long-term relationships. They
in effect suffer from three handicaps; the handicap itself; the
awareness of being handicapped; and the negative attitudes and
values shown to them by others.

Although normalization was originally interpreted narrowly
as encouraging handicapped people to have an existence as
close to normal as possible, and so has been associated with
moving handicapped people out of institutions into the
community and moving handicapped youngsters out of special
schools into mainstream education, Wolfensberger has pointed
out that normalization is not essentially about trying to make
all people 'normal' in this sense. It is certainly not about
thrusting people into the community or mainstream schools
willy nilly, without due care, preparation and support. Rather,
he would maintain that people, whatever their differences,
should be equally valued as full citizens with dignity and
respect as of human right; any differences in behaviour,
appearance or activity should be acceptable and worthy of
respect.

Wolfensberger now prefers to talk about 'social role
valorization' rather than normalization since this conveys the
need to reverse the process of socially devaluing people. He
looks at the whole social context of the handicapped person and
maintains that their social role requires enhancing. With social
role valorization the aim is to use culturally valued means to
establish, and/or maintain, valued social roles (not necessarily
normative roles). That is, it is argued that culturally valued
means must be used to convey dignity and social status to
handicapped people. In some cases this might involve giving
extra resources and better facilities to such disadvantaged

groups, in order to change attitudes and perceptions and so enhance their value in society.

For example, it is pointed out (e.g., in O'Brien and Tyre, 1981) that mentally handicapped people are often dehumanized by being treated in disrespectful ways as if they are not fully human. They may also be treated age inappropriately, as if they are perpetual children, in the way they are dressed, housed and spoken about. Or they may be rejected and treated as if they cease to exist, by being isolated from the community, either at home or at school. Putting the principle of normalization into practice would mean considering such things as the way mentally handicapped people are grouped, the buildings, facilities and physical settings in which they live; their personal appearance and their public image; the range of skills they are encouraged to develop and the work that they do; and the quality and variety of the choices in their life.

There has been a growing awareness that the various support services, (health, education and the social services) frequently fail to enhance the potential of their clients by having low expectations and treating them as if they were less than fully human. The philosophy of normalization provides principles which can act as a standard against which the quality and relevance of services for mentally handicapped adults and children can be measured and evaluated (see O'Brien and Tyre, 1981, pp. 24–6).

Categorization

Another fundamental issue tackled by the Warnock Report concerned the categorization of children in terms of their handicapping conditions. Under the 1944 Education Act, this process was necessary in order to assign children to appropriate special schools. Professionals involved in assessment were aware that, in point of fact, children's problems rarely fall neatly into a single category. Many children have more than one difficulty, making such categorizations of limited value.

Another concern about the old, rigid categorization system was that the notion of a handicap implies a permanent disorder, whereas many problems are relatively transient and shortlived, given appropriate help. For example, a child's learning difficulty with reading may be overcome after appropriate specialist teaching.

Furthermore, the categorization by handicap did not in itself reflect educational requirements or suggest appropriate action, so that children with a variety of different handicaps may have the same educational needs and, similarly, children with the same handicap may require very different forms of educational provision.

The Warnock Report also pointed out that the term 'handicap' is relative. Some children cope well despite considerable difficulties, if their home and school context is sufficiently supportive, and their attitude is positive. Clearly problems are more or less handicapping depending on the child's life situation, and if the right type of provision is given early enough, so that a minor difficulty does not become a major one. In this way the report emphasized the individual's needs within a particular context, rather than his handicapping difficulties *per se*.

A fundamental worry about the categorization process generally is the adverse affect of labelling difficulties and handicaps. Labelling can produce a self-fulfilling prophesy effect whereby parents, teachers and the child himself come to fix their expectations on the basis of that label rather than on the child's actual skills and potential. The dangers of this process have led to a great deal of professional disquiet in recent years, and it was hoped that it would be overcome by abolishing the categorization of children by handicap and redirecting attention to their needs.

Identification and assessment

Recent changes in the emphasis of special education have had considerable consequences for the type of assessments undertaken by professionals, although discontent with traditional methods of assessment had been growing for at least a decade prior to the new legislation.

Many educationalists have come to believe that the assessment of skills that have direct significance for the child, such as literacy and numeracy, should have the highest priority in any assessment of special needs. Curriculum-related assessment, where the child is assessed against predetermined learning objectives in order to find out what he has learned, has therefore come to be more important than normative assessment, where children are compared with others on a narrower range of standardized tests. Another adjunct to this new emphasis is that assessment has become increasingly prescriptive.

There has thus been a major change in emphasis from diagnosis to prescription; the emphasis now is on overcoming difficulties rather than attempting to establish their cause. Moreover, in order to remedy difficulties it is important to assess what the child can and cannot do, thus comparative or normative assessment is likely to be less useful than a close scrutiny of the child's attainments on various learning tasks. Normative assessment is waning in favour of criterion-referenced and curriculum-based assessment.

Identifying specific difficulties is seen as the first step in trying to improve them. A basic assumption underlying current thinking is that all children can profit from teaching and that progress can be accelerated by optimizing all the conditions for learning. In the not too distant past the term 'ineducable' was a legal category, and all too often a low intelligence test score was used as a justification for the child's lack of progress. The intelligence test could be positively harmful in limiting the teachers' and parents' expectations, and in providing a rationale for failure and inactivity.

Prescriptive assessment involves discovering the level of the child's skills and in arranging a suitable curriculum. This can be done using task analysis and precision-teaching procedures, and will be described in Chapter 7. In the USA, prescriptive assessment has been embodied in legislation and any child with learning difficulties must have a prescribed curriculum which has been determined by all the professionals involved with the child as well as the parents. This is known as an IEP (Individualized Educational Programme). Although British legislation does not go this far, the Warnock Report and 1981 Education Act clearly had American practices in mind.

Assessment is no longer seen as an end in itself, but as the first step towards meeting the child's needs, by setting educational goals and objectives. At the same time the responsibility for learning failure has shifted. If a child cannot master a task, it may be that the teacher needs to adjust his learning programme rather than blame shortcomings in the child.

It is recommended in the 1981 Act that the aims for the child be specific. In the past assessments tended to give generalized recommendations, but when an assessment is individualized and curriculum-based, prescription should be more specific and relevant to the teaching process.

As noted earlier, the Warnock Report proposed a staged model of assessment where teachers would usually be the first people to identify learning difficulties, usually using careful observations rather than formal tests. Concerns should be discussed with the headteacher and specialist teaching colleagues, and further information amassed. It might be at this stage that other outside specialists might be consulted, and in some cases, where difficulties are particularly complex or severe, formal procedures may be initiated under the 1981 Education Act. Teachers thus play an essential role in the identification and assessment of learning difficulties.

As a logical step in achieving a detailed assessment of the child's educational needs, the Warnock Report suggested that all professionals involved in the assessment should attempt to co-ordinate their recommendations. This idea was taken up by the subsequent legislation, so that teachers, educational psychologists, school doctors, and other professionals involved with the child exchange their assessment advice and share information. A true multi-professional approach may be difficult to manage in practice, but few would doubt its wisdom in theory.

Medical versus social models in education

Historically, children with special needs were primarily seen as the concern of the medical profession so that under the 1944 Education Act, children were ascertained by school medical officers as being in need of special educational provision. The very language of education is replete with medical references, such as diagnosis, prescription and treatment. This is a danger because, unlike physical illness, the root of the problem is frequently not within the child, and treatment at an individual level may not be appropriate. Prior to the Warnock Report the emphasis was on the cause of a particular condition, rather than on its remedy.

With some conditions, such as hearing or visual impairment, the medical model may be helpful for gaining a fuller understanding of the condition. But there are other problems, such as adjustment or learning difficulties, where the explanation may be social or educational, yet they are also frequently discussed as if the main cause of the problem were medical. A very active child, for example, may be diagnosed as hyperactive and explanations for his behaviour sought in his medical history, such as birth injury, lead poisoning, or food additives. Medical solutions involving drugs may be suggested whilst the social circumstances surrounding the child might be overlooked, although these factors may be the potent ones. This medical reification may lead to inappropriate and ineffective treatment, and obscure the true nature of the child's problems.

Furthermore, many educationalists now feel that dwelling on the causation of the condition, medical or otherwise, detracts from the real purpose of any assessment: namely, remediation. The remedy rarely results from a medical understanding of the condition, but solutions rest on an analysis of the problems the child is actually encountering. Educational treatment is thus predominantly concerned with the presenting symptoms. One of the frequently voiced objections to the notion of dyslexia (this being a medical term and an educational problem) is that the diagnosis makes no difference to the actual treatment of a child with reading problems. If the child is found to be dyslexic, he still requires sound remedial teaching.

It is at the point of issue of remediation or treatment that the medical model is least useful. It can be reasonably claimed that most teachers work with basically a hierarchical model of learning and development; be it with reading, numeracy, or other basic skills. The assumption is that the child should be put on the 'learning ladder' at the appropriate place, and then proceed at the right pace. This approach to overcoming learning difficulties is quite different from the medical one which seeks to diagnose in order to apply a specific treatment. When the emphasis is placed upon the fine detail of the educational programme, causation becomes far less relevant. If the pupil is failing to grasp number bonds, for example, the programme devised to help him to establish these will not be dependent on his underlying condition, but rather on how finely graded the programme should be to enable him to make steady progress.

Eventually when the process of learning and development are much better understood we may be able to describe each child in terms of the stages he has reached in a wide range of skill acquisition. A full educational description of this sort will probably decrease the need for other explanations. In the past a medical description alone could invoke educational provision. Since the 1981 Act, however, it is no longer sufficient to say the child is hearing-impaired and therefore needs a school for hearing-impaired children. What the child needs in educational terms is what now determines provision.

A final objection to medical reification is that it inevitably leads to categorization and labelling, since this is what diagnosis in medicine sets out to do. As we have already discussed, categorization is misleading and against the spirit of the new legislation. Categories are useful to administrators, students and textbook writers because they clarify and simplify human behaviour, but they usually detract from understanding individual needs.

Partnership with parents

In recent years, there has been a growing awareness of the important influence of parents in the educative process. During the last decade parental involvement in all procedures relating to their child's education has been given greater prominence, and parental rights on a number of fronts have been included in legislation. Under the 1980 Education Act, parents now have the right to choose their child's school, if a place is available, and there is a general trend for schools to be more accountable to parents. This is also one of the cornerstones of the recent 1988 Education Act.

The Warnock Report and the 1981 Act had a great deal to say about the importance of parents working in partnership with professionals and the LEA in the best interests of their child; frankness and openness on all sides was advocated as the best way to establish close relations. The 1981 Act pointed out that parents should usually be already aware that their child has learning difficulties before receiving formal notice from the authority. Parents generally have a right to be present at assessments, although classroom observations and some forms of psychological testing may need to be done privately. Even so, parents should be fully informed. When necessary, parents should be helped to make their own representations and professional advice given to local authorities should be available to them. Indeed, under separate legislation, parents and all citizens have the right to see computerized information kept on them and a general trend has been towards government departments giving access to confidential information.

Some educationalists have some reservations about the involvement of parents, although everyone welcomes in principle the general move towards the democratization of decision-making in education. Whilst acknowledging that parents are the prime educators and experts as far as their child is concerned, it is possible that some parents may lack knowledge and objectivity about their child's needs. Although their views are important, so too are the views of teachers and other professionals who know the child.

A second concern is that it is usually middle-class parents who are the most articulate, confident and vociferous about their child's education and, in a situation of scarce resources, the fear is that under their pressure more resources will be allocated to those who are already advantaged rather than to those children with less articulate parents.

It is probably true to say that at present the concept of partnership with parents is still in its infancy, and will require further development.

2
Learning difficulties

OVERVIEW

In this chapter the concept of learning difficulties will be discussed. Since all children with special educational needs have learning difficulties, the concept is now a fundamental one to special education. Traditional views of intelligence will be compared with the new broader concept of learning difficulties, and the growth of provision in ordinary and special schools to meet the various needs of children will also be considered. Chapter 3 will examine the factors thought to give rise to learning difficulties, and Chapter 4, the various physical and sensory disabilities which can give rise to learning difficulties.

INTRODUCTION

Over the years there have been various terms used for children who have learning difficulties of one kind or another. Deeply embedded in our educational system are expectations about how 'normal' children should learn and behave, so most of the terms imply the child is failing when compared to peers of the same age. 'Retarded', 'backward', 'remedial', 'slow learners', 'mentally deficient', 'under-achievers', 'mentally handicapped', 'subnormal', are just a few of the more commonly used terms. Labels tend to lead to stereotyped thinking and inappropriate expectations, but nevertheless, if we wish to distinguish between the varying learning abilities of children, then some terms are necessary.

The currently acceptable term, 'learning difficulties', is

intended to be less value-laden than some of the others previously used, and perhaps more simply reflects the notion that the child, for whatever reason, has difficulty in learning. Rather than the term being confined to those with mental or physical disabilities, the Warnock Report proposed that it should be used in a general sense to cover any difficulties children may have learning new skills. However, the 1981 Education Act defined learning difficulties in a more specific way, so it now has an additional legal meaning when used in certain contexts.

A major problem with the term 'learning difficulties' is that, like the others mentioned above, it places emphasis on the child failing to cope with the demands of school, rather than focusing on the shortcomings of the curriculum to meet the varying needs of individual pupils. Moreover, in trying to be non-specific some would say that it suffers from being vague and imprecise.

These issues will be returned to later, but in order to understand the various undercurrents to present-day attitudes and thoughts, it will be helpful to trace back our conceptualization of learning difficulties to pre-Warnock days, when intelligence was the key concept of fundamental importance when assessing which children required special education.

EARLY CONCEPTUALIZATION AND DEFINITIONS

As outlined in Chapter 1, the 1944 Education Act extended the duties of LEAs and required them to make suitable special school provision for children who were handicapped by 'disabilities of body or mind'; eleven categories of handicap were established. At this time, the handicapping condition itself was thought to imply a certain form of education, despite the fact that the degree of handicap could vary considerably, and children with various handicaps might benefit from a similiar curriculum.

As Table 1.1 illustrates, many of the legal categories were concerned with physical and sensory disabilities, and educational subnormality was a distinct grouping. For those children who were multi-handicapped, professionals were asked to categorize them in terms of their primary handicap.

Categorization of intellectual handicap

In order to determine whether children required 'special educational treatment' they were categorized principally by their measured performance on intelligence tests which were designed to be, as far as possible, independent of school learning. The intention was to measure the child's 'mental capacity' or 'intellectual potential', rather than his schooling experiences. The child with an intelligence quotient of 55–70 was said to be moderately educationally subnormal (ESN(m)), and those with quotients falling below 55 were categorized as severely educationally subnormal (ESN(s)).

From 1944 to 1970, only children ascertained as ESN(m) were acknowledged to benefit from special schooling; the small percentage of children with severe learning difficulties were considered to be unsuitable for education. It was not until the Education Act of 1970 that ESN(s) children also became the legal responsibility of the education department, and for the first time all children, whatever their handicap, had a right to be educated. Since the Act was implemented in 1971, special schools for ESN(s) children have also had to be provided by LEAs. Prior to this, the health authority had responsibility, and many children were cared for in hospitals or training centres, or otherwise stayed at home.

The concept of intelligence and its measurement

Until relatively recently, the assessment of children with various handicaps was dominated by the use of intelligence tests. Even when the child's intellectual ability was not in question, an intelligence test formed a major part of the assessment. It was assumed that intelligence was fundamental to every aspect of the educational process. Intelligence testing was viewed as an objective scientific tool for determining the child's intellectual functioning.

The originators of intelligence tests (Binet and Simon, 1905; Burt, 1909), were concerned to identify those children who would most profit from various forms of education. They attempted to find a means of measuring differences in ability and educability. It was assumed that variations in intellectual ability were similar to naturally occurring physical variations such as height. The distribution by height of boys of a certain age, for example, follows the normal distribution curve. The majority will be around average but a few at the extremes will be either very tall or very short.

In devising measures of intelligence, a large sample of children of a given age were tested on a range of skills believed to contribute to intelligence. These generally included memory, sequencing, visual and verbal reasoning, perceptual organization, general knowledge, vocabulary and arithmetic. The scaling of the test scores was adjusted or standardized to produce as closely as possible the normal distribution curve, with approximately 68 per cent of the population falling in the average range; 14 per cent above or below average; and 2 per cent very much above or below average. Most intelligence tests are thus arbitrarily constructed around the normal distribution curve, with a score of 100 representing average ability; a score of 70 or below indicating that the child is in the lowest 2 per cent range, and a score of 130 or above, the highest 2 per cent.

It was assumed that these tests validly tapped an underlying mental ability of intelligence. Originally this was conceived to be one general innate ability, fundamental to all mental abilities; later, intelligence was conceived to be a term denoting a variety of cognitive abilities including reasoning, memory, perceptual skills etc.

Mental age

Another concept related to standardized mental measurement is that of mental age. One of the fundamental principles of measures of intelligence is that skills develop with age. The above-average child could be said to have a mental age in advance of his chronological age, and conversely, if a child is less able, his mental age may be said to be lower than his chronological years. Scales were often constructed so that an intelligence quotient could be converted into a mental age. This lead to notions of 'underachievement'. The term referred to the difference between a child's intelligence quotient and mental age scores on basic skills tests, usually reading and number. Those with wide discrepancies, whose attainments were significantly lower than their intelligence quotient, were said to be underachieving or 'not reaching their potential'. This concept is questionable as it is difficult to know how someone's 'potential' might be estimated since it is not possible to measure 'pure intelligence' without the interplay of experience having its effects. It is also assumed that children should have an even profile of scores on the various skills measured, but most people have strengths and weaknesses, so an even profile of abilities is not to be expected.

Problems with the traditional concept of intelligence

The concept of intelligence is a confused and confusing one and various concerns have been expressed about it. Most people would now contend that it is impossible to separate innate from acquired components of intelligence, for the reasons just given. It is generally agreed now that a child's life experiences will determine the extent to which his intellect develops. It is also generally thought to be misleading to talk about intelligence as if it were one underlying mental quality. Intelligent behaviour can mean different things to different people, depending on the context, and according to one's values. Used in the context of schooling, it has been associated with success in public examinations.

A fundamental difficulty with normative intelligence tests is that they measure skills which are largely selected because of statistical and administrative convenience. Other important skills which might be termed intelligent are not included. Moreover, because they do not measure skills which are directly taught, it can be argued that they are not a measure of learning ability, and so have questionable use for teachers. An intelligence test also fails to distinguish between the variety of personality, motivation and learning styles that children bring to a task. Many uninterested or over-anxious children may be wrongly assumed to be of low ability. The test can only tell us how the child performed on one day on one occasion. Although children who do well on intelligence tests not surprisingly tend to be those whose academic attainments are also good, scores rarely correlate perfectly with academic performance. However, intelligence tests have probably retained their popularity as they are better predictors of later academic achievement than most other measures of attainment.

Recently devised ability scales (the British Ability Scales), which are often used by educational psychologists, overcome some of these criticisms. A range of intellectual abilities can be assessed and profiled, so that the emphasis has moved away from one generalized intelligence test score. This type of assessment device is probably of greater help in analysing the child's specific strengths and weaknesses on a range of intellectual skills, but it still does not give feedback to teachers about the child's performance on specific teaching objectives, or measure learning progress in a way which could inform teachers what skills need to be learned next.

Other assessment measures

Although the child's performance on an intelligence test was usually central to the categorization process, in practice, as the Warnock Report (1978) pointed out, attainments in basic literacy skills were probably highly relevant in determining school placement. For example, the Isle of Wight survey (Rutter, Tizard and Whitmore, 1970) found that of the 2.5 per cent of children with intelligence quotients less than 70, more than half attended ordinary schools. In addition, 20 per cent of the children attending special schools had intelligence quotients higher than 70. However, the distinguishing factor between the two groups was reading attainment. Children attending special schools were more seriously reading retarded, when reading ages were compared to chronological age, than those who were in ordinary schools.

The report quoted various other studies to emphasize the same point, such as Williams and Gruber (1967), who found that 45 per cent of children in the special schools studied had intelligence quotients higher than 70, and 10 per cent were higher than 80; and Marra (1981) who found that 49 per cent of children in the three special schools studied had intelligence quotients higher than 70.

In reality, many other factors were probably also influential in school placement decisions. Special schools were commonly perceived to be compensating for various types of disadvantage, thus views about the child's home circumstances might have been taken into account, as well as factors such as the ability and willingness of the ordinary school to adapt to the child's needs and circumstances.

Since there were no absolute criteria for categorization, Galloway and Goodwin (1987) made the point that it was the very act of transferring a child from ordinary to special school which conferred the status of educational subnormality, rather than there being any particular child characteristics of relevance.

PREVALENCE

Children with intellectual handicaps requiring special schooling

The 1944 Education Act envisaged that about 2 per cent of children would require alternative 'special educational treatment' to mainstream schooling, and the intelligence quotients mentioned above, based on a normal distribution curve, enabled selection to take place of approximately the right numbers of children to fit available provision. As noted in Chapter 1, the largest category of handicap was ESN(m), representing nearly half of the special school population, and only a small percentage (approximately 0.2 per cent) had a more severe mental handicap.

As far as special school placements were concerned, there have always been large regional variations. For example, the DES (1966) figures showed that nearly twice as many children were ascertained as ESN(m) in the south-east of England than in Wales (92.1) as opposed to 49.9 children per 10,000 in the population). This suggests a clear relationship between categorization and the availability of special provision, again emphasizing that the categories of handicap were not, in practice, as objective as many people considered them to be.

Children with remedial difficulties in ordinary schools

As well as those children who were considered to require special schooling, large numbers of pupils in ordinary school also had learning difficulties and received, or were thought to require, remedial help.

The Warnock Report (1978) quoted various surveys which suggested that many children were illiterate or semi-literate, a concern which was earlier discussed in the Bullock Report (1975). For example, Morris (1966), found that 14 per cent of 8 year olds were nearly illiterate and half continued to be poor readers in the secondary school. Start and Wells (1972), surveying the reading standards of 11- and 15-year-old children, showed that despite a growth in remedial services many children still had considerable literacy problems: for example, at 11 years, 9 per cent were 4 years retarded (i.e., obtained reading ages of below 7 years), whilst at 15 years 14 per cent were 4 years retarded (i.e., obtained reading ages of below 11 years).

Another large-scale survey, the National Child Development Study (Kelmer-Pringle, Butler and Davie, 1966), provided evidence about the extent of learning difficulties more generally. It found that by 7 years, 10 per cent of children had barely started to read. 0.4 per cent of children were already attending special schools, and 5 per cent received help in ordinary schools. A further 8 per cent of children were considered by their teachers to be in need of more help. In summary, 13 per cent of the 11,000 7 year olds were either receiving, or were thought to need, special help.

A follow-up study (Fogelman, 1976) of the same children at 16 years found that, by this age, 3 per cent of children had been assessed as in need of special education and 1.9 per cent were still attending a special school. In addition, 7 per cent of children in the ordinary school were receiving help and a further 2 per cent were thought by their teachers to need it. Moreover, 5 per cent of children were receiving help for behavioural difficulties, and it was thought that another 3 per cent might benefit. There was also a further 1 per cent of children who were getting help because of their physical difficulties.

To summarize, in total about 20 per cent of children were considered by teachers to need special help; of these, 11 per cent were perceived to have learning problems and 1.6 per cent of these were considered to have such difficulty that they would be unable to cope with reading a newspaper or completing forms and 2.6 per cent would have difficulty with everyday shopping activities.

The Isle of Wight survey (Rutter, Tizard and Whitmore, 1970) also looked at the prevalence of disorders, this time in children aged 9–12 years. Of the 2.5 per cent of children who had intelligence quotients less than 70, about half attended ordinary schools. 8 per cent of children had reading ages 28 months below their chronological ages on a Neales' Analysis of Reading test. It was found that about half these children had a specific problem with reading alone. When followed up 28 months later, these children had on average made just 10 months' progress on reading accuracy tests, and 13 months on the measures of comprehension. Most of the children reached a reading age of 9 years by the age of 15.

A comparative study in London (Rutter *et al.*, 1975), using the same tests and criteria, suggested that urban children have even more extensive difficulties. The study found that 19 per cent were retarded in reading, and of these, 9.9 per cent had specific reading difficulties.

Finally, a survey of 158 secondary schools conducted by the HMI in 1967–8 (DES, 1978) found that 14 per cent of children were considered to be slow learners by their teachers, and one school in seven estimated that 20 per cent of its pupils required special help.

The Warnock Report used these surveys as evidence for their more radical proposals about the nature and extent of learning difficulties, in particular, suggesting that approximately 20 per cent of pupils are likely to require additional resources and so could be said to have special needs.

READING AND SPELLING DIFFICULTIES

The majority of children seem to acquire literacy skills with little difficulty, despite a variety of teaching methods and teacher skills. In fact, research fails to establish the most effective method for teaching reading (DES, 1975). However, reading is a complex task and requires the acquisition of a wide variety of skills to become fluent; many children clearly have considerable difficulties. By outlining the normal development of reading skills it is possible to postulate why learning difficulties may occur, although the issue is taken up in more depth in the following chapter.

Most children acquire the basic skills of reading by 7 years, and they will then usually have acquired the basic skills of decoding print, and next need to learn more complex phonic rules and gain experience about language use and spelling irregularities.

As a symbol system, the English language is extremely complex, as there is no one-to-one correspondence between the visual display of letters and their sound values. Many phonic rules have exceptions which must be learned, and faulty teaching can confuse the child in his attempt to unravel the code. Many children also find spelling difficult due to the irregularities in the English rule system, the lack of correspondence between sound and letters, and the irregularity in the way combinations of letters are sounded.

The process of reading is still not properly understood, but it is thought to involve the coding and decoding of symbols using the auditory, oral and visual modalities which together yield information and meaning. Traditionally three aspects of the reading process have been highlighted, and reading difficulties are often thought to be associated with weaknesses in one of these areas:

a visual memory: remembering the visual pattern which represents the word;
b phonics: words are composed of single sounds in combinations and these have their written equivalents so that words can be deciphered on the basis of sounds;
c language: reading is dependent on, and ultimately limited by, the level of the child's understanding of language. Successful readers were found by Clark (1976) to extract meaning from print from the start. Reading can be said to be language in context.

When learning to read the child uses all these strategies and others including the probability of grammatical structures. The child's general vocabulary, interests, cultural background and language usage should accord with the reading scheme used for this reason, and many teachers use a language experience method initially, so that the child's own sentences are used for his first reading material.

The child usually first acquires a basic sight vocabulary of single common words. Some children require more rehearsal and repetition than others, possibly due to poor visual memory, lack of interest, or general developmental immaturity. Clay (1979) advocated the importance of writing as an allied motor activity to reinforce visual memory, with reading and writing proceeding together.

Reading schemes are frequently introduced at this stage, although rather than using structured published schemes, some schools prefer to use a 'real books' approach, encouraging children to choose nicely presented books which are of interest to them.

Traditionally phonic teaching starts once a basic sight vocabulary has been acquired, with the systematic establishment of the twenty-six sounds of the alphabet. These are learned until they become automatic. Decoding and encoding two- and three-letter regular words accompanies this. Encoding letter sounds to form words is called blending. Common consonant digraphs are usually introduced next (for example, br, gl, st, etc.). Family word lists may be taught so that the child can see the logic of the regularities. More complex blends are next undertaken, including vowel digraphs (for example, oo, oa, ee, ea, etc.). Finally the final 'magic e' may be taught as a rule; the final e makes the mid-vowel lengthen (for example, hop/ hope)

The successful acquisition of phonic strategies requires fine auditory discrimination and a sensitive ear. It gives readers a means of building and deciphering new words, although they still have to grapple with the daunting irregularities of language. Too heavy a reliance on phonics can hinder fluency and detract from using context and semantic clues when decoding print.

Phonics teaching is also used when a child has a spelling problem. Some children misapply phonic rules, and spell phonically inappropriately; others rely too strongly on visual cues.

REMEDIAL PROVISION

In primary schools

In the last couple of decades, remedial services to provide help for the large numbers of children with literacy difficulties in ordinary primary schools have mushroomed, and most LEAs now provide a specialist service.

The first remedial teachers were appointed in the 1950s, and by the end of the 1960s, 65 per cent of boroughs and 71 per cent of counties maintained a remedial service (Sampson, 1969). The traditional method of remedial teaching was for peripatetic teachers to visit schools on a regular basis and withdraw children from ordinary classes, to teach reading in small groups; lessons tended to be brief, lasting about twenty minutes. Some remedial teachers also taught children for more extensive periods in separate remedial centres, or in classes set up within ordinary schools.

The Bullock Report (DES, 1975), noted that three-quarters of primary and middle schools had withdrawal groups and most teachers listened to the poorest readers about three or four times a week. By the time children were twelve, 63 per cent of schools had withdrawal groups, 17 per cent had remedial classes for some lessons, and 52 per cent had remedial classes or streams for all lessons.

Half the schools had mixed-ability classes for the first year and one-third still had them in the third year. Since some children were often spending long periods in class without the necessary skills for independent learning, the report proposed that remedial help should be closely related to the child's work in class, and all teachers should have responsibility for teaching pupils, whatever their ability.

In secondary schools

Due to the autonomy given to LEAs, there has always been a variation in educational developments across the country, although there have been some general trends since the 1944 Act.

First, in many authorities, comprehensive schools replaced

secondary modern and grammar schools. Whereas children taught in these schools were usually segregated by ability at 11 years old, in comprehensive schools low-ability children are taught in the same school as their peers, although they may be set by ability within different subjects. Over the last two decades there has been a general trend towards mixed-ability teaching where children of all abilities are taught in the same class.

In addition, most secondary schools also developed their own separate remedial departments which offered full-time or part-time help for children with continued learning problems, with basic skills. As will be discussed later, in line with general trends, these departments tend to be extending their role from withdrawal remedial teaching into more general special needs work.

THE CHANGING CONCEPT OF REMEDIAL EDUCATION

A growing uncertainty about the role of remedial teachers developed in the 1970s and, in particular, questions arose concerning which group of children should be taught (Laskier, 1985). Commonly the target group was the children who were deemed to be underachieving or functioning below their potential, whose reading difficulties might be remedied with some intensive teaching on a short-term basis. Children who were considered to be dull or generally slow at learning, who were awaiting assessment, or whose parents had refused a special school place, were often omitted despite the fact that they may have had more profound learning difficulties and, arguably, a greater need for personal tuition. In fact, realistically, many of the so-called underachieving children, because of their circumstances, needed additional teaching help on a long-term basis. A short period of remedial attention was insufficient for them to catch up with their peers.

The aims of remedial teaching were also questioned. The stated intention was usually to raise children's reading ages to the norm. However, by definition, as many children must fall below average as those who fall above, so the objective was ill-considered. More precise teaching objectives in terms of literacy skills were required.

A further problem arose about the remedial teachers' role because of the magnitude of children with reading difficulties. Within the given staffing levels, it was not possible to teach in small groups with sufficient frequency all the children who required help.

In addition, the practice of providing what was essentially a remedial reading service was criticized for neglecting the teaching of other basic skills. Many children have numeracy problems, or more general literacy problems, requiring help with the spoken and written word, and not just the reading of print. The range and diversity of learning difficulties goes well beyond the failure to master basic skills.

Finally, and perhaps most importantly, there was growing criticism about the isolated nature of remedial teaching, which often operated regardless of the curriculum being taught in class. In some cases there was little liaison between the class teacher and the remedial teacher, so not only were skills taught out of the classroom context, but there was little continuity of skill development.

Along with this confusion over philosophy and approach, the effectiveness of traditional remedial teaching was also questioned. There has been considerable evidence of remedial help producing gains in phonic and word recognition skills, but comprehension skills are more difficult to improve. In addition, basic reading skills often regress once remedial help is withdrawn, unless children have attained reading skills equivalent to about a 9½-year level, when they are reading independently.

In 1979, the National Association for Remedial Teachers, reflecting these changing attitudes, endorsed an integrated approach to teaching children with learning difficulties and advocated broadening the role of remedial teachers. It suggested the new role should include supporting and advising colleagues, liaising with support services and parents, as well as teaching and assessing children. It was proposed that support might take the form of helping individual children within the ordinary classroom to do the work set by the teacher, or helping the teacher to adapt the curriculum to the needs of the child, by providing or advising on appropriate materials and resources (Smith, 1985).

Prior to this, the HMI in Scotland produced a progress report on the education of pupils with learning difficulties (Scottish Education Department, 1978), which was even more radical in its recommendations, arguing that up to 50 per cent of the school population experience learning difficulties. Unlike the Warnock Report which came out in the same year, the Scottish report placed the major responsibility for the creation of learning difficulties on the narrow way the curriculum is conceived and presented in schools, and concluded that 'appropriate, rather than remedial, education is required'.

The report recommended the extension of mixed-ability teaching, and the withdrawal of pupils for remedial teaching to be kept to a minimum. It suggested that a member of staff of the same status as head of department in secondary schools, and the deputy head in primary schools, should be responsible for children with learning difficulties.

The role of remedial specialists, in the report's view, should be to foster co-operative teaching and curriculum development. Inservice training for specialists and ordinary teachers was also strongly advocated.

THE WARNOCK REPORT'S CONCEPT OF LEARNING DIFFICULTIES

When the Warnock Committee was set up in 1974, as discussed earlier, there was an unease about the categorization of children by handicap, and an awareness that large numbers of children who received extra teaching help in ordinary school were not protected by legislation, but depended on the goodwill of LEAs.

Perhaps more critically, the philosophy of integration was gaining momentum with a growing belief that all children, despite their disabilities, have a right to be educated with their peers. In consequence, the belief was questioned that separate special schooling necessarily provides compensatory educational experiences. As well as this, the Warnock Committee's proposal for a changed concept of special education was inevitably influenced by trends in curriculum development, the growth of remedial provision and the changing philosophy in mainstream schools.

As mentioned earlier, after taking various surveys and studies into account, the Warnock Report recommended the abolition of the old distinctions between remedial, special and mainstream education. It recommended abandoning the old term 'remedial education', arguing that it is too narrow to cover all the learning difficulties children exhibit, and too optimistic, since the term implies that once the teaching remedy is given the child will catch up with his work. It was recognized that, although some difficulties are short-lived and respond well to intensive help, others require long-term support.

The report also recommended the abolition of the 1944 Education Act's categories of handicap, replacing them with the more general concept of learning difficulties. The concept of special education was broadened dramatically since children with special educational needs were to include the 18 per cent or so of children already receiving remedial help in ordinary schools, as well as the 1–2 per cent of educationally subnormal children in special schools.

Instead of categorizing children according to their deficits in intellectual, physical or sensory ability, the Warnock Report proposed the generic concept of 'special educational need'. It recommended that instead of attempting to isolate the causes of difficulties, the main thrust of assessment should be to describe the child's functioning in terms of a profile strengths and weaknesses, in order to identify the type of curriculum, teaching methods and educational facilities and resources required to meet the child's needs.

Rather than there being two distinct forms of educational provision for children with learning difficulties, special schools for those with more severe difficulties, and remedial help in ordinary schools for those with milder problems, the report recommended a continuum of provision to reflect the wide range of children's educational needs. Since there are not separate groups of children with clearly differentiating characteristics, it was argued that it is essential for provision to be flexible. This would include supporting children within ordinary classrooms; various part-time arrangements between special and ordinary schools; or full-time segregated provision in a special unit or school if the child's needs cannot be met within the mainstream. The report proposed that various forms of integration are possible, depending on the child's particular educational needs.

It was made clear that integration in mainstream schools should occur wherever possible, although the report also acknowledged the value of special schooling for some children, stating:

> In many respects, the special school represents a highly developed technique of positive discrimination. We believe that such discrimination will always be required to give some children with special educational needs the benefit of special facilities, teaching methods or expertise (or a combination of these) which cannot reasonably be provided in ordinary schools.

Degrees of learning difficulty

Although aiming to avoid categorization, the Warnock Report acknowledged that it is often necessary to have terms to indicate degrees of learning difficulty and thus proposed using the terms 'mild', 'moderate', 'severe' and 'specific'. These terms were intended to refer to the child's teaching and curricular requirements, rather than describe his intellectual characteristics or limitations.

SEVERE LEARNING DIFFICULTIES

Children with severe learning difficulties are defined as those who require a developmental curriculum, covering 'a range of educational experience but more selectively and sharply focused on the development of personal autonomy and social skills, with precisely defined objectives and designed for children with severe learning difficulties.' The report noted that these children are likely to require teaching programmes worked out in small steps to enable the acquisition of complex skills.

Since many children with severe learning difficulties are multi-handicapped, and are likely to require additional resources on a long-term basis, a careful assessment of their needs is required in order to decide what precise teaching methods, facilities and resources are required.

MODERATE LEARNING DIFFICULTIES

Children with moderate learning difficulties are defined as those who need a 'modified curriculum similar to that provided in ordinary schools but, while not restricted in its expectations, has objectives more appropriate to children with moderate learning difficulties'. These children may need well-planned individualized learning programmes to develop their abilities, and a more secure, less demanding setting, where they can form good relationships with teachers in smaller teaching groups. It was recommended that the curriculum should be comparable to that received by ordinary children, but the emphasis might need to be different.

MILD LEARNING DIFFICULTIES

The report suggested that children with mild learning difficulties can cope with the normal curriculum and most are likely to manage, with support, in the ordinary classroom. The support might include remedial teaching targeted to improve specific skills or help in understanding complex concepts. Additional resources might also be required, such as ancillary help, small teaching groups, or special aids and classroom facilities, depending on the individual child's specific needs. Thus children with mild learning difficulties might well require 'mainstream teaching, with support'.

SPECIFIC LEARNING DIFFICULTIES

The Warnock Report proposed that it would be useful to distinguish an additional group of children, those with specific learning difficulties, who may have learning problems in just one or a few selected areas of the curriculum. It may be, for example, that they have reading and spelling difficulties, but in other curricular areas they have no problems. These children may also require additional mainstream support or special facilities and resources, if they are to progress in school.

As noted earlier, by proposing that children with mild learning difficulties have some form of special educational need, the whole spectrum of special education was expanded. Although these children had frequently received remedial help, it had not been mandatory for the local authority to provide it.

The Warnock Report's distinction of a further group with specific learning difficulties is somewhat contentious as it carries with it some of the concerns about the concept of dyslexia. It is unclear why this group should be distinguished from those with mild or moderate difficulties, given the emphasis on meeting needs via the curriculum.

The dyslexia debate

According to the British Dyslexia Association's publications, 'dyslexia is a collection of specific learning difficulties which interfere with the acquisition of literacy and associated symbolic language skills including reading, writing, spelling and arithmetic'. It is stated that children may have an early delay in speech and language development, which is followed by a delay in learning to read and relative difficulty in spelling and writing. Characteristically, children may show a marked underachievement in one or more of these areas. given their age, general ability and competence in other areas; 'alerting signs' may include great problems with some of the following:

- skills requiring sequential or spatial ordering of letters or numbers (for example, they may muddle months of the year, or reverse numbers or letters);
- rote or short-term memory for letters and number (for example, they may have problems with remembering their tables, etc.);
- laterality (for example, knowing their right from left, body awareness and direction);
- sound blending;
- systematic visual scanning.

The controversy over dyslexia has revolved around whether or not there are a distinguishable group of children failing in reading, writing, spelling or arithmetic, who require special educational resources different from what is usually available in schools.

Hinshelwood (1917) originally proposed that some children have a congenital 'word blindness' present from birth. Later, Critchley (1970) referred to children with specific reading difficulties as 'dyslexic', defining this as: 'a disorder of children, who despite conventional classroom experience, fail to attain the language skills of reading, writing and spelling commensurate with their intellectual abilities'.

However, both the British Medical Association and the government committee under Tizard (DES, 1972) rejected the term 'dyslexia' because of its medical connotations, and suggest that the term 'specific learning difficulties' should be used instead.

In the United States, special provision for 'learning disabled' children has been available since 1969. In 1968, the National Advisory Committee on Handicapped Children defined learning disabled children as those:

> who exhibit a disorder in one or more of the basic psychological processes involved in understanding or in using spoken or written language. These may by manifested in disorders of listening, thinking, talking, reading, writing, spelling, or arithmetic. They include conditions which have been referred to as perceptual handicaps, brain injury, minimal brain dysfunction, dyslexia, developmental aphasia, etc. They do not include learning problems which are due primarily to visual, hearing, or motor handicaps, to mental retardation, emotional disturbance, or to environmental disadvantage.

The report also noted that such children display uneven development on a profile of tests, so that they have difficulty in specific skills. They are not generally slow in development but have learning problems in certain selective areas. It is usually assumed that these specific learning difficulties have a neurological basis, rather than resulting from adverse environmental circumstance, emotional problems, or physical or sensory disorders. The controversy over the United States definition has revolved around four main issues.

First, despite early work by Strauss and Lehtinen (1947), which suggested that some specific learning difficulties may result from neurological impairment or 'minimal brain damage', there is no sound physiological evidence to back this up. Most neurological investigations are negative, despite the fact that children may show symptoms similar to known brain-injured children. Thus in the absence of objective evidence, claims of neurological disorder are hypothetical.

Secondly, many people feel that in excluding, by definition, socially disadvantaged children from this group, special resources and provision could be claimed selectively for middle-class children. It would be unfair for this group, who are already advantaged in many respects, to receive special privileges. It is also illogical to suggest that children who are environmentally deprived cannot also have specific difficulties.

Thirdly, the notion of dyslexia relies on an outmoded concept of intelligence as a unitary mental quality, whereas intelligence is now conceived to be a range of intellectual skills and abilities, with all children having a variety of strengths and weaknesses.

Fourthly, it has been pointed out that even if there is known neurological damage, the education and remedial help given would be tailored to the individual child in the same way as for any child with learning difficulties. There is no reason to distinguish two groups of children as far as remediation is concerned.

Much of the above debate which has surrounded the notion of dyslexia has been diffused by the way the Warnock Report acknowledged that some children have specific learning difficulties in one area of the curriculum, without making assumptions about the reasons for this, or excluding any particular groups of children. By concentrating on a thorough assessment of the child's educational needs, much of the controversy is overcome. If certain children have significant learning difficulties so that they require special resources, then they too have special needs.

Comments on Warnock's concept of learning difficulties

The Warnock Report proposed a radically changed philosophy regarding children with learning difficulties. The principle of categorizing children in order to provide a special school environment to compensate for their handicaps and disadvantages, established by the 1944 Act, was replaced by the principle of integration and, with it, a continuum of provision in various settings to meet children's special needs.

Booth (1985) pointed out, however, that despite its good intentions, the report replaced one form of categorization by another. Having abandoned the terms educationally subnormal, moderate and severe, it instated similar terms, mild, moderate, severe and specific learning difficulties. Although the aim was to classify purely in terms of the type of curriculum required, in practice, it is presumably the learning characteristics of the child which would lead to recommendations for a certain type of curriculum.

Moreover, Warnock's definitions verge on circularity. For example, a child is said to have moderate learning difficulties if he requires a modified curriculum; but it is unclear how this is determined without referring back to his moderate learning difficulties.

Booth also pointed out the confusion in the report, where the statutory distinction between handicapped and non-handicapped is abolished, but at the same time expectations are raised about the existence of large numbers of pupils with learning difficulties. Teachers are urged to identify problems at an early stage with an expectation that in every hundred children approximately twenty will have special needs, and one or two whose needs cannot satisfactorily be met within the resources generally available will require a multi-professional assessment.

In addition, the way the Warnock Report used surveys of teacher opinion to argue the case for a broadened concept of special education has also been criticized. Although the surveys may represent a consensus of professional opinion, they are highly subjective in nature and the figure of 20 per cent has since gained a dubious respectability. Galloway and Goodwin (1987) argued that it is in fact a statistical artefact, based on what is essentially a political decision, reflecting the current provision of special and remedial education. The danger is that by providing teachers with an expectation that, by some inherent means, one child in five is likely to have learning difficulties at some stage in their schooling, schools are encouraged to identify large numbers of pupils who are likely to require some form of distinctive provision, rather than adapt their curricula to meet the needs of children. This can lead to a potentially unhelpful shift in responsibility away from ordinary schools. Some would argue that the report did not sufficiently stress that learning difficulties are relative to the context in which they occur; there is possibly as much a need to assess the school's ability to adapt the curriculum as there is to assess the child's functioning.

LEARNING DIFFICULTIES AND THE 1981 EDUCATION ACT

The 1981 Education Act, which followed in the wake of the Warnock Report, legislated for children with special educational needs and incorporated much of the Warnock philosophy. It was, however, in many ways much more limited and cautious. It backtracked from the broad definition of special educational needs being attributed to one child in five, presumably because of resource and financial implications.

By means of formal statementing procedures, as noted in Chapter 1, the Act is concerned to protect the rights of the smaller group of children identified by the Warnock Report, those with severe or complex learning difficulties who require additional provision to that normally provided in ordinary school. Since remedial support is generally part of the normal provision in schools, the circulars to the 1981 Act made it clear that it was not envisaged that children with mild learning difficulties would normally require a formal statement of their needs. A formal multiprofessional assessment is only required where learning difficulties are complex or severe.

Under the Act, definitions of the term 'special educational needs' hinges on the question of whether special provision is required for the child's learning difficulties; and to have learning difficulties they must be significantly greater than those of other children of the same age, thus introducing some notion of normative assessment. The Act makes no reference to Warnock's distinctions between different degrees of difficulty (mild, moderate and severe), and thus, although these terms have come into popular usage, they are not legal terms.

The Act specifically excluded from its definition of learning difficulties children whose problems arise primarily from the fact that the language spoken in the home is different from the language spoken in school. Such difficulties are not conceived to be special needs under the Act.

Although it is made clear that children with special needs should be taught in the ordinary school whenever possible, various exemptions are established; placement decisions must take into account whether the ordinary school can provide an appropriate curriculum, whether other children in the class will be adversely affected and whether it is an 'efficient use of resources'.

Comments

Further appraisal of the Act can be found in Chapter 9, but a few points are worth raising here. Although the 1981 Act has reformed the existing legislation relating to children with special needs, it creates new problems. The Act puts forward in its definition of learning difficulties various confusing messages. Professionals are asked, at the same time, to compare children with norms for their age, to look at available provision and also to consider the likely effects on the education of classmates within the same class. There may well be conflicting interests for each of these groups, and, in effect, the LEAs are given loopholes to avoid costly or unpopular placement decisions. It is possible to provide what they wish, and maintain the status quo. Thus although the principle of integration seems to be fundamental, and legislation states that children with learning difficulties, where possible, should be taught with their ordinary peers, provisos are built in to ensure that their classmates are not disadvantaged and that resources are managed efficiently.

Moreover, the emphasis on assessing the individual child may be misplaced. As Booth (1985) pointed out, to say that a child has learning difficulties if the school is ill-equipped, 'is stretching ordinary language considerably'.

DEVELOPMENTS SINCE THE 1981 ACT

Contemporary approaches to the assessment of learning difficulties

Cameron, Owen and Tee (1986) claimed that the 1981 Education Act has increased the urgent need to develop alternative assessment procedures, since a formal assessment is intended to be a means of giving a guide to the child's future education, and a basis against which to monitor progress, rather than as an end in itself. Curriculum–related assessment, which describes what pupils can do in relation to an agreed list of curriculum objectives, has thus to some extent taken over from the psychometric testing described earlier. It can provide continuous measures of performance, and be part of a teacher's usual record-keeping. Thus curriculum planning, teaching and assessment can be closely linked. It also means that assessment can be done by the teacher, who knows what information will be useful, rather than requiring the aid of outside specialists.

This type of assessment is not interested in measuring hypothetical constructs such as intelligence or personality, but aims to assess what the pupil has learned. Methods of assessment could include careful observations, checklists, or tests designed to sample skills, or find out how quickly children can acquire new ones.

Psychometric assessment can still have its place depending on what information is required. If the aim is to compare the child's ability on a certain test to an average population, or compare standards across schools, then they may also have a useful function. It is also possible to devise criterion-based tests which are standardized. This is one of the new proposals on assessment coming from the 1988 Education Act discussed in Chapter 9.

For children with complex or severe learning difficulties, the expertise of outside specialists may be required in assessing needs. Warnock's model of assessment, outlined in Chapter 1, suggested how the teacher should be the first person to identify difficulties, collect observations and make some initial assessment; but specialists within and outside school may be approached in due course, should concerns continue.

Supporting children in mainstream schools

Following the 1981 Act, in view of the new responsibility for schools in retaining children with learning difficulties wherever possible, the DES commissioned two major research studies to examine support in ordinary schools, and look at the implementation of the Act across LEAs. Both were completed by 1986.

The first study, conducted by the NFER, looked at ways of supporting ordinary schools in their task of meeting children's special educational needs (Moses, Hegarty and Jowett, 1987). Three aspects were looked at: outside support services, link arrangements with special schools and in-service training.

The study found that there was a general trend for schools to replace the concept of remedial education with support. Moreover, the traditional concern with reading problems has been extended to include a wider range of learning difficulties, and help for pupils was more likely to be given within the classroom than on a withdrawal basis. Services were now extending their help to all age groups, although concentration was still at the primary stage. Screening was the basis for selection in three-quarters of the LEAs. Support services aimed to work with teachers as well as pupils, and only a few were aiming to teach the 20 per cent who notionally have special needs. It was also found that the size of services varied considerably between authorities; nearly one-third had fewer than ten support teachers, whilst more than one in six had over fifty.

Three-quarters of the ordinary schools who responded to the survey had a link with special schools. In some schools this was a major form of support, and meant interchange of staff, the sharing of resources and a movement of pupils between schools. About one-third of special schools had staff going out to ordinary schools each week, to teach mixed classes of mainstream and special school children, advise mainstream colleagues and work with pupils from the special school. It was more common for pupils to move out of the special school; the majority did so as a group, for short periods each week.

All the LEAs in the study had learning and hearing-impaired services supporting mainstream schools; and two-thirds also had specialist support services for visually impaired pupils in ordinary schools.

The study found enormous variation in the structure and staffing of the support services and link arrangements; in fact Hegarty (1988) commented that extreme diversity was the abiding impression. Although this can lead to innovation, it was noted that the lack of a common framework can be arbitrary and make accountability difficult. It also means that staff can waste their efforts working out procedures and setting up structures rather than creating the provision.

The second research study, conducted by the London University Institute of Education (Gipps, Gross and Goldstein, 1987), looked particularly at changes in policy and practice in special education, particularly regarding the 18 per cent of children with special needs in ordinary schools. It was found that the economic squeeze had not adversely affected the support services generally: 'were it not for the changing climate towards special needs brought about by the Warnock report, remedial support services would, we suspect, have remained low status and been far more vulnerable'. It was found that nearly half the teachers questioned were dissatisfied with the form of service they now received, and many still needed to be persuaded about the changed roles.

Comments

These and other studies are helpful in giving feedback about changing attitudes and practices. If resources are to be decentralized for children with learning difficulties, then it is important that teachers in ordinary schools, who may presently lack expertise and confidence, receive the best form of support possible, since their responsibility for teaching pupils with special needs is increasing.

Changes in remedial methods rely on a lot of assumptions: for example, that the children with learning difficulties will get sufficient support in the mainstream class so that they are not merely contained, but make progress; also, that the ordinary curriculum, in its content and methods, is suitable.

Furthermore, training is required for both ordinary and support teachers if the changed role is to be fruitful; the skills of support and consultancy are different from the skills of small group teaching, and support teachers who have only expertise in reading may require additional training. Clearly, much understanding and negotiation is required for the substantial changes in role and responsibility.

Perhaps most important, the shift in role means that class and subject teachers are now clearly acknowledged to have prime responsibility for teaching children in their classes with learning difficulties, a responsibility which was in some ways blurred before.

However, although for some ordinary school teachers this is to be welcomed, others feel it is one more responsibility in a very demanding job, and wonder if it implies a loss of resources. Gipps, Gross and Goldstein (1987) found that most teachers felt that the best way to help children with special needs was to provide smaller classes; withdrawal help was the next most popular choice and in-service training was least popular.

Despite these objections, a likely result of the change in role is that it will demystify the notion that teaching children with learning difficulties requires some specialism beyond an ordinary class teacher's expertise. Classroom teachers will be encouraged to look at the suitability of the curriculum for all members of the class, and make the necessary adaptations for individual needs. Moreover, as Garnett (1988) pointed out, 'changing to the practice of supporting mainstream teachers within the class means the school is redefining the role of its remedial/special education teachers from working separately within a special or withdrawal group to working in partnership'.

PARENTAL INVOLVEMENT IN LEARNING

Finally, mention must be made of the importance of parental involvement in their child's learning.

Topping (1986) noted that there has been a lot of research involving parents hearing children read, and it is possible to conclude that a major factor in reading development is whether parents hear children read at home. Hewison and Tizard (1980), for example, compared reading progress using two programmes and a control group, i.e., parental involvement, help from an expert remedial teacher, and no intervention. The group which involved parents did significantly better than the group given extra help by a specialist teacher, and this result was maintained four years later.

Tizard, Schofield and Hewison (1982), studying inner-city multiracial schools, also revealed the effectiveness of parental involvement in learning, even with the most disadvantaged families. Collaboration with parents was found to be more effective for improving reading skills than even highly competent specialist teachers, and this was particularly the case at the time when children were beginning to fail at reading at the end of the infant school. Even with parents who could not read English, or in a few cases could not read at all, children made significant progress. Parents were found to value literacy as well as the contact with class teachers.

Paired reading schemes, discussed in Chapter 7, are also of proven effectiveness, although Topping concluded that long-term follow up is rare. Parents have also been trained to use other specialist techniques effectively, such as precision teaching and direct instruction, which are described in Chapter 7. Topping found in his literature review that there has been little systematic research of parental involvement in other school subjects.

Despite the findings of research about the effectiveness of parental involvement, Pugh (1981) found that although many schools now attempt to involve parents in supporting their aims, and most had open days and fund-raising events, few had open access to parents or were keen to collaborate with them in joint dialogue. If the partnership with parents advocated by the Warnock Report is to have meaning, then parents need to be involved with children's education to a greater extent. Wolfendale (1983) explored this further and set out various ways in which this can be accomplished.

3

Why do learning difficulties occur?

OVERVIEW

This chapter will consider some of the major factors which are thought to give rise to learning difficulties, with the main emphasis on the environmental influences on learning, including social class, home, neighbourhood and school factors. There will also be some consideration of individual child variables and task characteristics, which in turn raises questions about the nature of school knowledge and its assessment. The next chapter describes various physical and sensory disabilities which may give rise to learning difficulties. Although emotional and behavioural difficulties are treated separately in Chapter 5, this chapter is also relevant to the discussion.

INTRODUCTION

In attempting to understand why children experience learning difficulties, a distinction is usually made between organic and environmental influences; that is, factors arising from within the child himself, as opposed to those which are imposed upon him from his social environment. As a crude generalization, children with mild and moderate learning difficulties are usually thought to have predominately environmental causes for their difficulties. Whereas children with severe learning difficulties are more likely to have received neurological damage to the central nervous system during the time of brain formation, in the neonatal period or in early infancy, or to have genetic or chromosomal anomalies which adversely affect brain functioning. Craft *et al.* (1985) claim that recent surveys in Western countries show clearly that 'inheritance of recessive genes and chromosomal anomalies cause most of the severe handicaps, with environmental deprivation playing a major part in the causation of milder handicap'.

With the new conceptualization of learning difficulties mentioned in the previous chapter, this distinction is now less meaningful to educationalists. To state that a child has moderate or severe learning difficulties is to say something about the type of curriculum he requires, and something about what the ordinary school is unable to provide. A child with a severe physical handicap may only have mild learning difficulties (or none at all), for instance, if his brain functioning is unaffected, and the necessary adaptations to the school building are available. Thus the environment within which the child learns and develops will have an important effect on the extent to which disorders become handicapping. The physical environment (such as the availability of special equipment); the amount of additional resources (such as auxiliary helpers); as well as the attitudes and behaviour of other children, teachers, family members and society at large, may intensify or diminish the handicapping effects of disabilities. Thus theories which explain learning difficulties solely in terms of the psychopathology of the child, or deficits in the family or school, are in some ways conceptually naive. It is meaningless to consider the child in isolation from his social context, or to consider his learning difficulties in isolation from the demands of the task.

Learning is probably best conceived as an interactional process; the child is born with a capacity to learn which is to some extent determined by organic factors, but the quality of his experiences throughout life will in great measure determine what skills, attitudes and values he learns, and how he subsequently behaves. Learning difficulties may stem from a variety of sources, and frequently result from a combination of factors which interact. Although it may be possible to suggest why problems occur, and generalize about groups, it is usually not possible to be certain of the origin of difficulties in individual cases.

THEORIES TO EXPLAIN LEARNING DIFFICULTIES

Our understanding of the importance of various influences on pupil progress has radically altered over the years. In the 1930s and 1940s, low academic achievement was largely thought to result from biological determinants which made up the child's 'innate capacity', and certain groups of children were considered to be genetically inferior. The educational tripartite system, with its grammar, secondary modern and technical schools, was regarded as providing the variety of curricula suitable for children with differing abilities.

Sociological studies in the 1950s and 1960s highlighted the effects of the social and cultural environment on human abilities. Many surveys and studies looked at the social differences between people, and the stratification of society was seen as a crucial factor affecting children's life chances, and more pertinently, as the main cause of learning failure. Various studies suggested that children from certain social groups were more likely to be disadvantaged by their life experiences. The comprehensive school system was viewed as a way of redressing the balance, by attempting to give all children similar educational chances, rather than determining their future academic aspirations at the age of eleven. Various sorts of deprivation – cultural, social, emotional, and linguistic – were regarded as the root of failure. Compensatory education, and the availability of good nursery provision, were heralded as educational remedies for social disadvantage.

Attacks were made on this position in the late 1960s. Labov (1970), for example, argued against the notion of cultural deprivation, pointing out that linguistic differences in various minority social groups are not deficits. He pointed out that we can become preoccupied with the notion of language fluency and middle-class norms of standard English, whilst ignoring the effectiveness and complex structure of other language codes. The linguistic and cultural mismatch between home and school was also emphasized, as well as the demoralizing effect for some children of devaluing their culture.

In the 1970s, research into the factors influencing learning shifted from the family and neighbourhood to the school. Various studies (such as Power, Benn and Morris, 1967; Reynolds, 1976; Reynolds and Murgatroyd, 1977; and Rutter *et al.*, 1979), suggested that schools have a considerable influence on children's learning and behaviour and, what is more, these factors may be more amenable to change than home and community variables.

An alternative theory around this time stressed the importance of within-child factors; it was argued that some children with learning difficulties have cognitive deficits or problems with the cognitive processes thought to be necessary for efficient learning. Some went further to propose the notion of minimal brain dysfunction to account for intellectual difficulties which do not appear to arise from environmental disadvantage or from poor teaching.

Others have analysed the complexities of the learning task, for example the cognitive skills involved in language and number work, to see what abilities are required, and what teaching strategies best promote learning. A different approach has been to specify exactly what the pupil has to learn, in behavioural terms, rather than seeking underlying cognitive abilities. The emphasis, as far as educationalists are concerned, has shifted from the learner to the teacher, and from the home to the school environment. If a learner is having difficulties, then the teacher is being unsuccessful in his or her objectives, and the responsibility lies with him or her to help the learner achieve mastery. By conceiving learning difficulties in this way, the teacher's role becomes more clear.

An alternative view has questioned assumptions made about the nature of knowledge and suggested that learning difficulties are created by our conceptualization of school knowledge, rather than arising from the child's personal deficiencies. The problem lies with inappropriate curricula and invalid assessment procedures.

Finally, it must be mentioned that an emphasis on investigating the causes of learning difficulties has become relatively unpopular in recent years. The Warnock Report pointed out that in order to determine a child's special educational needs it is of prime importance to describe clearly what the child can do now, and what his strengths and weaknesses are, before establishing educational long-term aims and short-term goals. Past history, including considerations of difficult family circumstances, is only of incidental interest in so far as it affects the pupil's current needs. Under the 1981 Education Act, professionals are asked to make a clear assessment of the child's present functioning, and avoid hypothetical explanations about the causes of his learning difficulties.

There is much to be said in favour of this viewpoint, and it may be true that attempts to trace causative explanations for a child's problems are sometimes difficult to justify. We should concentrate on factors which are amenable to change. A careful analysis of the influential factors in the learning situation and an analysis of the task to be taught are usually much more appropriate and helpful for programme planning.

Nevertheless, there are questions to be answered about why some groups of children seem more likely to have learning problems than others. If we are to make any substantial progress in the field of special education it may be important to understand more broadly the various factors which can give rise to learning difficulties and school failure.

SOCIAL AND ENVIRONMENTAL FACTORS

As noted earlier, learning does not occur in a vacuum, and the context in which a child grows and develops will play a critical part in determining his ability to learn. In early life, the family and neighbourhood will play a central part in affecting a child's development, but the school will also be a significant influence as the child grows older. Much research has been conducted investigating environmental factors which enhance or hinder children's development, and the relationship between academic success and social factors has been firmly established.

Family and neighbourhood variables

Social and economic factors have long been central issues in discussing a child's educational performance and adjustment, since variations in material circumstances, parental life style, attitudes and values, fundamentally affect the child's learning achievement.

SOCIAL DISADVANTAGE

The concept of social disadvantage has often been used to explain why some children fail at school. A common factor with large proportions of children with special needs is that they come from socially disadvantaged homes. Many research studies have revealed that social disadvantage, behavioural difficulties, emotional disturbance, as well as mild and moderate learning difficulties, frequently occur together.

Research also suggests there is a close relationship between social disadvantage factors and the socioeconomic status of social groups, or social class. Social-class membership is most frequently defined in terms of the occupational status of the father, as this generally determines the family's income. The level of income will determine the type of house and neighbourhood the family lives in, and income will in turn be associated with standards of health, hygiene and nutrition. The classification by occupation is also linked to the attitudes and aspirations that parents have for their children, including their attitudes towards education.

Like any classification system, social class uses generalizations which can be misleading as far as individuals are concerned; nevertheless, in their national survey, Davie, Butler and Goldstein (1972) stated:

> social class is a convenient measure of many aspects of the child's environment, which will shape the way he develops . . . The father's occupation is therefore the most convenient consideration in determining social class membership and it has been found that the father's occupation correlates highly with all other factors, such as educational attainment, general health, housing standards, etc

The most frequently quoted social classification system is that used by the Registrar General for census purposes, with five basic groups, as shown in Table 3.1.

Table 3.1 Social class membership

Social Class	Occupation	%
1	Professional	5
2	Intermediate professional	14
3a	Skilled non-manual	10
3b	Skilled manual	44
4	Semi-skilled	17
5	Unskilled	6
No male head of household		3

Source: Davie, Butler and Goldstein, 1972.

Davie, Butler and Goldstein's survey of children's development looked closely at social variables and found that the proportion of children needing special education because of their intellectual difficulties was about seven times higher for children from social class 5 than social class 1, and the incidence of physical, sensory and behavioural difficulties was also much higher for the children in the lowest social groups. On teachers' ratings approximately 6 per cent of social class 1 children showed 'below average awareness of the world around them', compared to 50 per cent from social class 5. Approximately 12 per cent of social class 1 children had poor problem-arithmetic scores, compared to 40 per cent from social class 5. Reading test scores also showed wide differences; only 8 per cent of social class 1 children had poor test scores, compared to 50 per cent from social class 5.

Douglas, Ross and Simpson (1968) had similar findings for secondary children, suggesting that social and cultural differences continue to influence achievement in older children. In this study, the most significant factor was parental interest and aspirations for their child's education. It was found that children from lower-income families tended to leave school earlier, have fewer qualifications, and rarely go on to further education. Recent evidence at university level suggests that the trend continues at this stage of education. The ratio of middle- to working-class children in university in 1980 was about 11:1, and despite changes in the structure of education, this has remained static since 1944 and there is little evidence of an upturn in the figures (Halsey, Heath and Ridge, 1980).

Children who leave education young, tend to marry at an early age, and have low career prospects. They often have their own families young, and there is a tendency to have more children. Children of working-class parents, therefore, frequently perpetuate their own disadvantaged backgrounds.

Ethnic minority children are particularly disadvantaged in social and economic terms. The Swann Report (DES, 1985) states that they have an additional deprivation in the areas of housing and unemployment, as a result of racial discrimination and prejudice. This leads to an 'extra element of underachievement'. Certain cultural groups in Britain seem to be seriously underachieving, West Indian and Bangladeshi children in particular, whereas Asians show an average pattern of achievement. Mutual support and high aspirations amongst Asian families and communities are thought to be one reason for this.

FACTORS ASSOCIATED WITH SOCIAL DISADVANTAGE
The following factors associated with social disadvantage rarely occur in isolation as they tend to be interrelated. For example, if children are living in a very low income family it is likely that their housing will be poor and their general level of health and nutrition may be affected.

Income and poverty Poverty is a relative term, and is usually defined by the amount of money required to supply a family's basic needs and the income the family actually obtains. Until recent changes in the law, poverty was most frequently defined in relation to the person being at or below the supplementary benefit level. The state used to decide on the minimum that a family could be expected to live on and would supplement incomes accordingly; this minimum usually sets the poverty line.

Using this definition of poverty, according to 1985 statistics quoted in Selfe (1987), the following groups are usually most vulnerable:

(a) The unemployed (3.1 million, including 1 million long-term);

(b) The low paid (prior to 1988 this was usually defined as those earning less than two-thirds of the national average wage. 1985 figures suggest this amounted to about 1:10 males and 4:10 females);

(c) The elderly (3 million people claimed supplementary benefits);

(d) One-parent families (12.5 per cent of families);

(e) The sick and disabled (5.5 million people were estimated to qualify for benefits).

It can readily be seen that many children are members of low income families and this will affect them not only in material ways, standards of health, nutrition, housing, neighbourhood, etc., but, less obviously, in the educational experiences parents can offer their children and the families' attitudes towards education and their aspirations for them.

Poor housing Poor housing and overcrowding are frequently mentioned as a contributory cause of poor school attainments. A child from a poor home may well have less space for exploration and play, and he is unlikely to have a quiet place to read or do homework. Davie, Butler and Goldstein (1972) found that approximately 10 per cent of their sample were living in overcrowded conditions, and the figure was much higher in Scotland. At this time, 7 per cent of children did not have the full use of hot water, a bath, or inside lavatory; 4 per cent had no garden or back-yard for play.

Wedge and Prosser (1973) explained how the general amenities of the home and its immediate neighbourhood can detrimentally affect children. A dearth of space and amenities places a strain on other members of the family and can lead to frustrations and stress. Many disadvantaged children share a bed with the consequent problem of disturbed sleep, and bedwetting can affect the hygiene and social acceptability of those sharing the same bed. The smelly, dirty child may be shunned by others, and this can affect his attitude to school, self-respect and concentration.

Davie, Butler and Goldstein conclude in their study: 'quite apart from any readily measurable effects in terms of children's school attainments or adjustment, the impact of a lack of space upon the quality of life must surely call for strenuous efforts to remedy the present situation'.

Health The lowest social group still have poorer general health, despite the facilities of the national health service. Poor health contributes to learning difficulties since the child is likely to miss time from school, and he may be more apathetic and less able to absorb information when present.

From the outset of life, the chances of a baby's survival vary according to the occupational level of the parents. Davie, Butler and Goldstein (1972) showed that despite the fact that children from lower social groups lost more days off schooling, parents in social class 5 used preventive health facilities, such as child clinics and school dentists, less often than other parents.

The Black Report (DHSS, 1980), pointed out major inequalities in the health services. There are regional differences in infant mortality which show that poorer industrial areas have higher levels of mortality, and this remains greatest amongst unskilled manual workers. Unskilled workers are also statistically more likely to suffer injury or death in the course of their work with obvious consequences to their family and children. Their life expectancy is also shorter. In poorer industrial regions with higher, younger populations and where infant mortality and birth rates are relatively high, the number of general practitioners and community health workers is relatively low.

Single-parent families and low income Although being brought up by a single parent is not disadvantageous in itself, very often the family lives in poverty, as usually the breadwinner is a low-earning mother. Approximately half the total number of single-parent families live below the poverty line. The number of single-parent families has grown rapidly from approximately 9.3 per cent of families in 1965, to 12.5 per cent in 1985.

Unemployment Low-income, unskilled workers are far more vulnerable to unemployment and redundancies. The demoralizing effects of unemployment are well known; often the toll is paid in terms of confidence and the ability to make plans for the future. Children from unemployed or low-income families tend to have lower personal aspirations and leave school early rather than go on to further education.

Child-rearing practices Many studies in the 1960s and 1970s looked at different styles of parenting to see what effect they have on the child's development. Child-rearing practices vary between families of different social background, and these practices have been held partially responsible for differences in school performance between children (such as Newson and Newson, 1963, 1977; Chazan, Laing and Jackson, 1971).

Of particular significance seemed to be the way that parents use language when speaking to their children. The Newsons found that middle-class mothers tended to discuss issues and they placed more emphasis on the use of reasoning when disciplining their children, which in turn taught the children techniques of self-justification and self-expression which are useful in school. Wooton (1974) also found that middle-class parents were more likely to seize opportunities to extend their children's comments and questions, which result in the children acquiring a more elaborated language code.

The Newsons also reported that working-class parents in their study were often less knowledgable about how to pursue their children's interests and provide them with educational stimulation; they also comment that such parents were frequently hampered from doing so by financial restrictions. Tizard (1975) showed that middle-class parents were more aware that their own activities have educational significance for the child; working-class parents often felt that there was little that they could do to modify their child's development, and they were considered to be generally more fatalistic and defeatist in attitude towards their child's future scholastic performance. Chazan, Laing and Jackson (1971) found there were considerable social differences in the preparedness of children for school, teachers more frequently reporting children from the poorest homes to be least prepared.

Family size and birth order The size of families and birth order of children may also be significant factors in learning failure. Davie, Butler and Goldstein's study revealed that twice as many social class 5 families have more than four children, compared to classes 1 and 2. The study also showed that the eldest children usually have higher reading attainments. Douglas (1968), similarly found that vocabulary scores of children fall as a function of family size. Last-born children in large families are most disadvantaged.

Motivation, attitudes and emotional factors   Social disadvantage is not just a question of material disadvantage; it also can affect the child's emotional well-being and self-regard. Children quickly learn to assess their parents' social status, and comparisons are made on the basis of material possessions and academic achievements. Both children and adults can get caught up in comparisons of achievement and status; feelings of inadequacy and inferiority may result, and can be deeply embedded. It has been argued that these feelings can themselves cause a person to act in an incompetent and ineffectual manner, causing a descending spiral of negative self-regard and inadequate action. Holt (1969) argued that children who fail to learn easily become less confident and less adventurous in problem-solving to avoid the risk of getting the wrong answer, with the result that they tend to withdraw into themselves. Sennet and Cobb (1976) also argue that the effects of deprivation are as much a question of emotional well-being as of material and physical wealth, and this affects learning competence.

Emotional and behavioural difficulties will be discussed in more detail in Chapter 5.

Linguistic and cultural differences

Various explanatory hypotheses other than socio-economic status factors have been suggested to account for the learning difficulties experienced by many children from minority groups. These include notions of language proficiency and linguistic or cultural mismatch between home and school. However, as Cummins (1984) points out, 'we are still a considerable distance from a comprehensive theory of minority student underachievement because the interactions among social, educational, psychological and linguistic factors remain to be specified'.

The debate over whether ethnic-minority and working-class children have linguistic deficits or differences arose in the 1960s when Bernstein proposed that there are elaborated and restricted codes of language related to social-class membership. Bernstein characterized these in terms of differences in grammatical features, and suggested that there are essential differences between the codes, with the elaborated code being more explicit, and having its meanings expanded so that the listener can understand what is said, even if he does not share the same experience. Bernstein claimed that such differences in language might explain why working-class children achieve less well, since school predominantly uses the elaborated code and values more highly. Working-class children thus may have 'culturally induced backwardness' which is transmitted through the implications of the language process. Bernstein later modified his theory claiming he was referring to linguistic performance, not underlying competence, and that working-class speech is linguistically different, not deficient.

However, Labov (1970), in the United States, took issue with Bernstein, arguing that nonstandard forms of English have their own grammar, and are not substandard. He demonstrated that various dialects can be as abstract, logical and representational as standard English, and criticized middle-class linguistic codes for their verbose and redundant style. In his view no dialect is superior to another, and both should be equally acceptable in schools.

The debate about the effect of linguistic and cultural differences on pupil performance is even more pertinent when English is the child's second language. Although ethnic-minority children are unlikely to perform as well in English if it is their second language and their exposure to English has been minimal, Cummins maintains that bilingualism is often scapegoated for problems which are rooted more deeply in the social and educational conditions under which the children acquire their two languages. There is some evidence that bilingualism, in fact, can give cognitive advantages, by sensitizing children to differences in meaning as well as tuning them to finer auditory perception skills. Cummins, analysing research data from many countries, considers that cultural mismatch may be a more significant contributor to minority-pupil underachievement in many cases. He hypothesizes that children's cognitive and academic development is a direct function of their interaction with adults both in the home and at school, and whatever can be done to validate and strengthen this process of cultural transmission is likely to contribute to children's overall personal and intellectual growth. It is important that the child does not become alienated from his own culture, and that his culture is valued by society at large. It is important that the child is not underestimated and subtly devalued, and that speaking a different language is not perceived to be a 'problem': 'no child should be expected to cast off the language and culture of the home as he crosses the school threshold, and the curriculum should reflect those of his life' (Bullock Report, DES, 1975).

It would appear that the underachievement of minority children is more complex than mere lack of English fluency, and socio-political factors must be evoked for a more complete explanation.

SCHOOL FACTORS

Early research in Britain and the United States (for example, Coleman, 1966; Jencks, 1972) showed consistently that a pupil's intelligence, family and community background are highly influential variables for both learning and behaviour, and the quality of school experience has relatively little effect. School resources were shown to be very poor predictors of pupil performance, as compared to the socio-economic status of parents. Schools were widely regarded at the time as ineffectual in compensating for social inequalities.

However, Rutter and Madge (1976) suggested that the measures of the quality of schooling may be at fault; rather than assessing resources, other aspects of the school environment may be influential. More recently, factors such as school organization, teacher expectations and general 'school ethos' have been shown to be important variables. Many learning difficulties are probably the direct result of factors such as school absence and poor teaching, which fails to take account of the range of children's skills and abilities. There are also questions about the appropriateness of the curriculum for many children, and whether the way schools are organized helps to promote learning. Some of these factors have been closely scrutinized by research, but as yet others remain pure speculation. Because of the complexity of large schools, it is difficult to control variables, and conduct satisfactory research.

The impact of school factors on pupil behaviour is also discussed in Chapter 5.

Teacher Expectations

Children acquire feelings of self-worth and form expectations about their own possibilities from the way others treat them. Parents, being usually the most significant people in their early lives, thus have a central role in creating the child's views of himself and the world at large. Once the child starts school, for some this will be as young as 3, the school starts to play a highly significant role.

Teachers' expectations and attitudes are another important factor in academic performance. Pidgeon (1970) showed that teachers can unwittingly treat children differently, giving some more attention, more time, and more praise than others. Brophy and Good (1974) also found that teachers spend less time questioning and prompting low-expectation pupils and this produces passive, uninterested children. It has been found that teachers can have low expectations of children from minority groups or those who appear unkempt and inarticulate, and this can lead to a self-fulfilling prophecy effect, where low standards are expected and achieved. Low expectations can be unconsciously communicated to pupils, leading to an erosion of confidence and the development of negative attitudes towards school learning. Thus low expectations tend to be self-sustaining, and poor self-esteem is thought to be an important factor in under-achievement and poor performance in school.

The Swann Report (DES, 1985) noted that comparatively little research has been carried out on teachers' attitudes towards ethnic-minority pupils and the way this affects pupil performance, although there was some evidence that teachers tend to have have negative stereotypes of West Indian children, and positive ones of Asians.

The Fish Report (Fish, 1985), which looked at ways of promoting equal opportunities and combating underachievement in pupils in ILEA, explicitly recognized that difficulties are more or less handicapping depending on their social context and the expectations of others. It thus advocated the integration of children with learning difficulties in ordinary schools with all teachers enabled to meet children's needs via a network of advisory and support services.

The effects of streaming

Hargreaves (1967) and Lacey (1970) pointed out the polarizing effect of streaming children by ability in schools. In these studies, children in the lowest ability sets quickly became marginalized by the school, and formed their own counter-culture. Teachers' expectations of these groups are frequently low, and a downward spiralling of both school performance and behaviour can occur.

School 'ethos'

Rutter's study of twelve London comprehensive schools looked at the effect of school factors on children's academic performance as well as their within-school behaviour, attendance, and behaviour outside school in the form of delinquency. The study concluded that schools, even in disadvantaged areas, do in fact have an important influence on learning and behaviour. The physical aspects of schools such as size and age of buildings, as well as the pupil/teacher ratio, size of class, and formal organization of the school, are less important than other less tangible variables. The 'hidden curriculum', described generally as school ethos, may be more influential than the formal curriculum.

Rutter (1980) summarized his research findings about effective schools as follows:

(a) There should be a balance between intellectually able and less able pupils;
(b) There should be ample use of rewards, praise and appreciation;

(c)   There should be good general care of the buildings;

(d)   Children should participate in the running of the school;

(e)   There should be clear academic goals and a good use of homework;

(f)   Lessons should be planned in advance. Teachers should model good time keeping and a willingness to deal with problems. Discipline should be unobtrusive, and disruption dealt with swiftly;

(g)   There should be firm leadership, with all teachers feeling their views are represented.

The study has since been criticized for underestimating some intake variables, and also for giving insufficient attention to curriculum content and the relationships between teachers and pupils, which may have been responsible for some of the differences between schools. Nevertheless, other studies, such as Reynolds (1976) broadly support Rutter's findings, and the research has highlighted the importance of within-school factors.

Effective teaching

As well as looking for more subtle influences on learning of the hidden curriculum, there are many more obvious teacher-related factors which are likely to be important. An effective teacher is arguably able to analyse the demands of the task, (i.e., what exactly the child needs to be able to do), assess the existing skills of the pupil, and use various teaching strategies to help the pupil to learn. Curriculum planning and some specific teaching methods are discussed in Chapter 7.

Another relevant factor which has recently been the subject of research is the amount of time pupils actually spend on task. It has been suggested that the most successful pupils are, quite simply, those who spend more time engaged in learning. The effective teacher is likely to be one who engages pupils successfully and keeps them on task, where irrelevant time-wasting activities are kept to a minimum. This was one of the significant factors to come out of Rutter's study, described earlier. Peters (1970) also found, for example, that the successful teaching of spelling included the time spent on it.

Thus teacher variables are also relevant when considering why learning difficulties arise. There are various useful books published on the topic of classroom management (for example, Good and Brophy, 1978; Robinson, 1981; Laslett and Smith, 1984),

ORGANIC AND WITHIN-CHILD FACTORS

GENETIC/INNATE DIFFERENCES

Chapter 4 outlines some of the physical and sensory disabilities and disorders which can give rise to learning difficulties. In addition to those children who are clearly impaired by chromosomal or genetic anomalies or those who have received damage affecting brain functioning, some educationalists have proposed that there are innate differences between groups of children, which explains why working-class and ethnic-minority pupils, in general, fare worse at school.

Jensen (1973), for example, relying on data from standardized intelligence tests, proposed that certain groups of children are genetically less intelligent. This theory has been generally discredited (see Chapter 1), as it makes false assumptions about the nature of intelligence as well as the validity of intelligence or other ability tests, when used with children from different cultural backgrounds. Cummins (1984) pointed out the dangers of applying assessment procedures developed primarily to reflect the abilities of middle-class English-speaking pupils to pupils from linguistically and culturally diverse backgrounds. All intelligence tests, even the so-called 'culture-fair' ones, are biased towards children with good verbal skills. Tests which discriminate adversely against whole social or cultural groups must be interpreted with caution. There has been criticism at the over-representation of certain cultural groups in special schools which may well result from this process (Fish, 1985).

RATES OF MATURATION

Another way of conceptualizing learning difficulties is to discuss rates of maturation. Gesell, as early as 1940, pointed out the considerable differences between children of the same chronological age in various areas of development, and Tanner

(1961) more recently, showed that the physical development of a child of 10 years, as measured by bone and teeth age and primary signs of puberty, can vary by as much as eight years. Thus some children of 10 years have the physical development of an average 6 year old, whilst others are like an average 14 year old. However, we tend to group children by chronological age in mainstream schools, regardless of maturation and development. They must also start school by birth date, with little regard to their developmental readiness for school. Some developmentally immature children quickly sink to the bottom of the scholastic system as a result of this process. Special schools tend to be more flexible in this respect, and often have wider age-band groupings.

SEX AND AGE DIFFERENCES

As a general rule, for the majority of types of learning and behavioural difficulties, boys are reported to have more problems than girls. More boys than girls attend special schools. The DES 1982 figures gave a ratio of about 3:2 attending ESN(m) schools, and 5:1 attending schools for the maladjusted. There are all sorts of explanations for this phenomenon; there may well be physiological differences as well as a substantial cultural component. Gulliford (1985) also suggested that it may be because boys are poorer readers than girls, reading achievement seemingly being an important determinant in placement decisions about special schooling.

There are also found to be more children with summer birthdays in the lower streams in ordinary school, as well as in special schools (Bookbinder, 1967). Children who are young in the school year group, are naturally the most developmentally immature, and frequently attend nurseries and infant schools for shorter periods, so they start school with a disadvantage that can be difficult to ameliorate.

COGNITIVE PROCESSING OR NEUROLOGICAL DEFICITS

As discussed briefly in Chapter 2, an alternative theory to explain learning difficulties hypothesizes that some children have 'minimal brain damage' or neurological deficits, which adversely affect the child's ability to process information effectively. Frequently, there is no physiological evidence to back this up, although some children with learning difficulties do have histories of prolonged or difficult births, or there may be other family members who have experienced similar learning problems, which could suggest an inherited component. Others have some symptoms which might suggest neurological damage; for example, they may be clumsy, have poor pencil control, be late in establishing hand dominance, have poor laterality (that is, find it difficult to distinguish right from left), or have poor general body awareness.

Without necessarily postulating a physiological cause for learning difficulties, others propose that children with learning difficulties have cognitive skills deficits. On tests designed to assess the cognitive processes which are assumed to be necessary for learning complex skills such as number, spelling, handwriting and reading, various weaknesses may be revealed.

As noted in Chapter 7, no one yet understands how children normally learn to read although various models have been proposed to explain the process. One model, for example, assumes that a fundamental skill in decoding print is to be able to recognize and discriminate between letters, noting their relevant differences and similarities in terms of shape, orientation and spatial position. Some children seem to experience visuo-spatial difficulties with written symbols, so that they may reverse, rotate, invert or transpose the letters in words. This may affect their reading and spelling. Other children may have a weakness in visual scanning. Their eyes may not scan quickly from left to right and flick back at the end of a line systematically. Others may have visual or auditory memory difficulties. They may find it hard to remember words learned by sight, as they are unable to recall the key visual features of words. Or they may not discriminate between the essential features of the sounds making up words. In addition, some children with a restricted understanding of the meaning of words will be unable to read with understanding. Since the written word stands for a concept, these children may go through the mechanics of reading successfully without extracting the meaning from the print.

Although the sensory channels which pass on information to the child usually interrelate, some children seem unable to associate the input from their ears and eyes simultaneously; for example, they may be able to read aloud, but cannot interpret the written symbol silently. Others can spell in the written form but not aloud. Normally, if a child hears, we expect him to understand; if he can read silently, we suppose he can read aloud, and if he can read single words we expect him to read prose. Some children with learning difficulties seem unable to do these things.

The Plowden Report (DES, 1967) pointed out that there are many possible reasons for poor reading 'such as late maturation, ill-timed or poor teaching, sensory and speech defects . . . and emotional disturbance'. The report stressed the environmental factors influencing learning, and was unclear about other explanations. As noted previously, the Tizard Report (DES, 1972a) was also sceptical that a syndrome of specific symptoms exist, and maintained that there is a continuum of reading ability. The Bullock Report (DES, 1975), however, acknowledged that a few children seem to have reading problems rooted in visual and auditory discrimination and some may have a delay in the co-ordinating processes.

EMOTIONAL AND MOTIVATIONAL FACTORS
Others have suggested that some children have acquired a poor emotional response to reading rather than having a neurological deficit which affects their ability to learn to read. Reading is a prestigious skill, and reading failure can profoundly affect not only the child's attitude to learning and school generally, but also his own self-concept. As Sewell (1982) noted, 'learning to read is a highly visible social event with far reaching implications'. A late start at reading, for whatever reason, can quickly produce feelings of incompetence and failure. Maintaining a positive attitude, as with all learning, is likely to be crucial to ultimate success. There is some evidence (Lawrence, 1973) that a counselling approach, whereby the child's self-image is enhanced, can be an effective method for remediating difficulties.

Attitudes to the task are also important. The spoken and written language may not be valued or encouraged at home. The social context of learning was discussed earlier in this chapter.

LEARNING AND COGNITIVE STYLES

Rather than postulating neurological defects without medical evidence, other psychologists have proposed the notion of unhelpful cognitive styles to account for the differences between children. Stott (1978), for example, as mentioned in the previous chapter, preferred to conceive children with learning difficulties as having faulty learning styles. There may be constitutional origins for such differences in approach, but styles are likely to be largely learned and amenable to change. For example, he proposed that impulsive children naturally respond quickly but with high error rate, which consequently earns teacher disapproval. They may find it difficult to stay on a task, unaided, for more than a few minutes. It would be possible, when conceived in this way, for teachers to devise a learning programme which would encourage them to slow down, and think before committing thoughts to paper.

DIET AND TOXINS

The effect of poor diet and environmental toxins on children's learning and behaviour still remains a controversial issue. Apart from the accidental ingestion of a poisonous substance or long-term malnutrition, scientific research regularly uncovers a toxic substance or nutritional deficiency whose effects may be marginal initially, but are cumulative, and have a slow but deleterious effect on children's general health, academic performance and behaviour. The problem with such discoveries is that their relative importance on a child's wellbeing can become quickly distorted. Without doubt, low-level dietary deficiencies and toxic substances do affect performance, but to what extent is uncertain.

Undoubtedly, some substances are toxic and others are essential for good health but we are constantly faced with a bewildering welter of advice which is sometimes conflicting. Moreover, some educationalists feel that the predominance of this kind of explanation for learning failure or behavioural disturbance obscures far more potent factors.

Toxic substances   Accumulative poisons such as lead are known to produce considerable long-term damage. Lead was commonly used in plumbing and household paint, and is still present in most petrol exhaust. The effects of low level, cumulative lead poisoning are well documented (Davies and Stewart, 1987). The symptoms associated with such poisoning include lethargy, depression, kidney and metabolic dysfunction, high blood pressure and hyperactivity in children, although the evidence for this latter symptom is inconclusive (Rimland and Larson, 1983). Other metals known to be toxic include mercury and cadmium.

Other substances in everyday usage, such as aluminium and dental fillings, have been identified as possible low-level toxins. It is likely that minute quantities of toxic substances are also insidiously breathed in or ingested, and these can also cause various symptoms.

Diet Recent controversial evidence has suggested that the usual diet of schoolchildren is often insufficient in basic minerals, vitamins and protein, and this has been linked with poor academic performance and behaviour problems (Schauss, 1980). Moreover, there has been concern expressed about the flavourings, colouring and preservatives added to many highly processed convenience foods; tartrazine has been implicated in particular (Davies and Stewart, 1987).

Other studies have suggested that intellectual performance, weight and general health are grossly affected by prolonged malnutrition and the younger the child, the worse the consequences. By extension it would seem logical to suppose that an inadequate diet would have its effects, even if only in terms of the number of days lost at school through poor health.

THE NATURE OF 'SCHOOL KNOWLEDGE'

It is finally worth considering an alternative view, that learning difficulties are constructed as a result of the way we choose to define worthwhile knowledge, assess children and organize schooling.

Davies (1980), for example, argued that 'intelligence' is defined as a narrow range of middle-class skills with a high verbal component, and educational achievement is based on false premises about the nature of knowledge. She maintained that school-based learning which emphasizes speed, convergent thinking, memorizing facts, competitiveness and facility with the printed page are not necessarily worthwhile, nor the only way in which schools can be organized. She proposed that intelligence is a mechanism of social control, used to discriminate between children. In her view both intelligence and social-class background are not causal variables for explaining educational achievement, rather they are 'labels to justify and funnel selection'. The educational system is concerned with protecting the most able, and schools within both the ordinary and special sectors have been founded on the principle of selection. However, they do not need to be divisive in this way; a truly comprehensive system would cater for the needs of all children.

Cummins (1984) also argued that the underachievement of many children from minority groups is based on invalid assessment procedures, which are linguistically and culturally biased. He stated, 'the failure by educators and academics to critically examine the implicit acceptance of middle-class dominant-group values in the assessment and pedagogical process has served to perpetuate the educational (and societal) status quo in which cultural and socio-economic differences are frequently transformed into academic deficits'. Cummins maintained that special education categories are largely 'arbitrary, misleading and potentially self-fulfilling'. Arguably, rather than concentrating on the notion of learning difficulties, it may be more constructive to consider the diversity of children's needs, and teach accordingly.

4

Physical and sensory disorders and disabilities

OVERVIEW

This chapter outlines some of the major physical and sensory disorders and disabilities which may give rise to special educational needs. This includes organic disorders which primarily affect intellectual development and mobility; hearing and visual impairment; and speech, language and communication disorders. The main characteristics of the various conditions will be described and their incidence and medical treatment noted. The implications for teaching and resourcing are only briefly mentioned; they will be discussed further in Chapter 7, 'Meeting special needs'.

INTRODUCTION

Although the 1981 Act abandoned the concepts of physical and mental handicap as a means of categorizing children to determine school provision, it is clear that such disorders and disabilities must be taken into consideration when assessing a child's special educational needs, in so far as they have implications for the child's functioning in school and for the type of facilities and resources required to meet his educational needs. The Act states that a child has a learning difficulty if he has significantly greater difficulties in learning than the majority of children of his age; or if he has a disability which either prevents or hinders him from making use of school facilities in the area; or he is under 5, but would be likely to have such difficulties were he at school. Special educational needs would arise if the learning difficulties called for alternative or additional provision to that normally available in the mainstream school.

Prior to the Act, the Warnock Report recommended that existing ways of describing children with physical and sensory disabilities were still appropriate (para. 3.26).

One of the first points that needs to be made is that a child with a physical or sensory disability will not automatically have special educational needs. There are a number of conditions that have few, if any, implications for educational performance; nor is the child necessarily prevented from leading a full and normal life outside school. Epilepsy, for example, can be a serious condition, but if it is properly controlled by drugs and regular monitoring, the child can lead a full and normal life. He can follow the usual curriculum in an ordinary school and therefore may have no special educational needs. As Jones (1985) stated: 'The extent to which a disability becomes handicapping depends on its severity and nature, its prognosis and amenability to treatment, the extent to which it interferes with everyday life, and the attitudes of other people to it.'

These distinctions were elucidated by the World Health Organisation (1980). Impairment is defined as 'any loss or abnormality of psychological, physiological or anatomical structure or function'; disability as 'the restriction or lack of ability to perform an activity resulting from impairment'; and handicap, as 'the disadvantage for an individual that limits or prevents the fulfillment of a role that is "normal".' Thus it is worth remembering that treating children with disorders and disabilities as abnormal, and giving them segregated school provision, could mean that we are creating a handicap out of a disability.

When discussing various disabilities it is easiest to describe them as if they were discrete entities, but in reality many children are multihandicapped, and indeed the existence of one disorder often leads to other problems. For example, a hearing-impaired child is likely to suffer from delayed language development, which in turn will have consequences for reading and writing, and possibly for normal behavioural adjustment too. In Rutter, Tizard and Whitmore's Isle of Wight study of 9–11-year-old children (1970), 90 per cent of children with intellectual difficulties also had an additional handicap; 23 per cent had delayed language development, 45 per cent still had articulation defects and 30 per cent had co-ordination problems. The same point can be made from Shearer's study (1977). Assessments of 916 children in special classes and schools revealed that 7 per cent had some form of physical disability, 9 per cent had hearing or visual impairment and 20 per cent had speech disorders.

Any categorization system has its difficulties. In this chapter we are organizing various disorders and disabilities in a way which we feel makes most sense to educationalists, although the medical profession may classify these disorders in different ways.

ORGANIC DISORDERS WHICH PRIMARILY AFFECT INTELLECTUAL DEVELOPMENT

As noted in the previous chapter it is generally agreed that the major difference between most children with mild or moderate learning difficulties and those with severe learning difficulties is not just a question of degree. Frequently the latter group have an organic or physical basis for their learning problems (Craft, Bicknall and Hollins, 1985).

Elliott, Jackson and Graves (1981), in a survey of 450 severely handicapped children aged 3–16 years, obtained the following data:

%

26.5 Down's syndrome or other chromosomal anomaly
 9.0 Non-chromosomal abnormalities of the central nervous system
 6.5 Cerebral palsy
 2.0 Birth injury
 2.0 Infective, postinfective or immunological cause
 2.0 Nutritional or metabolic cause
 4.0 Psychiatric syndrome
 1.5 Cerebral anoxia
 1.0 Cultural-familial cause

%
1.0   Epilepsy
1.5   Heredofamilial degenerative diseases of the CNS
8.5   Other (including syndromes of unknown aetiology)
34.5 No known cause
(100.00 total)

Chromosomal anomalies

Chromosomes act as a biological blueprint which carry the genes of the individual. Sometimes these can be damaged, broken or muddled in some way so that from conception the biological programme for building the cells of the new human being is faulty. Chromosomal abnormalities can be inherited but can also occur randomly, although the risk increases as the mother ages. Some diseases and irradiation can damage the biological blueprint. The most commonly occurring of the chromosome disorders is Down's syndrome or mongolism, which affects approximately one child in 700 (22 per cent of all children with severe learning difficulties). Other rarer conditions also exist and usually involve a degree of retardation. Such conditions include Klinefelter's and Turner's syndrome. Chromosomal anomalies cannot be reversed.

DOWN'S SYNDROME

Normal children have twenty-three matching pairs of chromosomes in every cell. The child with Down's syndrome typically has an extra chromosome in the 21st pair making a total of 47 (Trisomy), although other abnormal arrangements in the chromosomes have also been identified.

Diagnosis of Down's syndrome is usually made at or shortly after birth, and relates to the appearance of the child and the striking hypertonia (floppy muscle tone). Down's syndrome is characterized in a number of ways. The eyes have a characteristic shape with epicanthic folds in the corner alongside the nose and are usually blue with a granular iris. The upper and lower jaws may be small so that the tongue appears too large and this is exacerbated by poor muscle tone so the tongue may protrude and the child may dribble. The skull is often round and flat at the back. Fingers and toes tend to be short and stubby and there is usually a distinctive crease along the palms and soles of the hands and feet. The skin and lung tissues are frail and children are more susceptible to colds and bronchial infections. Conductive hearing loss is common in Down's syndrome children. Finally abnormalities of the heart and circularity system occurs in about one-third of children with Down's syndrome.

Educational implications In the past Down's syndrome children were classed as ineducable. It is now recognized that Down's syndrome children generally have more learning potential than had been realized, and their range of ability, although usually well below average, is wide. Many Down's syndrome children are integrated in normal schools and most can learn to read and write although development of these skills is slower and may plateau in early adolescence.

Genetic disorders

It is a general principle of paediatrics that any major congenital abnormality carries with it the risk of severe learning difficulty. A small proportion of foetuses are abnormal from conception. These usually abort naturally and do not come to full term, but one child in 1,000 is born with a major congenital abnormality. Often severe mental retardation is just one of a number of handicaps which may result. With developments in medicine the number of abnormal births is falling. The incidence of such an occurrence can now be controlled, first by genetic counselling and secondly by screening *in utero* using amniocentesis, ultra-sound, foetoscopy and foetal blood sampling. Abnormalities in the unborn child can be detected and terminations offered. On the other hand, children born with a major congenital abnormality are also more likely to survive through improved health care, surgery and the use of drugs.

There are a number of rare disorders resulting in severe mental handicap which are genetically transmitted. The largest group are inherited metabolic or endocrine disorders such as phenylketonuria, homocystinuria, galactosaemia and cretinism. Some of these disorders can be treated and intellectual impairment may be avoided. For example, cretinism involves the absence of certain thyroid secretions and it is relatively simple to replace these providing the condition is detected immediately after birth. However, most genetic disorders are more complex and it will be useful to look more closely at the best known of these.

PHENYLKETONURIA (PKU)
This is a metabolic disorder in which the protein molecules break down forming unusually high concentrations of phenyl-alanine in the blood. Phenylalanine affects neural transmission and causes permanent and progressive brain damage. The level of phenylalanine can be controlled and brought to acceptable levels by reducing the amount of protein the child ingests. Babies are screened shortly after birth for abnormally high levels of phenylalanine in the blood (Guthrie test), and affected children are placed on a modified diet.

Despite dietary treatment affected children tend to have learning difficulties which are more severe in untreated cases. The low protein diet has to be maintained until the child is at least 12 years of age. and regular checks are made throughout life. Protein deficiency and frequent hospitalization are therefore problems, but severe retardation which once was inevitable can now be avoided. Children born to mothers with PKU are frequently damaged *in utero* by the mother's abnormal metabolic processes, unless the mother maintains a modified diet.

SKELETAL AND OTHER RARE INHERITED DISORDERS
Another group of rare inherited disorders affects the bone formation of the skull. These defects often lead to, or are accompanied by, severe mental retardation. Examples of these disorders are hypertelorism, gargoylism and Apert's syndrome. Similarly there are inherited disorders of the neurological tissue and the skin such as Sturge-Weber syndrome and tuberosclerosis. These conditions are often associated with a series of other abnormalities.

Infection, irradiation or immunological cause

In the main, the unborn child is protected against infections and diseases contracted by the mother during pregnancy.

A few viruses, however, can penetrate the placental barrier

and affect the growing foetus, the first weeks after conception being the most vulnerable period. German measles or rubella contracted by the mother during the early weeks of pregnancy can affect the unborn foetus causing severe mental retardation and abnormalities of the ears, eyes and other organs. As the foetus develops contact with the rubella virus becomes progressively less damaging but any contact is to be avoided and teenage girls are now vaccinated to insure immunity as a matter of course in this country.

Syphilis can also affect the foetus and is a particularly insidious disease because it may not show itself in the growing child but can emerge in its secondary phase when the child is in his teens. Brain damage may occur before diagnosis and treatment begins.

Severe toxaemia in pregnancy can also affect the foetus and unfortunately the pregnant woman is more prone to higher blood pressure which can predispose her to toxaemia. All pregnant women are given regular checks to ensure they remain healthy throughout pregnancy.

Rhesus incompatibility used to be a cause of mental retardation. If the mother's blood is rhesus negative and the baby she is carrying has rhesus positive blood, the mother's blood may produce antibodies which attack the foetus's red blood cells. The baby may be born prematurely and will certainly be anaemic or jaundiced at birth. This in turn may affect his ability to take up oxygen and a degree of brain damage may result. All pregnant women are now screened for rhesus incompatibility and the dangers can be ameliorated by the use of drugs and by blood transfusions after birth or even before birth.

Another cause of abnormality and mental retardation is exposure *in utero* to very high levels of radiation. Radiation can damage both the genes and the chromosomes and produce grave abnormalities. Again the foetus is at greatest risk after conception and in the early weeks of pregnancy. In hospitals precautions are taken to ensure that pregnant women are not X-rayed.

The child's vulnerability does not end at birth. For the first two or three years of life the brain continues to grow at a fast rate. There are a number of diseases which can cause brain damage and the younger the infant contracts the disease, the worse are the consequences.

The two most frequently occurring diseases which can cause varying degrees of brain damage are encephalitis and meningitis. Both are diseases in which the virus actually attacks the brain tissue. Not only is the brain damaged, but also pressure around the brain increases due to the production of antibodies to combat the intruding virus, and this pressure causes further damage. Severe pressure may result in hydrocephalus, and untreated hydrocephalus could cause severe brain damage, as discussed later. Encephalitis is usually more severe in its effects than meningitis which affects the outer covering membrane of the brain, but meningitis is also a cause of deafness.

Gestational disorders

Premature babies are regarded as at risk, and the more premature the greater the problems. The infant born before thirty-two weeks' gestation, for example, is prone to intra-ventricular haemorrhage as the membranes are so immature and may suffer from a degree of brain damage. Although even at this early stage mental retardation is not inevitable and all premature babies benefit now from improved post-natal care. Babies who were of low birth weight (under 5lbs) despite being full term, are also regarded as being at risk as are those who are born post mature. The danger in the latter case is that the mother's placenta may cease to function efficiently after the full term.

Birth injury

Despite vastly improved perinatal care, severe injury to the brain is still most likely to occur at the moment of birth through asphyxia or anoxia. There is a crucial moment when the oxygen supply from the mother's blood ceases and the baby must struggle for its first breath. If the brain cells are deprived of oxygen for more than about four minutes they will begin to die. The consequences of asphyxia at birth can be cerebral palsy and/or mental retardation.

The causes of asphyxia and anoxia are numerous. Sometimes

the umbilical cord gets caught around the baby's neck during delivery or, during breach deliveries, when breathing can be delayed as the head emerges last. There may be problems if the head is disproportionately large to the mother's pelvis.

DISORDERS WHICH PRIMARILY AFFECT THE CHILD'S PHYSICAL DEVELOPMENT AND MOBILITY

A common cause of severe mobility problems in children is damage to the central nervous system, that is, to the spinal cord or the brain. Damage may occur in the area of the brain controlling motor co-ordination, or to the spinal cord which means that nerve impulses are no longer transmitted to the brain. When the nervous system is damaged for whatever cause, muscular weakness or paralysis is a likely consequence. In some conditions, the child will also suffer intellectual impairment as a result of the disorder.

Cerebral palsy

The most common type of neurological impairment affecting mobility is cerebral palsy. The term 'spastic' is commonly used to denote this condition although spasticity is just one of a number of cerebral palsies.

The condition is the result of permanent damage to the developing brain usually before or during birth. Motor problems may well be accompanied by other effects of brain injury, such as intellectual impairment and speech or sensory deficits. Some children may be severely handicapped but others may have mild motor problems only. Many kinds of palsy are difficult to detect in the early months of life and, even when detected, the prognosis of the ultimate severity of the disability can rarely be made with any confidence.

The classification of cerebral palsy is complex. There are usually said to be three main types: spasticity, athetosis and ataxia. Many children do not fit neatly into these categories, and their symptoms may change as they grow older. Cerebral palsy is also classified medically in terms of the involvement of limbs. A child with monoplegia has one limb paralysed. This is a fairly rare condition. Hemiplegics have two limbs on the same side of the body affected: hemiplegia is the commonest form of spasticity. Paraplegics have only their legs paralysed, whereas triplegics have three limbs and quadraplegics or tetraplegics have all four limbs involved.

SPASTICITY

Spasticity is the most common of the cerebral palsies affecting 50–60 per cent of all children with cerebral palsy. Spastic children have increased muscle tone and rigid limbs. They tend to have exaggerated reflex activity and abnormal postures resulting from some muscles contracting too much while other muscles are too weak to counterbalance these. These postures may be exhibited even when the child is asleep.

ATHETOSIS

Athetosis is characterized by involuntary, jerky, writhing, uncoordinated movements. As with other types of palsy the baby's early primitive reflexes tend to remain, rather than disappearing in the course of normal development during the first months of life. Children with athetosis tend to be floppy with weak muscle tone. They have problems with the control of movement due to the interaction of successive groups of muscles and in many cases the muscles involved in speech are also affected. Frequently there is a high tone deafness, all of which makes it difficult for athetoid children to communicate verbally. In this type of palsy the abnormal movements are not displayed when the child is asleep. About 25 per cent of cerebral palsied children are of this type.

ATAXIA

Ataxia is a much rarer condition than the two previously described types of palsy. Only about 2 per cent of children with palsy are categorized in this way. The child's ability to balance and to integrate spatial information is usually impaired. Characteristically the child has an unsteady gait with flaying arms and uncoordinated legs. He also has problems with fine motor movements. Ataxia may improve as the child grows older.

INCIDENCE

Wide variations in the incidence of cerebral palsy are reported internationally due to the fact that diagnostic criteria vary. The reported incidence in Britain is about one in 350 births. There has been a decline in the incidence of cerebral palsy in this country due to improvements in pre-natal and perinatal care but more severely damaged babies now survive.

CAUSES AND MEDICAL TREATMENT

In approximately 20 per cent of cases, no cause can be identified (Craft, 1985) Strong relationships exist, however, with a number of adverse pre-natal and perinatal events. In most cases, damage to the brain is thought to occur during birth when the oxygen supply to the baby's brain is cut off. This can happen for several reasons; for example, sometimes the placenta can become detached too early, the baby's head is too large for the mother's pelvis, or the umbilical cord becomes entwined around the baby's neck.

Prematurity before thirty-two weeks' gestation, when the immature brain is susceptible to haemorrhage, can also result in cerebral palsy. Rubella virus in the expectant mother has been implicated in cerebral palsy as well as maternal toxaemia and rhesus incompatibility. It is also thought that some kinds of dysfunction of the brain are congenital.

Most children acquire the condition in the pre-natal and perinatal period but some may do so post-natally through accident or infections such as meningitis or encephalitis.

Surgery is not usually recommended and drugs are of limited use. Physiotherapy is probably the most useful form of treatment, the aim being to increase the child's mobility and improve his muscle tone either to decrease it with spasticity or increase it with athetosis. Primitive reflexes which prohibit growth can be reduced and normal posture and motor development encouraged. Therapists usually try to work with parents and the goal is usually to encourage the child towards independent motor skills. Some children will also require the help of the speech therapist.

EDUCATIONAL IMPLICATIONS

Cerebral palsy can have widely varying effects – some children are only slightly handicapped whilst others have severe multiple disabilities. Children with cerebral palsy are likely to have accompanying learning difficulties because damage to the brain often has a reverbatory effect. More than one-third have visual problems frequently with peripheral vision and about half are reported to have sensory impairments with a diminished sense of pain or feeling. About one-third of cerebral palsied children have a hearing problem and a large proportion have speech problems caused not only by deafness but by poor control of speech muscles. A significant number suffer from epilepsy.

Thus although many cerebral palsied children are of normal intelligence, they frequently have learning difficulties. Lack of motor experiences in the early years can lead to difficulties with perception, and delayed language development can have consequences for the development of literacy skills. What is more, they may be handicapped not least because of their restricted opportunities for normal social experiences with others.

Spina bifida and hydrocephalus

A child born with spina bifida has a congenital malformation of the spinal column where the arches of one or more of the vertebrae have failed to fuse, causing a gap in the column encasing the spinal cord. The term spina bifida refers to two main conditions, the least handicapping being known as spina bifida occulta (hidden). It has been estimated that as many as 50 per cent of the population have a faulty spinal column, but because the surrounding membranes do not protrude through the gap that the defect is likely to remain unnoticed and has no consequence.

The more serious type of spina bifida is known as spina bifida cystica. The child is born with a cyst like sack on his back. Spina bifida cystica is divided into two types. The less serious form is known as meningocele, where the sack containing the fluid and the meninges does not retain the cord itself. About one in six cases of spina bifida cystica are of this type. Physical handicap is an unlikely consequence and intellectual ability is also rarely affected.

Myelomeningocele is most common and more serious, since the spinal cord intrudes into the sack which is filled with cerebro-spinal fluid. Damage to the cord results in irreversible damage to the central nervous system. The degree of paralysis depends on where the malformation of the spine occurs: the higher up the spinal column the greater the damage. Paralysis will occur below the level of the lesion where the nerves are affected. About one-third to half of myelomeningocele children are totally paraplegic. Some children may have normal lower-limb function yet may still be incontinent. Myelomeningocele frequently leads to further complications such as hydrocephalus.

INCIDENCE

In England and Wales, about 1,500 children are born each year with myelomeningocele and there are currently about 2.4 per 1,000 babies born with spina bifida cystica. This varies according to region, it being as high as 6.5 per 1,000 in South Wales and as low as 1 per 10,000 in Japan.

CAUSES AND MEDICAL TREATMENT

The cause of spina bifida is not yet established; it is probably largely genetically determined although environmental factors have been implicated. The disorder is thought to originate in the growing foetus at about five weeks after conception when the neural tube fails to form and fuse properly; why this should happen is not yet clear. The genetic link seems strong since spina bifida tends to run in families. There is also believed to be an environmental factor in spina bifida; there are more spina bifida births in the lower socio-economic groups and there are regional differences. Diet, for example, might be implicated.

Children with spina bifida cystica usually have an operation at birth to enclose the exposed cord or remove the cyst of redundant membrane. Delay in surgery can result in secondary problems of hydrocephalus where cerebro-spinal fluid builds up within the brain causing brain damage in some cases. In fact in two-thirds of cases of myelomeningocele, hydrocephalus is already detectable at birth.

Surgery may also be required in the older child to correct deformity of the limbs, dislocated hips or unstabilized joints. Many children require corrective surgery of this type up to the age of 12 or so. Physiotherapists also play an important role in treatment. Their function is to ensure that the child gains maximum use of his limbs and retains movement in his joints. Parents need advice about the best way to promote mobility in their child; moreover, they need to be informed about ways of avoiding pressure sores in children with no lower trunk sensation where the danger signals of discomfort and pain are not felt.

Incontinence is an additional problem for most children with damaged spinal cords due to the loss of sensation in the bladder and sphincter control. The social problems are obvious but health problems are also a hazard since kidneys can be damaged if urine is retained. Advice is given to parents on the urinary devices available. Boys can usually manage satisfactorily if they can be taught to manually express their bladders. The problem is more acute for girls. They may use incontinence pads or protective pants but this is troublesome. An alternative is to have a urinary diversion operation so that the bladder is bypassed and urine is brought to the surface of the body, usually at the abdomen, where a plastic bag or stoma may be fitted to collect the urine. It is important that the stoma does not become infected and careful hygiene is essential. Bowel incontinence is likely to be a further problem, but most children may acquire regular bowel habits with systematic and persistent training, although parents again need help in establishing such routines.

The treatment of spina bifida infants remains controversial. At one time mortality rates were very high, only 15 per cent of children surviving, although some were very severely afflicted. In the 1960s, improved surgery techniques were applied unselectively to all children and 50 per cent of children survived beyond 5 years of age. Although more children survived, many had both physical and intellectual handicaps and their quality of life was poor. At present in most areas of this country selection now occurs and about 50 per cent of children are given surgery, thus reducing the number of children surviving with severe handicap. However, there is a chance that some babies who are given no surgical intervention will survive, and consequently such children are likely to be severely physically handicapped.

EDUCATIONAL IMPLICATIONS
Spina bifida children may have normal intellectual abilities, although those who have had the accompanying hydrocephalus tend to be be delayed in their development. Due to early restricted mobility these children often have perceptual and visual motor problems which may cause learning difficulties.

About 75 per cent of spina bifida myelomeningocele babies are born with some hydrocephalus and appear to have associated cranial abnormalities. However, the two conditions are not necessarily associated.

Hydrocephalus

Hydrocephalus results when there is too much cerebral fluid in the ventricles of the brain, the brain tissue becomes impacted and permanent damage can result if pressure is not relieved. The baby's head may become grossly enlarged by two months of age if no action is taken and the areas of brain controlling limb movements may be affected, paralysing the lower and sometimes the upper limbs. The child's eyesight can be affected if the condition is untreated. He can also experience fits. In mild conditions, however, the problem may right itself and intelligence and physical development may not be affected. The head may be near normal in size by the time the child is a few years old. Damage is likely to be most severe when older children get hydrocephalus since the head cannot become distended and thus brain damage is more likely.

CAUSES AND MEDICAL TREATMENT
There are various causes of hydrocephalus. In some, a congenital defect at birth means that the cerebro-spinal fluid does not circulate naturally. In other cases, there is haemorrhage at birth or afterwards due to disease or accident, and a prime cause can be due to infections such as meningitis where the pathways in the brain become congested.

Where hydrocephalus is rapidly progressive, surgery may be necessary. A shunt procedure is commonly used where a unidirectional valve is inserted into the cerebral ventricles and the excess fluid is taken to the heart or abdomen. This serves to decrease pressure and remains permanently in place.

Muscular dystrophy

Muscular dystrophy is a hereditary, sex-linked, disease where there is a progressive degeneration of the muscles as the fibres in the muscles swell and become replaced by fibrous tissue and fat. Although muscular dystrophy is caused by a recessive gene, it can occur in families with no history of the disease, as the gene appears to be susceptible to mutation. There are various forms of the disease, the Duchenne type being the most severe. Common to all types is a progressive muscle weakness displayed in slowness in walking, an inability to run and difficulties in getting up after falling. In its early stages the child has a clumsy waddling gait, the disease commencing in the pelvic muscles, the buttocks and the thighs.

The Duchenne type begins as early as 2 years in some cases; the child is often unable to walk by 11 years of age and becomes confined to a wheel chair. The child becomes progressively weaker until he can no longer move the muscles in his body. He then becomes highly susceptible to pulmonary complications and most do not survive beyond adolescence. Boys only are affected by Duchenne muscular dystrophy.

There are, in addition, various types of muscular dystrophy which affect both boys and girls equally. They are very rare and generally slower in developing, usually starting in adolescence and becoming progressive, leading to death in middle age.

IMPLICATIONS FOR EDUCATION
Muscular dystrophy does not affect intellectual functioning. Despite continued research there is no known cure, and life expectancy is limited usually to late teens or 20s. Physiotherapy is the main form of treatment.

Cystic fibrosis

Cystic fibrosis is an inherited metabolic disorder characterized by chronic digestive and respiratory problems. The endocrine glands become blocked and distended, the pancreas shrinks and the lungs become infected and abscessed. Cystic fibrosis is known to be due to a single recessive gene and it is the commonest genetically determined disorder affecting children in the United Kingdom. Frequently there is a family history of the disease.

Originally many children died of pneumonia, but advances in treatment have made the outlook much better. In most cases, as the pancreas fails to function properly, pancretin, a substitute, has to be taken with every meal throughout life in a carefully controlled dosage. A high protein diet and an adequate supply of vitamins are also necessary. Physiotherapy is also important and is usually taught to parents to aid the child's breathing and help to clear congestion. There are no associated intellectual difficulties.

Haemophilia

Haemophilia is a rare disorder of the blood which is transmitted through a recessive gene. The blood is deficient in a clotting agent called Factor 8, which means that relatively minor knocks can result in both internal and external prolonged bleeding. The blood can enter the muscles of the joints and permanent crippling and severe pain may result. The child may need intravenous injections and blood plasma to treat the condition.

Approximately one person in 8,000 has a form of haemophilia. Most children can cope well in mainstream school.

Asthma

Asthma is an intermittent condition rather than a permanent handicap, in which the child has wheezy breathlessness and coughing. Some types of asthma are allergic, and run in families with a history of hay fever and eczema. Non-allergic types of asthma may be caused by bronchial infection. An asthma attack usually has a sudden onset and is characterized by wheezing and rattling as expiration and inspiration make breathing very difficult. In very severe attacks the child may turn blue and can be at serious risk. The attack usually ends suddenly although it may be followed by a period of coughing when the child clears his lungs.

It has been estimated that 130,000 children in England and

Wales suffer from severe asthma at some time, with the consequent loss of schooling. Treatment involves the use of anti-histamine drugs and decongesting inhalants, Breathing exercises may be given to help to develop the lungs.

Diabetes

Diabetes occurs in both children and adults and can begin at any age. There are estimated to be over 1 million people with diabetes in the UK and approximately 30,000 are under the age of 16 years. Early symptoms in children include excessive thirst, frequent passing of urine and loss of weight. Secondary complications which can arise are visual impairment, heart trouble and kidney damage. In most cases the basic cause of diabetes is the failure of the pancreas to produce insulin. This results in an abnormally high level of sugar being produced in the blood (hyperglycaemia). Insulin injections are needed although excessive amounts of insulin too can cause problems. The diabetic who does not receive regular insulin injections may fall into a diabetic coma.

Apart from regular insulin injections, treatment involves dieting and exercise. With regular monitoring, the child can live a normal life.

Epilepsy

A child with epilepsy has recurrent attacks of temporary disturbance of brain functioning known as fits or seizures. They are caused by a sudden discharge of electricity in the nerve cells of the brain and may take many forms. Some children have disturbances of consciousness which are scarcely noticeable, whereas others have severe seizures with convulsions. The cause of seizures are various, such as brain damage, scar tissue, severe inflammation of the brain resulting from diseases such as meningitis, tumours, raised temperature during fevers, etc. Even pulsing or flashing lights can trigger the electrical discharge.

INCIDENCE
About 1 person in 200 takes regular medication for epilepsy, but the incidence is probably higher. Epilepsy can start at any age, but it most commonly starts in childhood.

TYPES OF EPILEPSY
Epilepsy can take various forms. Some children experience a slight loss of consciousness with or without a seizure. Some have seizures which occur only at night or in the early morning. Some seizures come with good warning; others have no prior symptoms. Attacks may respond well to medication, but some are hard to control.

Since the focus of epilepsy may be in any area of the brain, many different types of seizure are encountered. A generalized seizure involves the whole brain. Partial or localized seizures initially involve limited areas of the brain, but often these generalize as the discharge radiates throughout the entire brain.

(a) *Major fit, clonic-tonic seizure or grand mal*   With grand mal, the seizure progresses through various observable stages. First there is often, but by no means always, an aura lasting from several hours to a few seconds, announcing the onset of the fit. The aura may take the form of a visual hallucination, tiredness, depression or elation, or a headache. This is followed by the clonic stage, where the muscles go into rigid contraction which can last about half a minute. The child may fall and breathing may be affected, although the heart continues to beat. Next, the tonic stage follows, with rhythmical jerking of the muscles of the body and face. The jaws tend to clench and the tongue may be bitten. Finally comes a period of complete relaxation and unconsciousness which frequently moves into sleep. This state of unconsciousness may cause the bladder or bowel to relax causing incontinence. Ultimately, the child wakes, often with no after-effects other than confusion, embarrassment and possibly a headache. Since the child in unconscious throughout the fit he has no memory of it, in fact, he may also forget the preceding events. This is called retrograde amnesia.

The only real danger in grand mal is damaging the head or limbs when falling, or swallowing the tongue and choking.

The most serious form of epilepsy is called status epilepticus which occurs when one major fit follows another without the child regaining consciousness. In this case permanent damage may occur if the brain is starved of oxygen.

(b) *Psycho-motor attacks* In these seizures only part of the brain, usually the temporal lobe, is affected by the discharge. The child most usually reports various hallucinations of sensation. He may smack his lips, sniff the air, hear voices or become strangely frightened for a few moments. He may also have strong feelings of *déjà vu* or memories of past events. Sometimes an action will be repeated in a stereotyped manner which had begun on onset of the attack. The child may appear to be in a dream-like state; these minor lapses of consciousness often pass unnoticed, and last only a few seconds.

(c) *Absences or petit mal* Unlike the previous forms of epilepsy, petit mal is generalized across both brain hemispheres. The child may seem to experience brief losses of awareness lasting a few seconds, with no convulsive movements. The hallmark of this condition is lapses in concentration which may occur many times a day. Sometimes the child may lose colour or balance, or pass urine. Attacks may be brought on by breathing deeply or by excessive visual stimulation.

CAUSES AND TREATMENT OF EPILEPSY
Most people have a high threshold against epileptic seizures, but given abnormal conditions, anyone can have a fit. Certain stimuli may lower thresholds such as fever, flickering lights, emotional stress or drugs. Many different metabolic and endocrine disorders, such as diabetes and kidney disease, may give rise to epileptic seizures. Low blood sugar levels, and disturbances in mineral balances when dehydrated, can also precipitate a fit. There may also be more obvious causes such as severe head injury, birth trauma, stroke or tumour. It can also occur spontanteously, and may depend on genetic factors.

With modern advances in medicine, it is possible to prevent or reduce the frequency of seizures for most people with epilepsy. Drugs such as Epilim and Tegratol are very effective, and neuro-surgery is reserved for rare cases. The development of anti-epileptic drugs is ongoing and the side-effects of some of the earlier drugs have been substantially reduced. Epilepsy is more difficult to control where the cause is a progressive, degenerative disease, where brain states are not stable. Changes in body states at puberty may also cause problems in drug control.

EDUCATIONAL IMPLICATIONS
Most children with epilepsy lead normal lives and there may be no major educational implications. However, because epilepsy may involve frequent lapses of concentration or occur in association with other neurological disorders, it can give rise to learning difficulties.

Accidents

In England and Wales in 1978, accidents, poisoning and violence accounted for 56 per cent of all deaths in the age group 1–19 years (Forfar and Arneil, 1984). Death rates reveal only a small part of the accident problem. US statistics show that for every fatal accident there are between 100 and 200 non-fatal accidents. Many of these will be trivial, but it is estimated that one out of forty causes permanent disability. Road traffic accidents form by far the largest category of accident.

Young children are obviously more physically vulnerable to all types of accident due to lack of co-ordination, foresight and physical strength. In addition, they are curious and enjoy exploration, heedless of danger. Children have a predisposition to accidents which can only be offset by continuous supervision by parents. Mortality from accidents is highest for children under 5 years of age, and generally declines with age although certain types of accidents are more common with older children. Road traffic accidents account for three out of four fatalities between the ages of 15 and 19 years and 80 per cent of those killed are boys. Other causes of accidents, in order of incidence, include burns, drowning, inhalations, falls, poisonings, assaults and suicide. The loss of a limb and spinal injuries are the most common cause of permanent disability.

Accidents as a result of drug or solvent abuse are discussed in the chapter on behaviour problems.

Spinal injury

A few children receive spinal injuries resulting from accidents. This can lead to partial or full paralysis if the nerve fibres are broken or damaged in the spinal cord. Sometimes vertebrae are broken, but the cord is undamaged; however, it may take eight weeks or so for the spinal cord to recover from the shock of injury. The severity of the paralysis will depend upon which sections of the spinal cord were damaged. The higher the damage the more extensive the paralysis. Most spinal cord injuries affect the bladder, the bowels and the sexual organs because the nerves in these organs stem from the lower regions of the spinal cord. The most obvious result of paralysis is the loss of movement and the loss of sensation in the limbs and body below the lesion. Temperature control and heat regulation are consequent problems.

Minor conditions affecting mobility

There are several minor conditions which may affect the child's mobility which are either congenital or acquired after birth as the result of disease or injury. A relatively well known congenital problem occurring in about 2 in 10,000 children is clubfoot or talipes, where one or both feet are turned at the ankle in an abnormal way.

Curvature of the spine or scoliosis is another condition which can be congenital, but can also be acquired through poor posture.

Dislocation of the hip can occur in approximately 1.5 in every 1,000 births, with many more girls than boys being affected. The defect is probably genetic but can usually be overcome using corrective measures. Untreated dislocation of the hip can lead to arthritis and mobility problems.

SENSORY DISABILITIES

Hearing impairment

Hearing impairment may range in severity from mild to profound. Hearing loss can be a major handicap, not only because of the obvious problems of communication, but because of the implications for language development which, in turn, can adversely affect intellectual development.

A profoundly deaf child has a disability which precludes him from processing linguistic information through the sense of hearing, with or without a hearing aid.

In audiometric terms, those whose loss is in the range of 30 to 50 decibels (dbs) are classified as moderately deaf: 50 to 80 dbs, as severely deaf; and those who do not respond to sound higher than 80 to 100 dbs, as profoundly deaf. To give some indication what this might mean, an ordinary conversation is usually conducted at about 65 dbs. A telephone rings at about 85 dbs, and loud pop music is about 110 dbs.

In addition to the loudness of sound, audiometry measures the pitch or frequency of sound. Vowel sounds, for instance, have frequencies mainly below 1,000 cycles, whereas many consonant sounds are much higher, some with frequencies between 6,000 to 8,000 cycles. High frequency deafness means that the child may go unrecognized as deaf, but in fact he has difficulty in distinguishing consonants and his own speech will be faulty. Deafness can also be unilateral or bilateral, that is, affecting one or both ears. Clearly unilateral deafness is not as handicapping as bilateral deafness although a child with a unilateral loss may have difficulties in locating sound sources and in selective attention.

The degree of handicap caused by deafness will depend on the severity of the loss, but also on whether the loss has taken place before or after the acquisition of language. Children who are hearing-impaired from birth or babyhood are likely to have many more problems than those who became deaf post-lingually. In the latter case, although speech may deteriorate, language competence is likely to be maintained.

TYPES OF HEARING LOSS

The ear consists of an outer passage ending in the ear drum or tympanic membrane behind which is the middle ear. Within the middle ear there are small bones called the malleus, the incus and the stapies which conduct sound waves to the inner ear. The inner ear consists of a snail-shell-like structure called the cochlea which holds millions of sensory cells which are stimulated by sound waves. These translate sound into nerve impulses which are sent to the brain via auditory pathways. Hearing loss can occur when there is damage or blockage in any of these structures and pathways.

If the outer or middle ear is damaged or blocked the resulting loss is called a conductive one. If the sensori-neural pathways which start at the cochlea and continue through the auditory nerve and associated brain cells are damaged, the deafness is known as a sensori-neural hearing loss.

Conductive losses are usually acquired during infancy or early childhood but some develop in adult life. Sometimes the outer ear can become blocked; however, the majority of conductive hearing losses are located in the middle ear. Inflammation of the middle ear (otitis media), can result from persistent colds which block passages from the middle ear to the nose and throat. The condition can become chronic leading to damage of the eardrum and the ossicles. If left untreated, fluid caused by inflammation of the middle ear becomes thick and gluelike (hence commonly termed 'glue ear') and impedes the conduction of sound. This may be alleviated by the surgical removal of the adenoids and drainage of the fluid from the middle ear.

Congenital conductive deafness is rare; conductive losses tend to be of a lesser degree than sensori-neural losses and as such may not be detected early. Conductive hearing losses can also be of an intermittent nature, which again makes diagnosis difficult.

CAUSES AND INCIDENCE

Forfar and Arneil (1984) report that the incidence of severe sensori-neural deafness is 1 in 2,000 children. Maternal rubella was the cause in 30 per cent of the sample. A similar percentage were caused by hereditary factors. In contrast to the low incidence of severe deafness, 20 per cent of all children suffer from some conductive hearing loss during childhood. The diagnosis of the milder forms of deafness can be difficult, and only 50 per cent of children with partial hearing loss are diagnosed by three years of age.

In 1977 there were 4,000 children in schools for the profoundly deaf in England and Wales, 6,000 children in schools for the partially-hearing, with an additional 20,000 hearing-impaired children educated in ordinary schools, supported by a peripatetic service (DES statistics, 1977).

MEDICAL TREATMENT
Where the hearing impairment is located in the inner ear and auditory nerves, there is very little that can be done medically. Conductive deafness caused by infection can be treated with antibiotics and there is a certain amount of surgery which may help.

There has generally been a great advance in aids for deaf children. Hearing aids designed to magnify sound tend now to be small and fit closely into the ear. Many do not require a connecting flex between the amplifier and the ear-piece and babies under 12 months can now be given hearing aids. During school years, when listening is essential but sometimes difficult, other resources are available such as loop systems which amplify sound for the partially-hearing. The phonic ear apparatus may also be worn where the teacher speaks to the child through a microphone, and the pupil wears headphones and a small amplifier on the chest.

Visual impairment

Although the terms blind and partially-sighted are still widely used, most professionals now prefer the term visual impairment. One reason for this is that many misconceptions surround blindness. Only a minority of so called blind people are completely sightless. Gillham (1986), quoted an incidence of 10 per cent of the blind who are unable to see anything at all. 'Blind and partially sighted' are legal categories, rather than precise medical terms.

Visual impairment tends to be defined in terms of visual acuity but it may be easier to think in terms of a person's ability to read print. In fact, the majority of the registered blind read print rather than braille.

The degree of visual handicap is usually attained using a measure of distance acuity, such as Snellen's Chart. A ratio figure is given which represents the distance in metres at which the tested eye can read compared to the normal eye. A registered blind person, for example, can read print at 6 metres which a sighted person can read at 60 metres. Someone with a ratio of 6:24 would have difficulty reading newspaper print. Another measure which is frequently used is the type size the child can read. N18, for example, means that the child can read type 18 with near vision and this would imply severe visual difficulties.

Usually only the Snellen Chart for distance acuity is used for routine purposes in school medical screening. A child who appears to have more complex problems is likely to be referred to the opthalmologist for a more detailed investigation. As with partial deafness, it is easy to overlook signs of milder visual handicap in a young child. Signs of visual fatigue, bumping into objects or holding objects at odd angles may all be symptomatic.

CAUSES OF VISUAL IMPAIRMENT

Frazer and Friedman (1968) made an extensive survey of 776 British children in special schools for the visually handicapped to determine the incidence of types of blindness. There were five major categories:

● heredity/genetic;
● pre-natal;
● perinatal;
● post-natal;
● a combination of heredity and environmental causes.

Heredity/genetic   About 42 per cent of the visually impaired children in the study had genetically based defects. There are a number of hereditary diseases which can result in visual impairment, for example, retinal blastoma, a malignant tumour of the eye may occur in infancy or may be inherited. Another hereditary cause is infantile cataracts which cloud the lens of the eye, and may also result from a disease affecting the eyes such as diabetes. Abnormalities of the optic nerve and visual cortex may also be inherited.

Pre-natal   Radiation and drugs may possibly cause blindness pre-natally; however, maternal rubella is the most common causal agent and about 6 per cent of the children in the study were affected in this way.

Perinatal   Over one-third of the children in the study were visually impaired as a result of too much oxygen being given at birth to prematurely born babies, the result being retolental fibroplasia. Once the cause of this type of blindness was detected, improvements in perinatal care has led to a dramatic decline. A very small risk remains, however, for very premature babies.

Post-natal   In the study about 11 per cent of children had become visually handicapped as a result of accident, infection or disease in infancy.

Heredity/environment   The remaining very small proportion of children had suffered from poor social circumstances where eye conditions have been neglected or exacerbated by disease. The majority of the children in the study described above had lost their sight before birth or in very early infancy. The vast majority of blind people are elderly, and the commonest causes of blindness are therefore, accident, degeneration and disease.

INCIDENCE
Since registration of the child with defective sight as blind is voluntary, it is difficult to get reliable official statistics. In 1976, there were approximately 100,000 registered blind people in Britain and a further 42,000 registered as partially sighted, but the vast majority of these people are adults and over 70 per cent were over the age of 65 years. In the Third World blindness, due mainly to disease, is common and it has been estimated that there are a staggering 40 million blind people in the world today.

The DES (1968b), predicted that 1,000 children would require special schooling for blindness in 1980. There has been a marked downward trend in the registration of blindness and partial sight in children. However, there is also a proportional increase in the blind with multiple handicaps. 35.2 per cent of blind children in 1970 had severe mental handicap and over 50 per cent had more than one handicap.

LESS SERIOUS VISUAL IMPAIRMENT

The vast majority of visual impairment in the Western world is not seriously handicapping, and corrective spectacles or low-vision aids, such as magnifiers, can help the child considerably.

Short-sightedness The most common defects are focusing and refraction errors. Myopia or short-sightedness is the most common visual problem. The child is best able to see near objects and has difficulty with distance. The reason for this is that the child's eyeball is too long from front to back so that light is focused in front of the retina rather than on it. The result is an inability to focus on distant objects; in the classroom visual aids will be difficult to see unless the defect is corrected by a concave lens which focuses the light back onto the retina. As the child grows older, myopia usually progresses but may become noticeable only at the growth spurt at around 10 to 14 years and the condition usually stabilizes in late adolescence. In extreme myopia, the retina may become detached by injury or violent movement. It was once advised that children with this tendency should avoid physical exercise. Nowadays, however, although care is advised, the child is not usually limited in this way as secondary problems may unintentionally accrue.

Far-sightedness Far-sightedness or hypermytropia means that distant objects are seen well but near objects present difficulties. The eyeball is too short from front to back, thus accommodation of the lens for focusing on the retina is faulty. A convex lens is used for correction purposes.

Other disorders Another common problem is astigmatism. Here the cornea or lens of the eye is irregularly shaped so that the image may be distorted or out of focus, and reading print horizontally and tables and graphs vertically may present difficulties. The condition is corrected using a cylindrical lens. Squints or strabismus are again relatively common, and may be of varying severity. Here one eye turns inwards or outwards so that the two eyes do not focus properly. Double vision can result, or a problem known as 'lazy eye', where vision from the weak eye is suppressed by the brain to avoid interference. The result is that the child sees only monocularly, apart from using the weak eye for peripheral vision. It is important to treat a lazy eye early since visual acuity of that eye may deteriorate. A further disorder of eye movement is nystagmus, where the eye oscillates in a jerky manner.

Despite their odd appearance, many of the children manage quite well in school. Spectacles, exercises and sometimes surgery may help all these conditions.

LEARNING DIFFICULTIES ASSOCIATED WITH VISUAL IMPAIRMENT
Vision and mobility are clearly very important for learning processes in the early years. There are marked delays in the locomotor development of blind babies. Norris, Spaulding and Brodie (1957) found that only about 50 per cent of blind babies can walk independently by 24 months. Many blind babies never crawl. A degree of mobility is necessary for the child's growing concept of space, and mobility should be encouraged in the blind infant if other aspects of development are not to be retarded. Some blind children indulge in internal stimulation such as rocking, finger flicking and head banging. Many of the usual avenues for learning, such as imitation, are closed to them, and imitative play, which usually develops at about three years, may well be absent.

Another problem is that children learning to read braille tend to learn much more slowly than those reading print. In 1970, the DES survey of braille-reading found that 36 per cent of visually handicapped children had not mastered the mechanics of reading by 11 years of age. A comparison of matched groups of normal and visually impaired older children found that although their comprehension skills were similar, the sighted group read at twice the speed. Some blind children can learn to use auditory stimulation, that is, changes in the pitch or echo of sound to detect obstacles. The pitch of a sound rises as you move towards an obstruction. Thus, to some extent, the visually impaired can compensate for their loss of vision by using their other senses. Similarly, given the incentive to overcome their handicap, blind children are likely to make better use of the senses they do have. Some become accomplished musicians because this represents an avenue for achievement.

The child who has sight before he becomes blind is not likely to be as retarded intellectually, since he may retain visual imagery and many concepts which are grounded on the sense of sight, such as colour, will have meaning for him. However, he will have to adjust to his handicap and relearn many skills. Many children find this an easier task than their parents would suppose. The child born blind is less likely to suffer the emotional problems associated with readjustment, but his experience may be so narrow that unless his parents are able to offer a great deal of stimulation, he may become intellectually limited.

SPEECH, LANGUAGE AND COMMUNICATION DISORDERS

Language is a highly complex skill which distinguishes human beings from all other animals. It is a system of verbal symbols which can represent objects, actions, attributes, events, ideas, etc., through which we communicate with one another. Language and social life are interdependent, and culture and science are transmitted via language. Our very thought processes are embodied in language, so it is one of the fundamental characteristics of intelligence. The child's ability to use language, his verbal expression, his general vocabulary and his comprehension, will all set the limits of his reading ability. Language is thus a necessary prerequisite for scholastic attainment.

Language development is often judged in terms of the child's spoken utterances, but it is usually the case that much more can be understood than spoken, and comprehension generally precedes language production. When language development is delayed or absent, the cause may be physical or environmental. In this chapter we are concerned with the physical causes; in the previous one we discussed some of the associated environmental factors.

Normal language development

In order to understand language difficulties in children it may be helpful first to provide a framework of normal language development.

In normal development, in the first weeks of life the baby begins to respond socially by listening to the human voice and trying to bring his eyes into focus on the face in front of him. By the fourth month of life he is able to play some small part in the social exchange that is going on around him. He responds with smiles, kicks his arms and legs with pleasure when people talk to him and he begins to discover his own voice as it emerges in cries, coos and gurgles. At around 6 months the baby will begin to babble and will continue to expand his repertoire of sounds. First words appear at around his first birthday (Crystal, 1985).

After the appearance of the first few words there is usually a long plateau. Research has shown that language development accelerates at around 18 months of age, so that, by the age of 2 years the average child has a vocabulary of about 250 single word utterances. At around this age, the two-word utterance or holophrase emerges. It is this development of the embryo sentence that is often the crucial difference between normality and serious handicap. Two-word utterances mark the beginning of grammar, syntax and the facility to generate many new sentences from a fixed number of words.

Many children with severe learning difficulties can acquire a considerable vocabulary of single words but fail at the holophrastic stage. Brown and Bellugi (1964) analysed samples of two-word utterances in babies and found that one word acts as a pivot for the generation of many sentences. Examples are 'Ball gone'; 'Dinner gone'; 'Mummy gone'; the word 'gone' is the pivot to which many words in the child's vocabulary can be attached. The child can now comment on the world around him and join in conversation at a much more elaborate level. By the age of 3, four-word sentences are usual and from this time on language increasingly reflects experience rather than biological determinants.

Classification of disorders

The distinction is usually made between speech, which involves the production of sounds, and language, which involves comprehension. Language can be further subdivided into grammar or syntax, and meaning or semantics. This classification can be useful when describing different problems.

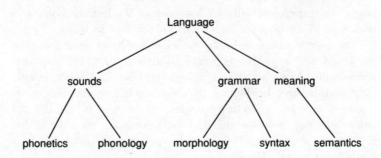

Source: Garman, 1980.
Figure 4.1 Levels of linguistic analysis.

Crystal (1980) used another classification:

a Pathologies of reception: deafness, partial hearing and auditory discrimination;
b Central pathologies: aphasia, agnosia, dysphasia, dysarthria and developmental language disorders;
c Pathologies of production: fluency, voice and articulation.

Harding (1986) proposed a simpler model for teachers and other non-specialists:

a Receptive difficulties: deaf and partial hearing, auditory discrimination;
b Speech problems: voice, fluency (stuttering and stammering), articulation;
c Language difficulties: developmental language disorders.

RECEPTIVE DIFFICULTIES
As mentioned earlier, children with hearing difficulties are likely to have problems also with speech and language. As far as auditory discrimination is concerned, many young children of 3 or 4 often make errors in the discrimination of speech sounds but usually grow out of it. As Harding points out, many children with speech and articulation difficulties beyond the age of 7 or 8 also have problems with the discrimination of speech sounds. In particular they may have difficulty discrimin-

ating between ck/g, b/p, t/d, and this is also frequently reflected in their reading errors. Auditory discrimination difficulties can also occur in children who hear normally.

Bryant and Bradley (1985) found in their research that the significant difference between poor and young readers was their awareness of sounds. This problem predated their reading problems, and when given specific training in sound awareness, using exercises in alliteration and rhymes etc., their reading skills improved considerably. Bryant and Bradley recommended training poor readers in sound awareness using multi-sensory methods as discussed in Chapter 7.

SPEECH PROBLEMS

The sound structure of language is usually defined in terms of phonetics and phonology. Phonetics refers to the sound quality of speech, that is, the pitch and loudness of the voice. Phonology refers to the speech sounds. Whereas normal children may have articulation difficulties, partially hearing children are likely to have problems with the voice.

Stuttering and stammering   Some children with a stammer or stutter have problems with speech production, that is, the motor aspects of speech. Stuttering is characterized by repetitions of sounds, stops and gaps. Andrews and Harris (1964) found that 79 per cent of the children in their study had periods of fluent speech before they became stutterers. Van Riper (1973) has made an extensive study of stutterers, and Crystal (1980), has analysed the problem in some depth. One of the problems in remediation is deciding on the root causes of the stammer. Some prefer to treat the stammer directly through speech therapy, whereas others prefer to tackle the cause of anxiety. Van Riper points out that the Western approach is to work indirectly by encouraging parent and child to communicate and help to relieve anxiety. Whereas the Eastern approach is to give speech training, with stress on rhythmical activities.

Articulation problems   Ingram (1976) quoted in Harding, gives a useful table of the average age acquisition of English speech sounds. 90 per cent of children can produce most sounds by the age of 7 or 8. The most difficult sounds to reproduce are 'z' (as in measure), 'th', 'v', 'j', 'c' (as in ceiling), 's', 'r' and 'l'. The position of the sound in the word is also probably important. Some children also have difficulty with polysyllabic words.

Harding suggested that teachers can give the following test, devised by Sheridan (1945), to assess roughly whether a child's speech is abnormal, and if referral to a speech therapist may be required. Pringle, Butler and Davie (1966) found that most 7 year olds can articulate them correctly:

Say after me: Mary had a little lamb (practice)

1   Carol threaded a needle with wool.
2   She mended her sister's frock.
3   Roger grasped a bundle of sticks.
4   Eating porridge gives him strength.
5   My brother rode his bicycle to school.
6   Philip had scrambled eggs for breakfast.

Many children's speech problems will be overcome with time, although some require speech therapy.

LANGUAGE DIFFICULTIES
Peripheral language disorders (involving tongue and palate)   Some children suffer with difficulties of speech production through physical problems associated with the tongue and palate. Tongue thrust affects clear sound production, and children born with a cleft palate have great difficulty in making speech sounds until their palate is repaired. Children with these articulation difficulties are disadvantaged in subtle ways apart from the obvious problem of making themselves understood. After initial failures, they tend to avoid further difficult communications. The child is thereby denied opportunities to practise speech and to develop his comprehension. Secondary emotional problems can accrue.

Central language disorders (involving the brain)

DYSPHASIAS   Clinical observations of adults suffering from speech problems caused by strokes or similar types of damage to the brain have led researchers to argue that children with similar severe characteristics may be suffering from a developmental form of the same condition. However, other commentators point out that it may be misleading to draw any comparison between the adult damaged brain, where functions are fully developed, and the undeveloped infant brain. There is a group of children with severe and intractable language difficulties who display average intelligence in other areas of ability and developmental dysphasia is frequently discussed, if less frequently diagnosed, in such cases. Most children have difficulties in one area which are only slightly more marked than difficulties in another.

There are two main types of dysphasia:

RECEPTIVE DYSPHASIA The child with this rare and disabling condition has great difficulty in discriminating between speech sounds although he is not deaf. He often cannot distinguish between the sound of a bell and the sound of a tambourine although he may demonstrate average intelligence on some visual and perceptual tasks. Apart from discriminating sounds, the child may also have difficulty in symbolization, that is in learning that words can stand for objects or actions and in understanding a temporal sequence. Severe emotional difficulties can arise from the frustration that this condition can bring about and such children are frequently misdiagnosed. The condition is baffling and poorly understood.

EXPRESSIVE DYSPHASIA With expressive dysphasia, the child comprehends speech normally but has great difficulty in organizing and sequencing his reply. Sometimes dysphasic children can be taught expression and improved comprehension through pictures or through reading, and occasionally a manual signing system helps. Often, however, other associated learning problems exist and teaching has to be undertaken on a specialist, individualized basis. Expressive dysphasia is sometimes known as Broca's aphasia, after the neurologist who also gave his name to the area in the brain involved with speech production.

DYSARTHRIA Dysarthria is a disorder of articulation, rather than language. It involves the movement of lips, tongue and palate with laryngal involvement resulting in an abnormality of the voice, and possibly an associated effect on the rhythm of speech. The commonest cause of dysarthria is through a cleft palate, which is due to an anatomical lesion. There is also neurological dysarthria usually associated with cerebral palsy. Children with cerebral palsy sometimes lack the necessary motor control of their tongue and palate and speech is consequently impaired. Dysarthria can also result from brain injury. Alternative communication systems such as Bliss symbolics which employs pictograms or a manual signing system are usually taught. Dysarthria is rare, affecting fewer than 1 per cent of children with language disorders, and is the specialist province of the speech therapists.

INCIDENCE OF SPEECH AND LANGUAGE DISORDERS
In a study by Calnan and Richardson (1976) up to 16 per cent of all children showed some degree of speech defect. They found that the incidence of boys to girls was 2:1. The vast majority of these children have a temporary articulation disorder. Only 10 per cent of all the speech disorders actually involve language usage rather than speech production. Children with long-term severe speech disorders such as the dysphasias constitute a tiny proportion of children with language problems.

Language disorders and severe learning difficulties

Spreen (1965) showed that there is a strong correlation between learning difficulty and language disorder. 90 per cent of children in schools for children with severe learning difficulties have severe language disorders. It has been demonstrated that within the range of intelligence scores in the severe learning difficulties category, language development correlates strongly with intelligence. Although not all thinking is linguistic, language development appears to be crucial if intellectual capacities are to be maximized.

Some aspects of language development appear to be more affected by intellectual impairment than others. Children with severe learning difficulty may have a large vocabulary of single words but they generally lack the ability to form categories, give descriptions or explanations and describe a logical sequence. Gillham (1986) also reported that such children fail to learn incidentally, that is, they fail to pick up those words and phrases that parents use which are not directed entirely at them. In any assessment of language delay the possibility of a more general mental retardation is always considered.

AUTISM

Autism is a particularly severe and distressing phenomenon. It is fortunately a rare condition affecting approximately four children in 10,000, and is seven times more common in boys than in girls. Autism is generally found in association with severe mental retardation although there are some more intelligent autistic children. Autism was first described by Kanner in 1943, when he identified a group of children as having 'autistic disturbances of affective contact'; later Kanner adopted the term 'early infant autism'. Historically the terms 'infantile psychosis' and 'childhood schizophrenia' have been used interchangeably with autism, but most investigators now view autism as distinct from forms of childhood schizophrenia. The diagnosis remains difficult, however, since it rests on behavioural symptoms, rather than on a known neurological condition.

Kanner described twelve symptoms of autism. A child may have a number of these symptoms but not all of them and thus not display the same behaviours as another autistic child. Increasingly, the failure to communicate through the flexible and fluent use of language, and the lack of social responsiveness, have been seen as the hallmarks of autism.

Characteristics of autism   Autism is probably present from birth and most investigators believe that it results from organic damage to the brain. The autistic child is often reported to have been a very good baby because, being unresponsive, he does not actively seek his mother's attention. As a result, autism is not always recognized in babyhood. It may not be until the second or third year of life, when the autistic child has failed to develop language, that the parents seek medical advice.

Rutter and Schopler (1978) suggested that the symptoms of autism can be separated into four groups of primary symptoms. These are: delayed language development; profound problems of relating to other people; obsessional and ritualistic behaviours; the early onset of the above symptoms together with disturbances of developmental rate.

DEVIANT AND DELAYED LANGUAGE DEVELOPMENT The autistic child usually has problems in understanding the prerequisites of language, for example, in imitating others, in gesture, pointing and in the body language of social interactions. Speech development is almost always delayed and fixations in language use may occur in the course of development such as echoing the last word or words of a sentence just heard, misuse or reversal of pronouns and telegraphese. Some autistic children fail to develop language at all, whilst rudimentary language develops very late with others. Their language is usually both poor in quality and content and contains many rigidities, oddities and obsessions. Typically, it fails to convey subtle emotion, imagination or humour and is tied to concrete observations, often of the associative type.

DISTURBANCES IN RELATING TO OTHER PEOPLE One of the distressing and notable symptoms of autism is the child's seeming lack of interest or response to other human beings. Characteristically, the child avoids eye contact and has delayed or absent social responsiveness. The child may also have an aversion to physical contact and he is as uninterested in other human beings as if they were merely part of the furniture. Autistic children generally look perfectly normal so that strangers are likely to have standard expectations of them in their initial contact. The stress imposed on the child by such expectations is likely to be extremely high and could help to account for the fact that autistic children find social encounters difficult, but the problem appears to be more fundamental than a learned response to stress, and the comprehension of social behaviour is drastically impaired.

OBSESSION AND RITUAL Autistic children characteristically develop obsessional interests in certain activities such as running up and down on the spot, flapping their hands and walking on tiptoe; and in certain objects such as tin cans, stones, watches, washing machines, trains and calendars. They may also have particular and seemingly irrational aversions to everyday activities and objects. The autistic child may also show unusual responses to sensory stimulation. His reaction to sound, sight or touch may be alternatively exaggerated, absent or diminished. He may walk into objects as though he did not see them, but show intense interest in tiny points of light or flashing objects. He may respond with fright to ordinary everyday sounds; equally he may seem oblivious to very loud noises. These exaggerated, diminished and bizarre responses can lead to embarrassing scenes where the child can become besides himself for no apparent reason through his excessive interests or aversions.

EARLY ONSET   Kolvin (1971) investigated a large number of psychotic children and identified two distinct groups; those who had an early onset of their symptoms and who were characterized by language disorders; and a late onset group characterized by hallucinations and delusions, who were more appropriately labelled as psychotic. Kolvin concluded that autism begins before 30 months, and subtle signs of autism that were present in babyhood can usually be elicited by careful history-taking. Autistic children also show a disordered development with spurts and plateaux, and their abilities can be very uneven with 'islets' of skills which can sometimes be highly developed and above average for the normal child (Selfe, 1983).

Causes and treatment   The cause of autism is not known. There are no known factors in the psychological development of the child that give rise to the condition. It afflicts children in all parts of the world, of all racial and ethnic backgrounds, and is found in all families across the full spectrum of intelligence, social class and personality type. Recent evidence supports the theory that autism results from damage to the brain through injury, disease or some other factor, but the locus is unknown (Rutter, 1978). Autism also appears in conjunction with other diseases and autistic features are regularly seen in children who are known to have neurological damage such as those who are victims of maternal rubella and retolental fibroplasia. A significant number of autistic children develop epilepsy as they grow older, confirming the theory that brain dysfunction is the likely cause.

The treatment of autism is at an experimental stage; most autistic children will need specialist teaching as the majority have severe learning difficulties, but some cope well in ordinary schools. Educational programmes for autistic children tend to stress language development and the modification of the unacceptable behaviours that the child may exhibit. Training in social awareness and social skills is also attempted.

5

Maladjustment, emotional and behavioural difficulties

OVERVIEW

This chapter discusses some of the ways adjustment difficulties are conceptualized, and considers some of the influential factors affecting behaviour and emotional development. The focus of maladjusted behaviour has widened in recent years from a focus on child characteristics to a consideration of the total context of behaviour, as this chapter will reflect.

INTRODUCTION

Many children cause concern to their parents and teachers because of emotional and behavioural difficulties. It may be that they behave in ways that are difficult for adults to manage, or in ways which suggest they are unhappy or distressed. The way we describe such problems belies our own attitudes and conceptual framework, so whether we describe the children concerned as 'maladjusted' or 'deviant', 'disruptive' or 'disaffected', 'disturbed' or 'disturbing', 'troubled' or 'troublesome', not only reflects the way we view the problems, but is likely to influence the way we react to them.

Most early accounts of maladjustment talk as if the child had a problem akin to an illness, which requires expert treatment. The personality characteristics of the child were analysed, and explanations were sought for their behavioural difficulties, in terms of the effect of past events on their emotional and social development. More recently the influence of the context in which maladaptive behaviour takes place has been emphasized, and explanations have focused on the interaction between the child and his environment. It is now recognized that people behave differently in different situations, so if problems are to be resolved it might be more appropriate to analyse the influence of the context in which the behaviour occurs than attempt to change the individual child in isolation. This chapter looks at some of these issues in more detail.

EARLY CONCEPTUALIZATIONS AND DEFINITIONS OF MALADJUSTMENT

The 1945 Handicapped Pupils and School Health Regulations, which were published after the 1944 Education Act, officially recognized the category of maladjustment, and for the first time made it a legal duty for LEAs to provide suitable educational provision for children with adjustment difficulties.

Maladjusted pupils were defined as those 'who show evidence of emotional instability or psychological disturbance, and who require special educational treatment in order to effect their personal, social and educational readjustment.' The definition is circular and thus not very helpful as it remains unclear how to identify emotional instability or psychological disturbance, or what the treatment might consist of. However, it was officially established that some children are unlikely to benefit from ordinary education because of their emotional and behavioural difficulties, and some alternative form of special education was needed to remedy their problems.

Laslett (1983) points out that this regulation must have been confusing to teachers at that time, as there were no trained specialist teachers, nor courses or literature available, to explain what the specialist educational treatment might be.

Since this time there has been much confusion about the

term 'maladjustment', as well as soul-searching about the best methods for identifying maladjusted children in order to determine who should receive special educational provision. Galloway and Goodwin (1987) claim that this search for a group of children whose behaviour is qualitatively different from others reveals a misunderstanding of semantics. They point out that the term was largely invented as an administrative label to invoke an alternative form of schooling under the 1944 Education Act, and the term does not refer to a clearly defined set of characteristics. 'Maladjustment', they maintain, 'is a ragbag term to describe any type of behaviour which teachers, psychologists or doctors find disturbing.'

The next official report concerning maladjustment was not until ten years after the 1945 Regulations, when the Underwood Committee reported on the medical, educational and social problems of the maladjusted child. The Underwood Report (DES, 1955), elaborating on previous definitions of maladjustment, stated: 'a child may be regarded as maladjusted who is developing in ways that have a bad effect on himself, or his fellows, and cannot without help, be remedied by his parents, teachers and the other adults in ordinary contact with him . . . they are characteristically insecure, unhappy, and they fail in their personal relationships . . . receiving is as difficult for them as giving'.

Behavioural symptoms

In order to help in the identification of these children, the report went on to group behavioural symptoms under six main headings:

1   Nervous or emotional disorders: these difficulties are sometimes referred to as neurotic disorders and include children with excessive fears and anxieties and those who are very quiet and withdrawn.
2   Habit or developmental disorders: an example might be enuresis occurring in an older child.
3   Behavioural or conduct disorders: these are sometimes referred to as antisocial or acting out behaviour; for example, stealing, aggression, vandalism or truancy.

4 Organic disorders: these have a physiological origin, such as temper tantrums which result from some forms of epilepsy.
5 Psychotic behaviour: some rare conditions such as childhood schizophrenia may present symptoms such as abnormal fears, delusions and hallucinations.
6 Educational and behavioural difficulties.

The report made clear the difficulty of categorizing these symptoms since there is no absolute distinction between normality and abnormality. It suggested that factors such as the intensity and duration of the problem, as well as its developmental appropriateness, would need to be taken into account. Thus, whereas temper tantrums are usually regarded as a normal developmental feature in a 2 or 3 year old, they may suggest an adjustment problem if they continue into adolescence. Although the report acknowledged that external factors might be understood to cause the stress, and so would need to be considered in evaluating the severity of the problem, the problem was seen to reside within the child, and it was the child who might consequently require special educational treatment.

The confusion between educational and psychiatric terms

It is evident that conceptions of maladjustment at this time relied heavily on the medical notion of a psychiatric disorder, and it is difficult to distinguish between them. Rutter and Graham (1966) defined a psychiatric disorder as 'an abnormality of behaviour, emotions or relationships sufficiently marked and sufficiently prolonged to cause persistent suffering or handicap to the child and/or distress or disturbance to the family or community'. They pointed out, however, that although many children with psychiatric disorders could be regarded as maladjusted, the two terms are not synonymous. Maladjustment is an educational not a medical term, and is used to indicate that a special form of schooling is considered desirable.

Rutter *et al.* (1975) argued that in most cases children with disordered behaviour do not need to be treated by a psychiatrist as they do not have a mental illness. They stated that few problems are qualitatively different from the norm, but rather they 'constitute exaggerations of or deviations from the normal'. They also pointed out that in fact most children show isolated psychological problems at some time, and 'to a considerable extent this is part and parcel of growing up and they are not in themselves the cause of concern'.

Rutter suggested that in deciding whether behaviour is abnormal, consideration should be given to:

a whether the behaviour is age and sex appropriate;
b its persistence;
c the child's life circumstances;
d the social-cultural setting;
e the extent of disturbance (number of symptoms);
f the type of symptoms;
g the severity or frequency of symptoms;
h changes in behaviour;
i the situation specificity (what happens before and after the behaviour).

Decisions should also take into account the degree of suffering caused, the extent of the interference with the child's development, as well as the effect on other people. He also pointed out that concern about behaviour does not necessarily imply that it is the child who has the problem and requires help. When making an initial assessment it is important to determine the answer to questions such as who is concerned, why they are, and why they have sought help at the present time. The problem may reside with the parents, the family or the school. Thus not only the child but the social context needs to be assessed.

The overlap between educational and psychiatric terms probably reflects the fact that in the past psychiatrists and school medical doctors played a dominant role in diagnosing and treating emotional and behavioural problems presented at school, as well as making recommendations about special schooling. A survey of child guidance clinics in 1974 found that psychiatrists alone were responsible for about 64 per cent of the recommendations for placements in maladjusted schools (Laslett, 1977).

Since then there has been a steady shift in professional roles and responsibilities. Educational psychologists are now more likely to be consulted about behavioural difficulties presented in school and they also have a more central role in defining special needs and making recommendations about the most suitable educational provision for children with these difficulties (Circular 2/75, DES). The emphasis has consequently shifted from conceiving adjustment problems in terms of a personality disorder, to focusing on the child's needs relevant to schooling.

THE FREQUENCY OF ADJUSTMENT DIFFICULTIES

It is difficult to estimate the number of children with adjustment difficulties at any one time, partly because of the problems of definition, and partly because of the different ways in which data is collected.

Laslett (1983) draws attention to the diversity of figures arrived at in various surveys between 1946 and 1975. The 1944 Act suggested that approximately 1 per cent of children need special schooling because of maladjusted behaviour, whereas the Underwood Report (DES, 1955) suggested that between 5 and 12 per cent of children might require special schooling because of adjustment problems. Davie, Butler and Goldstein (1972), in a national survey of 11,000 7-year-old children, found that teachers regarded 14 per cent of pupils as maladjusted, with a further 22 per cent 'unsettled'. Rutter, Tizard and Whitmore (1970), found 12 per cent pupils to have adjustment difficulties in their Isle of Wight survey, but as many as 25 per cent in their London survey (1975). Since the range given seems to be between 1 and 25 per cent, clearly figures are somewhat arbitrary.

As noted earlier, much of the data was arrived at by asking teachers to complete questionnaires which reflected their perception of the child's problems. However, teachers' perceptions are likely to be coloured by many factors: some may not like to admit to teaching difficult pupils for fear it might reflect adversely on their own ability; others may feel identification could argue for additional resources in their school. In addition, their skills, attitudes and tolerance levels will affect their views. What is unacceptable behaviour to one teacher may be tolerated by another. A child who is difficult to manage might represent an interesting challenge to one teacher, but might be the final straw to another. Behaviour which is considered normal in some schools or homes, may be regarded as extreme in others. It could be said that deviance, like beauty, lies in the eyes of the beholder.

The problem is not just to do with the subjectivity of perceptions. As noted earlier, people behave in different ways in different circumstances. Children are affected by their teachers and by other children, and they may well behave differently at home to school. In the same way, pupils who are perceived as problematic in secondary schools may have behaved appropriately in the junior school, and vice versa. The point is an obvious one, that behaviour is a complex interactional process and it is misleading to describe children as if their behavioural characteristics were an unchangeable aspect of their personalities. Few children are difficult all the time, with everyone. Their behaviour changes in different contexts, and it varies with circumstances and with age. When problem behaviour is described it is therefore important to avoid generalizations and to be explicit about the difficulties and the context in which they occur.

For all these reasons, it is difficult to estimate the prevalence of emotional and behavioural problems, or to know if they are increasing in frequency.

THE GROWTH OF PROVISION

Special schools and units

Whatever the truth about the numbers of children with adjustment difficulties, indiscipline in schools would seem to be a growing problem and there is no doubt that there has certainly has been a notable expansion in special provision in the last few decades. Between 1955 and 1975, the number of places created for these children in residential special schools, day schools and special classes and units rose considerably, despite falling rolls in education generally, and widespread financial cuts.

Table 5.1   Full-time pupils attending special schools for the maladjusted

1950	1960	1970	1978	1982
87	1,742	6,093	14,406	14,017

Sources: DES, 1966, 1978, 1982; Welsh Office, 1978, 1982.

On- and off-site units in mainstream schooling

In addition to the increase in special school provision for maladjusted pupils, during the 1970s there was a huge increase in small segregated units, on- and off-site, which were generally for secondary-aged pupils in ordinary schools who were causing control problems for teachers. This developed as a way of catering for disruptive and disaffected pupils as well as poor attenders.

Difficult pupils were isolated from the rest of the class to relieve the stress on teachers and the school system generally, offer containment and hopefully provide a more therapeutic setting for the youngsters concerned. A national survey in 1978 (DES, 1978b) revealed that nearly 4,000 places were available in 239 units, across 69 local authorities. Over 80 per cent of these had been established since 1973. By 1980, there were 339 units for 6,791 pupils (Advisory Centre for Education, 1980).

It is unclear why there was this sudden expansion in unit provision in the 1970s. Some suggest it was necessitated by a breakdown in discipline in the secondary schools; others, that it was a response to the raising of the school leaving age from 15 to 16 years, and to allay teachers' fears about comprehensive education and the abolition of corporal punishment. Tattum (1982) sees their establishment as arising from social and political pressure to resolve the conflict in schools created by an educational system based on cultural inequality, which prefers to offload problems rather than adapt to them.

Since the provision was part of ordinary mainstream provision, either on-site of the secondary school, or as a central off-site unit provided by the authority for a number of local schools, there was no problem in finding candidates to fill the places. The units were usually controlled by headteachers, and were used as a quick and convenient answer to discipline problems. There was a minimum of administrative fuss, and placement could often be an internal matter for the school, without involvement by the educational psychologist. As the intention was not to make them attractive alternatives to the classroom, the units were often punitive in philosophy, and so were regarded as 'sin bins', housing unmanageable children.

The pupils who entered these units tended to be older, and were perceived to be disruptive rather than maladjusted. Unlike pupils who go to special units as a result of lengthy assessment procedures, where parental rights are safeguarded and parents have a say in the choice of provision, pupils in disruptive units were often placed there without ceremony. Although their stay was usually intended to be short-term, classroom teachers were frequently reluctant to accept them back into normal classes. Surprisingly, the legality of removing children in this way was not questioned until the Rampton Report (DES, 1981). There was clearly a risk of arbitrariness, parental rights of appeal were unprotected, and the child's needs were not examined.

Other problems became apparent. Because of the small size of units, the curriculum was usually very limited, and frequently amounted to basic skills work; resources were also limited progress with learning, and reintegration rates were poor. boys referred, and in London, at least, an over-representation of ethnic minority pupils.

Topping (1983) found that pupils who attended units made limited progress at learning, and reintegration rates were poor. Moreover, their subsequent adjustment after attending a unit tended not to improve. Evidence suggests that behavioural units were positively harmful for those pupils who attended them, and they were educationally unsound.

There is often a conflict of interests between the needs of mainstream teachers to remove a pupil speedily from class, and the needs of unit staff to control and balance admissions. There are also problems about the limitations of the curriculum and reintegration difficulties which frequently arise. With careful planning of policies these problems are not insurmountable, but alternative schools and peripatetic support teams are possible alternatives.

The support service approach

In response to changing attitudes about segregationalist policies, various local authorities are now establishing peripatetic support teams to consult with teachers, liaise with parents, and offer advice and support to pupils with behavioural difficulties in school. Depending on the philosophy and size of the service, sometimes pupils are withdrawn from lessons and given individual or small-group help. Long (1988) reports on one such scheme where a behavioural problem-solving approach is used in schools with an emphasis on establishing good liaison between home and school. Reporting systems are refined to overcome the frequently negative effects of report cards, and pupils are involved in monitoring their own behaviour. Research suggests that involving the pupil in their own assessment increases their awareness and promotes behavioural change (McNamara, 1979). In addition, reward systems are set up involving parents at home, as school-based reinforcers are more difficult to establish and sustain.

THE CONCEPT OF MALADJUSTMENT
IN THE WARNOCK REPORT
AND THE 1981 ACT

As noted earlier, the Warnock Report reviewed the whole field of special education and made many wide-reaching recommendations. It therefore came as some surprise when all the 1944 Act categories of handicap were abolished, with the exception of maladjustment. The committee noted that they considered recommending various alternative terms such as 'emotional and behavioural difficulties', but on balance they decided that 'maladjustment' was still useful and should be retained. The committee recognized that the term can stigmatize a child unnecessarily and that it is so relative as to be meaningless without details of the child's circumstances. They also accepted that the term may falsely imply a permanent condition as well as fail to indicate the type of special educational provision required. Despite these objections, the committee argued that the term itself implies that children are poorly adjusted in relation to their circumstances, and that this outweighs other considerations.

Nevertheless, the term seems to be becoming outmoded since it has negative connotations, and frequently confers all sorts of unhelpful and inaccurate attributes. It still suggests a medical model of difficulties which focuses on the child and largely ignores the social and environmental context in which behaviour occurs. The danger, as Tattum (1985) noted, is that 'concentration on the social pathology of the individual permits us to ignore deficiencies in the system'.

Thus, although the Warnock Report pointed out that 'the underlying problems may derive from or be influenced by the regime and relationships in schools, and many children may simply be reacting to these', the committee and the Act which followed seem to have paid scant regard to this important factor. For example, formal assessments are geared to assessing the functioning of individual children, rather than considering why difficulties arise by looking at the curriculum or school system in depth.

Galloway and Goodwin (1987) also pointed out that although the report and the Act support the principle of integration, there is also an underlying assumption that some children who are difficult for their teachers to manage will need to be removed from the school, for the good of the rest of the class. The 1981 Act, for example, created clear loopholes which can be used to enforce segregation rather than integration. The Act requires that LEAs must consider the best use of resources and the good of the rest of the class when deciding on provision. The danger is that, rather than creating a climate for integration, the Act may create a demand for increased segregated provision.

Furthermore, the 1981 Act has increased the conceptual muddle over terminology and in effect created new categories, by proposing different legal procedures for different groups of children. It is made clear that pupils who are disruptive in class, who require alternative schooling as a short-term measure, may be removed and taught in special units without the 'protection' of a statement. In contrast, other children who undergo formal assessments, can only be given special educational provision after a lengthy multi-professional assessment, when their needs are determined and parents are fully consulted.

It is important to remember that there is often no behavioural difference between pupils described as maladjusted or those termed disruptive. Galloway and Goodwin argued that the labels say more about the age of the child and the teacher's attitudes than about the child's characteristics. They claim that the term maladjustment is most frequently used when teachers wish to convey that the child has reached the limit of their tolerance, and they want him removed to an alternative school. In addition, younger pupils are also more likely to be described maladjusted, formally assessed, 'statemented', and placed in special schools. Older pupils are more likely to be labelled disruptive, and suspended from school and/or removed to a disruptive unit.

Galloway and Goodwin raise the question about whose needs are being met by using these terms. They suggest that schools and units for disruptive pupils exist more for the benefit of teachers and children in ordinary schools, than for the pupils they claim to help. This is not to say that a teacher's needs and those of the rest of the class are not important, but rather that, whilst they are not being overtly recognized, the nature of the difficulty may be incorrectly identified and the wrong type of help provided.

In their view the solution to the problem of terminology is relatively easy: 'the Committee could have adopted the easy, and honest, solution of calling these children "disturbing" rather than "maladjusted"'. In their opinion, this would give recognition to the importance of school factors in any analysis of behavioural problems, and would not necessarily imply that the only helpful solution is to remove the child from ordinary school.

Thus both the child's difficulties and the influence of environmental circumstances need to be acknowledged: 'many disruptive pupils do have exceptional personal needs which cannot be ignored in a comprehensive treatment plan. Equally important though . . . responses to disruptive behaviour must not only recognise the importance of factors in the pupil and his background, but also the relevance of factors in the school itself.' (Galloway *et al.*, 1982.)

It could be said that recent reports and legislation reflect the general mêlée of ideas about adjustment difficulties, but in many ways they do not provide a sufficiently clear philosophy upon which to build new, innovatory practices.

FACTORS INFLUENCING EMOTIONAL AND BEHAVIOURAL DIFFICULTIES

It would be impossible in one chapter to summarize all the research attempting to identify the factors associated with emotional and behavioural difficulties in children. All we can do is to draw attention to some factors which seem to be particularly relevant. It is worth remembering that most research studies only suggest that certain factors are associated with adjustment difficulties, since behaviour is a complex interactive process, and it is difficult to establish any causal relationships. Although for the sake of clarity this chapter is distinct from Chapters 3 and 4, there is much overlap between the factors which influence learning and behaviour.

Individual differences, temperament and health factors

With a few children, impaired neurological growth or damage to the central nervous system may affect their behaviour, so that they may have a limited attention span and an intolerance of frustration. Sometimes there is no hard physiological evidence of impairment, but 'minimal brain damage' is postulated in the absence of any other explanation, particularly if they have other symptoms associated with neurological dysfunction such as perceptual or language problems, or poor co-ordination. Diet, and toxins in the environment, are also put forward as possible causative factors particularly for hyperactive behaviour.

There are also likely to be constitutional differences in the degree of stress that individuals can tolerate, and it seems likely that there are some sex differences which may also be constitutional in origin, although they may be acquired characteristics. For example, boys are generally found to be more dominant and active than girls. Rutter *et al.* (1975), for example, found a 4:1 ratio between boys and girls for conduct disorders, and this figure is common in many studies.

Stott (1978) postulated that constitutional differences may underlie the differences between boys and girls, although the differences can be largely attributed to faulty learning styles, culturally acquired. Society encourages and expects different behaviour from males than females, and starts to shape this from the cradle.

Stott also found an association between the child's general health and maladjustment. Children with several physical disorders were found to be three and a half times more likely to have symptoms of maladjustment than healthy children. Children with delayed development may also take longer to achieve independence, and have more difficulty in controlling their impulses than other children. Children with delayed language, for example, may show their frustration over communicating by outbursts of temper. The same can be said of children with impaired hearing, or with some physical disorders.

Research also suggests that there are temperamental differences in children from birth, and children who frequently cry or who fail to thrive may quickly develop a negative mood that makes them difficult to manage and unrewarding to parent. Rutter *et al.* (1975) studied the temperamental differences in 3–7-year-old children, and found those with features of 'low regularity, low malleability, negative mood and low fastidiousness' were most at risk of developing disorders in the next four years. Children with at least two of these adverse temperamental features were three times as likely as other children to develop problems. They were twice as likely to be the target of parental criticism when their parents were depressed, and become the butt of marital stress and the focus of discord. Because of their negative behaviour, these children are at risk of being rejected when parents are under stress themselves.

Studies of adopted or fostered children of adult criminals suggest that some children may be constitutionally vulnerable, and are likely to succumb to environmental stress. It is always difficult to separate constitutional from environmental influences, but it seems possible that an interaction of factors may place some children at risk.

Family and community factors

There is little doubt that behaviour is largely shaped by the social context. From their earliest days, children learn about acceptable and non-acceptable behaviour from modelling others and from the way they are themselves treated. Socialization is the process of inducting a child into the social and moral rules of the family, and by means of this process children acquire a system of rules to regulate their interpersonal behaviour. It is important that children internalize the rules and do not just keep to them when forced to do so.

SOCIAL DISADVANTAGE

A variety of social disadvantage factors have been associated with adjustment as well as learning problems. Chapter 3 deals with these factors in more detail. In their national survey, Davie, Butler and Goldstein (1972) found about four times as many children rated as maladjusted came from social class 5 compared to social class 1. Crude measures relating to parental employment give no clear indication of what aspects of culture and lifestyle might increase the likelihood of difficulty, but more detailed surveys pinpoint some of the stresses that come with poverty and unemployment.

For example, Rutter *et al.* (1975) found that emotional disorders, conduct disorders and specific reading retardation were twice as common in the inner London area than in the Isle of Wight. Four variables were found to be associated with disorder: family discord, parental deviance, social disadvantage, and certain school characteristics, such as high teacher turnover, high absenteeism, and low teacher–pupil ratio. Rutter *et al.*'s study revealed that children in the inner city are often subjected to a multiplicity of stresses, and their families are more likely to have several difficulties to contend with at once.

Rutter pointed out that the number of stresses a child has to contend with is significant. Children with only one chronic family stress generally coped well, but with two or more stresses the psychiatric risk increased (Rutter and Quinton, 1977). They isolated six family adversity factors which seemed to be correlated with emotional and behavioural difficulties in children:

1 Father in unskilled/semiskilled job.
2 Overcrowding or large family size.
3 Marital discord or 'broken home'.
4 Mother depressed/neurotic.
5 Child 'in care'.
6 Father – any offence against the law.

Davie, Butler and Goldstein (1972) also found birth order to be important. The youngest child in a large family seems most at risk, which may be because material poverty is likely to be higher, or because the child may receive less attention and control from parents. Alternatively, he may be over-indulged by the family, and kept as the baby, so that his emotional needs as a growing adolescent remain unmet.

Chazan *et al.* (1983), also note a variety of home factors which they believe can lead to emotional and behavioural difficulties in young children:

1 Basic needs being unmet (physical abuse or neglect will
2 Unsatisfactory housing conditions and poverty can lead to stress and ill-health.
3 Lack of routines may mean that the child gets overtired or restless.
4 Prolonged separation from mother may slow down development and can lead to acute distress followed by apathy.
5 Domestic crises and parental disharmony can affect children's emotional well-being.
6 Parental illness can adversely affect children if, through ill health, parents are erratic or moody or children are anxious about them.
7 Unsatisfactory parental attitudes and practices: children's emotional development is likely to suffer if they are rejected or overprotected, or if parental discipline is inconsistent so that it is unclear what behaviour will result in praise or reprimands.

PARENTAL STYLES AND PARENT–CHILD RELATIONSHIPS
Styles of parenting have been studied to see how behavioural expectations are transmitted. According to Wright (1971) an internalized rule system is most likely to develop in the child if:

1 there are strong ties of affection between children and parents;
2 parents make strong moral demands on their children;
3 sanctions are used consistently;
4 punishment is psychological, rather than physical (for example, the withdrawal of love);
5 reasoning is extensively used.

Studies have repeatedly shown that the quality of family relationships, and parental styles in managing the child, are important determinants in the learning of socially acceptable behaviour.

Early work by Bowlby (1952), when he reviewed the effects of mother–child separation in early life, suggested that the bonds of affection formed in the first years of life have far-reaching effects on the emotional development of the child. Bowlby maintained that the mother–child relationship should be warm, intimate, consistent and continuous, for healthy personality development. He argued that failure to form affectional bonds could lead to irreversible damage in later life.

More recent studies (such as Kelmer-Pringle, Butler and Davie, 1971; Rutter, 1972; Tizard, 1975; and others), suggest that Bowlby was too sweeping in his generalizations. Rutter, for example, found that children with a warm and positive relationship with one parent were one-third less likely to develop conduct disorders than children with poor relationships with both parents. Similarly, children who had suffered stressful separations in early life were found to develop well with improved family circumstances in middle and late childhood. Rutter claimed that 'the damage done by early stresses cannot be undone, but it can be considerably modified by experiences when older'.

The quality of care received in childhood seems to be more important than who mothers the child. Studies of mothers who go out to work, finding substitute caretakers for their children, supports this finding. Davie, Butler and Goldstein (1972) found no evidence of emotional problems when substitute care is of a high quality.

Patterson, Littman and Bricker (1967) also concluded that parents of aggressive anti-social children tend to behave inconsistently towards their children. Assertiveness is often encouraged and punishment erratic. Unless children are consistently shown that certain behaviours are unacceptable to their parents, they will be unlikely to learn appropriate social behaviour. Other studies also emphasized the importance of warmth in the relationship between child and parent, marital harmony and the importance of close parental supervision of children.

It is unclear from these studies what factors are operating. It may be that the children are modelling themselves on their parents, so they are learning the same response to stressful circumstances shown by their parents. Or it may be that parents who are cold and rejecting do not form the affectional ties with their children needed for good social adjustment. What does seem evident is that certain personality traits are more likely to develop in certain social circumstances.

THE DEVELOPMENT OF A POSITIVE SELF-CONCEPT
In terms of emotional development, in order to develop positive feelings of self-worth it seems to be important that the child feels an interest is taken in him, and that he is held in warm regard by his parents. Some children only experience feelings of rejection from parents which may take various forms but in each case is likely to damage their feelings of self-worth. Some children receive overt hostility, or material and/or emotional neglect. Others may be rejected in more subtle ways. Parents may adopt perfectionist attitudes towards their offspring, making unrealistic demands so that the child can never win their love and respect. In other cases, by overprotecting the child and smothering their natural development, parents may create in the child feelings of anxiety which hinder their emotional growth.

Some parents may be inadequate to the task of parenting for various reasons. There may be mental or physical ill-health in the family. The pregnancy may have been unwanted or there may be marital disharmony. The parents may be immature themselves, and if they have also had inadequate parent models, they may be unaware of the needs of young children or incapable of giving the unselfish love demanded by young children. Parents who abuse their children tend to have been victims themselves as children (Rutter and Madge, 1976). Poor relationships thus tend to become self-perpetuating and, as with material matters, it is difficult to break the cycle of disadvantage.

For example, Farrington and West (1971) found in their study of aggressive delinquents, mentioned in the next chapter, that the boys were more likely to have criminal, alcoholic fathers, and to have experienced cold, harsh and rejecting parenting between the ages of 8 and 10 years. They were also more likely to have been separated from their parents, that is, to have been in care. Thus, unfortunately, factors which seem to predispose aggressive behaviour in young children are likely to predispose young adults to criminal violence. Aggression was found in this study to be a fairly stable personality characteristic between the ages of 8 and 18 years, possibly because social circumstances rarely change dramatically in the family. Poor supervision and criminality in the parents were also significant factors.

Stott (1978) proposed that adjustment problems are learned styles of response. Some children learn from an early age that they will fail in life. Due to lack of encouragement, they develop what he calls an 'effectiveness deficit'. At school they may well be withdrawn and isolated. Other children are distractable and lack concentration. They are likely to find it difficult to defer gratification of their immediate needs for the sake of worthwhile long-term goals. Others have what he called a 'social attachment deficit'. They have learned to mistrust adults, not to expect help or attention, and greet the world with hostility and aggression. Stott believed that these styles of learning are not permanent personality attributes, but they are capable of change with positive planned experiences by a good teacher. He maintained that about 10 per cent of children have written off adults by the age of 7 years, so the intervention needs to be early. However, rather than improve matters, schools often increase the alienation between children and adults, so problems may well multiply in school, rather than diminish.

Wider social and economic factors

Recent opinion surveys suggest that emotional and behavioural problems in school children have increased due to a general deterioration in social values in society at large. The DES survey (1978b), for example, explained the problem of indiscipline in school in terms of 'family breakdown, lack of respect for authority, a fall in moral standards and a widespread lack of discipline'.

The Pack Report (Scottish Education Dept, 1978) on truancy and indiscipline in schools in Scotland made similiar points about the permissive society and parents expecting schools to enforce values they do not hold themselves. They doubted whether schools could deal with problems associated with social trends.

The National Union of Teachers (1976) also argued that indiscipline is associated with poor educational stability, which in turn relates to academic failure, low parental interest, low literacy at home, social deprivation and poor material standards. Schools with their over-large classes, poor resources and inadequate staffing were not thought to be capable of coping with these problems.

The popular view that lax social standards are to blame for lowered behavioural standards in school seems to be supported by rising crime figures and an apparent increase in the incidence of violence and aggression in society at large. However, the statistical figures are open to interpretation, and Lloyd Smith (1984) argues that the media is unhelpful in promoting understanding and tends to 'mythologise the complex question of causation'.

Nevertheless, the values of society at large are bound to affect the socialization of children, and influence their attitudes, values and behaviour. Coffield (1986) drew attention to the fact that there are still huge social inequalities in all regions of Britain and Europe and, in particular, that lack of any prospect of employment is causing a long-term crisis for many young people and their parents. Many youngsters are forced to remain emotionally and financially dependent on their families into adulthood, because of unemployment. Twelve million young people in Europe and EEC countries are excluded from becoming adults because of this, and there are growing numbers in the long-term unemployed. Work, Coffield argued, has great psychological significance. Not only does it signal a passage into adulthood, it imposes an important time structure on daily life, and the enforced activity ensures that skills are exercised regularly so that the young person achieves competence. With it comes a sense of identity and self-worth. Work also has an important social function, in that through work contact is made with other people, so that feelings of isolation are overcome; and finally, the wage is a vehicle for independence, providing freedom to make personal choices.

Coffield proposed a model of adolescence as a growing-up process, in which the youngster must come to terms with various factors in life: adolescence can be a difficult time for some youngsters in adjusting to the pressures from within himself, the family, the peer group, the neighbourhood as well as political and economic factors from the region where he lives and the country at large.

Coffield found in his interviews with working-class youngsters in a region of high unemployment that there was at best high concern or, at worst, resigned passivity about the problem of finding work. He also found a worrying cynicism about politics being able to affect their situation and deep-seated fears about nuclear war. Thus large numbers of young people are living on the margins of society, and feel powerless to improve their lot.

Given this social and economic context for many of our young people, it is hardly surprising that school is seen as irrelevant to their situation.

School factors

The development of children's behavioural responses and social interaction skills will depend on a variety of influences in the family, the community and the school. Whereas research in the 1950s and 1960s centred on factors within the family which might cause low achievement and emotional and behavioural problems in children, more recently the school as an institution has been investigated, and there is evidence to suggest that 'the structures and processes which characterize these contexts are as important as any analysis of factors relating to individual characteristics of pupils or backgrounds' (Lloyd Smith, 1984).

It has long been recognized that schools are likely to influence behaviour and that uncongenial teachers and work of the wrong standard can give rise to problem behaviour in class. Schools are understood to be an alien culture for a significant proportion of our children; the values and standards of the school, and the curriculum, may have little intrinsic interest for them. Many bored and alienated young people are forced to stay within the classroom until they are 16, creating problems for those who teach them. However, many of these views have been difficult to put to the test. Attempts to isolate significant factors within the school environment which might influence behaviour is no easy matter. Schools differ in many respects, including intake of pupils, facilities, teaching methods, curriculum and discipline methods, so variables are difficult to control when research is conducted.

The socializing effect of school was illustrated in a study by Patterson, Littman and Bricker (1967), who showed that at the start of nursery school most children were fairly passive. However, they quickly learned to become more assertive as this type of behaviour was reinforced by teachers and fellow pupils. They quickly learned that aggression pays.

A great interest in the effect of schools arose with a spate of research in the late 1960s and early 1970s which suggested that there can be large differences in the behaviour and attitudes of children with similar home backgrounds attending different schools. Power, Benn and Morris (1967), for example, found that social-class differences could not account for the range of delinquency rates, between 7 and 77 per 1,000 children, in some inner-city schools serving the same area, and suggested that the school itself must be an important determinant. Baldwin (1972) pointed out that since some schools are more willing to accept 'at risk' pupils, this could account for the differences noted in the earlier study.

However, Reynolds (1976), in his South Wales study, also found consistent differences between schools serving similar catchment areas, so it became of great research interest to try to determine the characteristics of a 'good' school.

TEACHER–PUPIL RELATIONSHIPS AND TEACHING STYLES

A study by Finlayson and Loughran (1976) found that the teachers in schools with high delinquency rates were perceived to be more authoritarian in style although not less caring.

Reynolds and Murgatroyd (1977) concluded that in schools with low truancy rates, class teachers were given responsibility for the pastoral care of pupils, whereas deputy heads were more likely to do this in schools with high rates. Presumably attendance difficulties were dealt with quickly, in a more personal and less formal way, in schools which had least truancy.

Reynolds (1976) also found that schools with more disruption had inflexible teacher–pupil relationships, whereas more successful schools were characterized by what he termed a 'truce'. In these schools there appeared to be a common understanding; neither teacher nor child made unreasonable demands on one another, nor created confrontations unnecessarily.

SCHOOL ETHOS

As mentioned in Chapter 2, a wide-scale piece of research into school variables was conducted by Rutter *et al.* (1979). A large number of 10-year-old pupils were studied and followed up at 14, when they attended ten different comprehensive schools. Rutter's study found that controlling, for home background factors, pupil behaviour on several different measures, varied considerably according to the school attended. Differences were found not just in teacher perceptions about the difficulty of their behaviour, but also in more objective terms, such as rates of attendance, attainments and measures of delinquency. The most successful secondary schools had good teacher–pupil relationships, emphasized academic progress, had clear rules of behaviour, prompt starts to lessons, school uniform, low punishment rates, and there was greater care of the buildings. The actual quality of the school buildings was not found to be relevant, contrary to commonly held beliefs, nor was class size or school organization.

Rutter *et al.* claimed to have indicated some of the factors which contribute to that nebulous concept of a positive 'school ethos', and to have established that home factors alone cannot explain differences in pupil behaviour. They proposed that schools themselves can make a difference to children's academic performance and behaviour; well-run schools can, to some extent, compensate for disadvantaged or stressful homes.

Whether these aspects of the 'hidden curriculum' are the most critical aspects of schooling remains unknown. Running a well-controlled, large-scale study presents various difficulties, and many of the hypotheses we may have about the way schools might promote academic achievement and personal adjustment remain to be put to the test. As noted earlier, Rutter's study has been criticized on methodological grounds, but has generally found acceptance.

Other research has continued on a smaller scale. Lawrence, Stead and Young (1984) reported on two whole-school studies they conducted between 1977 and 1981. In particular they looked at the nature and seriousness of disruption and its 'symbiotic relationship with aspects of the school system'. Disruption was defined as 'behaviour which interferes seriously with the teaching process and/or seriously upsets the normal running of the school'. Incidents were monitored over a three-week period. The research team did not observe lessons, but relied on staff interviews and informal discussions and meetings. In the first study, younger teachers reported most disruptive incidents and, in particular, the fourth-year pupils became substantially more difficult by February in the school year. Teachers were particularly concerned with the difficulty of engaging some pupils. To overcome these difficulties, the research group suggested changes in the timetable, length of day, utilization of rooms, movement about the building and improved equipment for the less able.

In the second study, recommendations were made about improving the visual display of work, continuity of staffing for first-year pupils, changing the role of senior staff, etc. In other words, to counter disruption, Lawrence, Stead and Young attempted to promote structural change in schools; that is, changes in their organization, pedagogy and curriculum. From their research, they were able to itemize the features of a 'difficult school' as follows:

1   A large number of 'untreated' maladjusted pupils.
2   An unstructured environment – that is, deficient senior management with poor communication between staff.
3   A number of staff who are unsympathetic to children.
4   Support services not used.
5   Absence of school liaison with parents.
6   Faulty curricula, such as lack of choice.
7   Inadequate remedial assistance.
8   Poor morale amongst teachers – lack of trust.
9   Large number of social priority factors, that is, where many children come from socially disadvantaged homes.
10 Erratic use of sanctions.
11 High staff turnover.
12 Lack of good teaching – classes out of control.

It was suggested that the difficulties which teachers experience should be more open to discussion and less a cause of shame and embarrassment because they are regarded as a sign of professional incompetence. Interestingly, the type of disruption encountered was not usually extreme, but constant interruptions gave rise to frustration and irritation. This resulted in strain and stress both on teachers and pupils.

Lawrence, Stead and Young concluded that disruptive behaviour can be viewed as 'an opportunity to review the adequacy of educational aims and the appropriateness of the means available to achieve these'. Schools are never likely to be disruption-free, but while some of this is unavoidable, some can be ameliorated. Lawrence identified a need for staff support and development, as well as a need for every school to monitor behaviour in an ongoing way and develop an agreed school-behaviour policy.

Coulby and Harper (1985) looked at the elements of schooling likely to encourage disruptive behaviour and, in particular, at aspects of the curriculum, pedagogy, school organization and peer group. They accepted that there may be elements within a child's home background which generate a predisposition towards anti-authority or troublesome behaviour, but 'these predispositions are either fulfilled or frustrated within the social contexts of the school and the classroom' (Coulby, 1984). As noted above, research has shown that schools vary in the way they encourage or discourage these predispositions, and professional experience suggests that some teachers within the same school are more likely to encourage disruptive behaviour. By examining these processes, the aim is to highlight alternative procedures to minimize difficult behaviour and suggest what might be good practice.

CURRICULUM

As far as the curriculum is concerned, Coulby suggested that Midwinter's (1977) maxim is helpful: that a curriculum should be useful, first-hand, developmental, interesting and under-standable. However, much of what is taught in school would not meet these criteria. In some schools, the culture of some children is belittled or ignored. This can lead to lack of interest in schooling and possibly resentment by some children when they do not see the relevance of much of what is taught in schools. Some would argue that a practical curriculum, which is more closely allied to the job market, might be more valued by some children and their parents.

As Leach and Raybould pointed out (1977), when children are perceived as failing to meet the demands of school, teachers need to review their demands: 'It is not the setting of goals, standards and rules which creates a problem child, but the interpretation of his failure to meet them, and the course of action taken.' The problem label, they maintain, is usually applied to a child in response to the number of resources the child possesses (such as his appearance, social skills, etc.) and the number of resources the school possesses. Children with few personal resources need more compensation from school.

PEDAGOGY

Good pedagogy can itself prevent the emergence of many behavioural difficulties in class, so Coulby argued that teachers can themselves create well-behaved pupils. Much has been written about good classroom practice recently, as discussed in Chapter 3. Factors such as good preparation of lessons, good time-keeping by teachers, vigilance so that difficulties are 'nipped in the bud', clear classroom rules, positioning of the teacher and the desks, etc., etc. – all contribute to good practice, so that classroom control can be established quickly.

Teachers can also affect the performance of some children by the quality and quantity of their attention. Observational studies suggest that they tend to give attention to bright, hardworking, well-behaved children, or those who actively misbehave. Other children, actively rejected by some teachers, are seen as time-wasters and receive mainly criticism (Good and Brophy, 1972).

Good classroom management skills should thus not be underestimated. By presenting interesting and well-organized lessons, and managing a large group skilfully, teachers are doing all children a service, including those who for various reasons are potentially difficult to manage.

SCHOOL ORGANIZATION

There are also various aspects of school organization which can encourage disruptive behaviour. Hargreaves (1967) pointed out that streaming can have an adverse effect on some low-ability children, whereby their attitudes to school can quickly become negative, resulting in the formation of a deviant 'anti-school' peer subculture. The examination system is also partly responsible for the apathy and rebellion of those children who are excluded from it. Offering an alternative curriculum in itself may help little, if teachers and pupils regard it as inferior.

There is a considerable overlap between low attainment and difficult behaviour, and this may be due in part to the negative attitudes resulting from low status and lack of success. It may also be partly due to the self-fulfilling prophecy of poor teacher attitudes. Once teachers view a child or group of children as non-academic or uninterested, they may be reluctant to set them homework, or make the necessary effort to plan stimulating lessons. Nash (1973) reported on various ways negative teacher attitudes can perpetuate difficulties.

Other aspects of schooling may well encourage or discourage disruption. For example, the school building, the corridors, break and dinnertime supervision, and the use of temporary classrooms (often of poor quality, set up in the school grounds but isolated from the patrol of senior staff), will all affect the running of the school and the behaviour of pupils.

A further aspect of the hidden curriculum is peer group relationships. Schools provide a forum for children to cooperate or compete with one another and this can advance or deter their social development. In the socializing process of schooling, roles quickly develop, so some children learn to behave as the class clown, bully, or leader. If pupils are reinforced in their roles, by their peers or by teachers, their behavioural patterns will become more permanent. It is also important to remember that the social aspect of schooling is probably the most important one for most non-academic pupils. Much of their disruptive behaviour in class is done for fun, in order to gain the respect of their peers. Again the way schools handle this will, in effect, either encourage or discourage difficult behaviour.

There is little doubt, then, that the school environment, teachers' classroom management skills, the curriculum, the quality of pastoral care, the overt and covert messages given to children about themselves, are all likely to affect children's attitudes and behaviour. In Coulby's view, disruptive behaviour 'must be seen as the product of the interaction of various elements – pupil, peer group, teacher, school organisation – within a specific social context, and not as the inherent result of the character of one participant'. He suggests that rather than talk about disruptive children, we should think of 'children whose behaviour is in some contexts disruptive to the teachers' perception of academic progress'.

A recent study by Reynolds, Sullivan and Murgatroyd (1987) supported the hypothesis that school organization affects both pupil attainments and behaviour. They compared pupils from a small community in Wales over a four-year period who were identical on entry to their comprehensive or selective schools. The study found that the comprehensive pupils did worse on both academic and social grounds, particularly on measures of delinquency, attendance and locus of control (that is, perceived responsibility for actions). Closer analysis showed that this was largely due to the poor results achieved by the middle third of the ability range, who would normally be top of a secondary modern school. It was found that the bottom two-thirds of the ability range were more delinquent in the comprehensive school and the bottom third were worse attenders. However, the top third of the ability range did as well as the grammar school pupils on measures of attendance and delinquency.

The research team postulated reasons for this. It was felt that comprehensive schools had minimal commitment to both formal and informal links with parents, and pastoral care had relatively low priority. The teachers were more likely to stress academic skills at the expense of social development, and the schools were 'pseudo comprehensives', trying in effect to be grammar schools for all. Reynolds and his team argued that the comprehensive schools failed because of poor management for their large size. They noted that few LEAs have yet considered how to cope adequately with this problem.

The differences between the ways schools cope with disruptive behaviour was studied by Bird (1984) who looked at the pattern of referrals to the educational psychologist by six schools in two Outer London boroughs between 1977 and 1981. Distinct differences were found between the schools in the number and type of pupils put forward for referral, and the differences could not be explained by extra resources available, the number of vacant places in the units nor pupil characteristics. No two schools were found to use outside welfare and educational specialists in the same way, although most teachers recognized their worth. Bird concluded this was due to three interwoven reasons:

(a) no two schools responded to their exceptionally difficult pupils in the same ways or shared the same ideas about the causes of disaffected behaviour;
(b) no two schools shared the same idea about the merit of referring to outside agencies as compared to containing the child themselves and offering some alternative education/support within school;
(c) each school had a different capacity for adapting to or coping with disruptive pupils.

One school, for example, regarded all disaffection as irrational. A referral to the educational psychologist was seen as a soft option, and instead attempts were made to bring the child firmly back into line. Another school saw disaffection as the consequence of limited educational expectations held by most working-class parents. To counter this, attempts were made to make the curriculum more challenging, and to better engage parents. A third school assumed the disaffected child to have major personal problems. The school responded by counselling, or referring to the educational psychologist for treatment.

All schools were found to use various official and unofficial strategies for coping. Thus referral to outside agencies was just one of a number which might be used, and the schools' attitude to disruption affected their choice.

Gillham (1981) is critical of professionals who explain pupils' behavioural difficulties in terms of individual or home differences. He uses the analogy of managers in a factory having trouble with the workforce. Presumably they would be unlikely to call the workers maladjusted, blame their home backgrounds or suggest they should see a psychologist or psychiatrist. Occupational psychologists who tackle problems in industry are more likely to look at the communications operating within the factory; see if the workers are getting their needs fairly recognized; check whether the tasks are suited to the workers' skills; and investigate how the foremen are supervising the workers.

Is the concept of maladjustment an artefact?

Another perspective on the question of behavioural difficulties has been offered by Coulby (1984) and Galloway and Goodwin (1987), who pointed out that the construct of a disruptive or maladjusted pupil is an artefact, since both the type and amount of special provision available will largely determine the numbers of children 'discovered' to have behavioural problems. If there is a unit for disruptive pupils, candidates will be found with no difficulty; however, in its absence the same pupils will have to be contained within ordinary classes. It is argued that educational psychologists, school doctors and others who continue to place children in these schools unwittingly help to establish the construct. As Coulby remarked, 'the giving of institutional validity to the category of disruptive pupils may be regarded as a major contribution to their creation'.

Burt (1937) made it clear, from the earliest days of assessment, that the cut-off point for children ascertained to require special schooling was an administrative convenience.

Statistically, there is no reason why any particular intelligence test score should be taken to indicate that a different form of education is required, but it will reflect the amount of provision available.

Galloway and Goodwin argued that, in the same way, professionals who are now responsible for recommending alternative local authority provision are subject to various pressures and will largely make decisions based on practical contingences. Of prime relevance will be the amount of provision locally available. Even under the 1981 Education Act, where professionals must give advice to the local authority about the child's special educational needs, recommendations are likely to be affected by what provision they feel the administrators will give, and LEAs who produce the statements will be influenced by their own economic and political pressures.

Although there is some validity in this position, by abolishing special provision, emotional and behavioural problems will not be instantly eradicated. For many varied reasons, some children will continue to have difficulty adjusting to their life situations at home or at school. Some pupils cannot or will not adjust to the demands made upon them either in class or in the family, and the structures of families and schools are difficult to change. Moreover, some parents, and teachers, find it difficult to manage children.

The fundamental questions in the debate over emotional and behavioural problems revolve around the locus of the problem, whose responsibility it is to change, and how improvements might best be achieved.

6

Some behaviour problems of social concern

OVERVIEW

This chapter discusses some specific behaviour problems involving young people which are currently of general social concern. Delinquency, truancy, substance abuse, and sexual abuse have been selected because of their topical interest.

DEVIANT BEHAVIOUR AND DELINQUENCY

Definitions

The apparent rise in crime figures and the involvement of young people in delinquent activities is of major public concern at present. Delinquency can be defined as criminal behaviour by 10–17-year-old young people. There are two major types of criminal offence: indictable offences, which are serious offences, punishable by law, which must be brought to court by the police (examples of these offences are theft, burglary, robbery, and assault). Non-indictable offences are less serious crimes which tend to be punished by fines (for example, motoring offences, underage drinking or malicious damage to property).

Rather than using the term delinquency, many writers prefer to talk more generally about deviant behaviour. Deviant behaviour is unusual or uncommon behaviour, although the term usually refers to disapproved behaviour, which can include both legal and illegal acts. Becker (1977) defines deviancy as the infraction of some agreed rule. Much so-called delinquent behaviour, which does not break the law, is more accurately described as deviant.

Cohen (1971) pointed out that deviance and crime are relative concepts. For example, taking what does not belong to you can be shrugged off as borrowing without asking, 'fiddling' or stealing. Horseplay amongst a group of adolescents can be seen as fun, or as menacing aggression. However, once a young person's 'deviant' behaviour is reported to the police or he goes to court, it becomes labelled 'delinquent'. This can alter the perceptions of all concerned and, rather than deterring bad behaviour, it can have the opposite effect. In fact the experience of being publicly caught is one of the critical steps in a delinquent career, according to Becker. Once the youngster views himself as criminal, problems amplify and are likely to snowball.

Prevalence of criminal offences

The bulk of offences are not serious, and motoring offences are most common. However, roughly half of those found guilty of serious offences are young people. Theft and burglary are the most common serious offences, with crimes of violence being relatively rare, despite popular fears. Boys are most frequently involved in all types of crime, with the exception of shoplifting, where girls are nearly as often involved.

Criminal activity would appear to be most common in adolescence and early adulthood. In 1977, 8 per cent of boys aged 14–17 were found guilty or cautioned for offences, and 1.6 per cent of girls. 15 was the peak age for boys, 14 for girls. This compares with only 0.7 per cent of men and 0.2 per cent of females aged 30 or over, who were either found guilty or cautioned. Recent studies in London reveal that half of all arrests were aged under 21, and a quarter were under 17 years (Marsh, 1978).

Table 6.1 gives the number of young people found guilty of offences; there are approximately seven times this number of

Table 6.1 Young people found guilty of offences in England and Wales, 1985 (numbers in thousands)

age	boys	girls
10–13	13.8	1.4
14–16	77.9	7.5
17–20	337.5	31.5
21+	1389.6	212.8

Source: adapted from *Social Trends*, no. 17.

reported offences, but only small numbers are proceeded against.

It is important to note that official statistics can be misleading. They are collected by the police and are liable to bias for various reasons. Criminologists estimate that only about 10 per cent of crime gets reported to the police, since much crime goes undetected, or unreported.

Hough & Mayhew (1983) recently conducted a survey of 11,000 households and asked about both the crimes the family members had committed, and those they had been subjected to. The study found that four times as many crimes were claimed to have been committed than were reported to the police. Various reasons were given for non-reporting, including the view that the crimes were too trivial to waste police time, or the fear that the police would do nothing, etc. The study suggested that there could be twelve times as much theft and twice as many burglaries than are officially reported. However, it also noted that the average person is only likely to be burgled once in forty years, and crimes of violence are extremely rare. Marsh (1978) notes that the Hough and Mayhew study relied on self-report and only looked at certain types of criminal behaviour. For example, stealing from work and shoplifting were excluded. Marsh concluded that the actual crime figures could be even higher.

There are other reasons why police figures are likely to misrepresent criminal behaviour. Some argue that girls are more likely to be given 'help' than punishment, which means that they are less likely to find their way into criminal statistics. Similarly, middle-class youngsters are probably under-represented in the statistics, as they are less likely to engage in the type of criminal activity which the police monitor. Middle-class, 'white-collar' crimes such as stealing from work, bribery and corruption, or the breach of workplace regulations, often pass unnoticed, are less likely to be detected, and in any case are more likely to be treated informally without making reports to the police. 'White collar crimes' are often an accepted part of business life.

Policing practices also vary between regions, and over time, and there are occasional changes in the law which can affect what is deemed to be an offence. In the past minor offences, for example, were either prosecuted or no action was taken. Now formal cautioning is used much more frequently, so larger numbers of youngsters find themselves included in official statistics.

Explanations of delinquency

HOME FACTORS

Various attempts have been made to explain delinquent behaviour using social-class variables. Sutherland (1961), for example, emphasized the role of socialization in the development of a propensity to commit criminal acts. He stressed that many delinquents have little discipline and control at home, and frequently there is an absent father figure. In his view, many middle-class children are brought up in an atmosphere of controlled care, whereas for working-class children the street as a playground lacks this dimension. He proposed that socialization in most middle-class homes is conscious, rational, deliberate and demanding, whereas the working-class child more often grows up in an atmosphere with little restraint. Middle-class culture tends to stress the importance of the family as a social unit and accepts responsibility for the behaviour of the family members. In some working-class families, the family is a less effective agent of social control during a child's development. The street gang has its own rules and norms, but may well lead to conflict with society.

Other more recent studies support the view that family factors are highly relevant. Rutter and Madge (1975), concluded that seriously disturbed family relationships in early and middle childhood are associated with an increased risk of delinquency in children. As far as divorce and separation are concerned, the discord prior to separation may be more significant than the rift itself. Delinquent children often come from families where there is a lack of affection, persistent quarrelling or inconsistent discipline. Discipline may be too severe, too lax, or just ineffective. Many delinquents have a history of being placed 'in care' during family crisis (Power *et al.*, 1974).

Yablonsky (1967) put forward the view that many hardened delinquents have genuinely defective personalities, and in conditions of poverty and urban congestion these boys are most likely to become the central core of a gang.

There have been several large-scale studies attempting to verify these theories and find some common characteristics of those young people who become delinquent. West and Farrington (1973) made a longitudinal study of over 400 London children born between 1950 and 1952, following them up to adulthood.

Five major factors were found to be linked with delinquent behaviour:

1 Low family income.
2 Large family size.
3 A parent with a criminal record.
4 Unsatisfactory child-rearing practices.
5 Low intelligence.

In this study, nearly half the boys with criminal fathers acquired delinquent records, and 63 per cent became delinquent when both parents were criminal. There was also a strong link between becoming criminal and having a brother who was criminal. Low income was associated with poor parental supervision, separation, parental conflict, and large family size. Rutter and Madge (1976) also concluded that harsh discipline, rejecting attitudes and poor supervision make up the unsatisfactory child-rearing practices which can give rise to delinquency. West and Farrington also examined a variety of motives given by young people for their delinquent acts and concluded that there is a recognizable delinquent personality profile. They claimed that their study demonstrated 'unfashionably but irrefutably' that the individual characteristics of the offender are important. For example, convicted delinquents were not typical of their social class, but seemed to be a particular subgroup which had poor home relationships. It was found that young people who become delinquent are more likely to come from broken homes or homes with an absent father figure where there is presumably less parental control.

Earlier, a national longitudinal survey also revealed that social–class factors are highly correlated with delinquency. Douglas, Ross and Simpson (1968), analysing the official statistics of 1,200 children originally born in the same week found that there were three times as many children offending from social class 3 than social classes 1 and 2. Moreover, there were seven times as many from social class 5. These differences were even greater when only serious crimes were considered.

More recently, Ouston (1984), has analysed the data in Rutter *et al.*'s (1975) study. To see if intelligence and social class are valid correlates of delinquency, and the resulting study broadly confirmed West and Farrington's findings. Children who were most likely to become officially recorded delinquents came from lower–social–class homes, were more troublesome in school, and were less able academically.

The study found that it was possible for teachers to predict potential delinquents at the age of 10, because of their troublesome behaviour. Children who were poor attenders, and had more difficult behaviour and lower educational achievements, were more likely to become delinquent by the age of 14.

In early studies, delinquency was found to be very much a predominantly male activity, but the trend appears to be changing. In the Ouston study, the ratio of delinquency between boys and girls was nearly 5:1. It is unclear why there should be this sex difference but various hypotheses have been suggested. It is likely that different socialization experiences mean that girls tend to adopt more passive roles than boys, and they are likely to be more closely supervised by their parents. In addition, boys are encouraged both overtly and covertly to be aggressive and tough. It has also been suggested that, when caught, girls are generally treated more leniently by the police and the courts. Even when convicted, fewer girls get custodial sentences, and, as noted earlier, they are more likely to 'need help' than require punishment. In 1979, 143,000 men spent some time in prison compared to 8,000 women. This difference between men and women may not be an artefact of police statistics, however, as self-report studies reveal similiar alleged differences between the sexes.

To conclude, most youngsters who become part of the official delinquency statistics are predominantly boys, live in urban areas where there is widespread social disadvantage, overcrowding, low income and unemployment.

PEER GROUP AND CULTURAL FACTORS
In contrast to these explanations of delinquency which stress the importance of individual and family factors, some sociologists maintain that delinquent or deviant activities are a normal part of growing up. Belson (1975), for example, interviewed a cross-section of 1,425 London boys aged 13–16 years. He found that 88 per cent claimed to have stolen at some time from school, and 70 per cent to have done so from shops. From these self-reports, it has been estimated that an average boy in London is likely to commit more than a hundred petty thefts before he leaves school, although much of this goes undetected and so does not become part of the official statistics. Belson also found that delinquent behaviour is normal across all social backgrounds, and in his study it was not predominantly a working-class phenomenon.

Matza (1964) argued that the delinquent act is seldom well thought out or deliberate and young people may drift into crime whilst seeking a thrill. For some youngsters, trouble is a part of everyday life and the delinquent is usually not deliberately opposing the established values of society. Many youths totter on the fine line between horseplay and criminal acts, and it is largely a matter of chance how their behaviour becomes labelled. As noted earlier, adverse labelling of behaviour is seen by some as a potent factor in the criminal career.

Others conceive delinquency as a reflection of working-class values which are acted out inappropriately. Working-class culture is said to value toughness, aggression and excitement, and delinquency gives a vehicle for these qualities. An alternative view is that many working-class youths behave delinquently because of the structure and culture of their environment. It has been argued that those who cannot achieve success through legitimate means, will turn to illegitimate methods. It has also been suggested that society holds out goals and rewards which are beyond the reach of the poorer sections of society (Wilmott, 1966). Advertising regularly parades material possessions in front of young people who have no means to obtain them legally. Wilmott stressed that there is widespread disenchantment and frustration amongst young people in deprived areas, and law-breaking is seen as a legitimate way of obtaining material possessions. Delinquency is seen as a way of hitting back at the family or society which appears to have rejected them.

Cohen (1955) similarly argued that working-class youths reject middle-class values because of frustration over their lack of status in society. Disenchanted youths who live in an area of organized adult crime may join this group, the 'subterranean subculture' of gangs, or retreat into another subculture of drugs or alcohol.

In an early study in America, Shaw and McKay (1942) added a different dimension by explaining delinquency in terms of environmental factors. They found that delinquency rates are highest in those areas closest to the city centre, where there is a declining population and also physical deterioration in the neighbourhood. They proposed that such community factors influence the behaviour of the inhabitants. British research suggests that high delinquency areas tend to be poor, overcrowded and the inhabitants of low social status (Rutter and Madge, 1976). It is unclear what it is about the area which predisposes crime; whether it is the social mores and neighbourhood pressures, or personal living conditions.

By institutionalizing youngsters, either by placing them in residential care, or by sending them to penal institutions of one sort or another, we may be hardening their attitudes and behaviour. Residential settings can become places where youngsters learn delinquent behaviour rather than the socially acceptable modes of living they are intended to acquire. The peer group in such institutions tends to reward criticism of adults, aggressive behaviour and rule-breaking, and punish behaviour which deviates from delinquent norms.

SCHOOL FACTORS

The studies by Power *et al.* (1972), and Rutter *et al.* (1979), mentioned in previous chapters, suggested that schools themselves seem to have a significant effect on delinquency rates. In Rutter's study, significant differences in both delinquency and attendance rates were found between the twelve comprehensive schools studied which served similar catchment areas. The research team concluded that home-background factors cannot alone explain high delinquency figures and that the characteristics of schools as institutions can help or hinder the process of socialization. Ouston (1984) argues that schools with proper mixed-ability classes and a balanced intake from all neighbourhoods may prevent the formation of a delinquent subculture in the school, provided that the school is also able to offer potentially disaffected pupils a suitable curriculum and teaching resources to go with it. Interestingly, the size and type of school seemed to make little difference, but various aspects of school organization appeared to be significant in creating a positive school ethos.

A relationship has also been found between delinquency and poor educational attainments. It may be that failure in basic subjects such as reading is a potent form of discouragement and loss of esteem; alienation from school can quickly follow.

CONCLUSIONS

To conclude, there is no single explanation for delinquent behaviour, although most studies agree that, as far as reported crime is concerned, youngsters, particularly boys, from poorer social backgrounds, in congested urban areas, are most at risk, especially when they mix with a delinquent peer group. Many people maintain that social adversity is usually combined with personal vulnerability. More sanguinely, some would argue that it is also a matter of bad luck that some get caught. Much delinquent behaviour never enters official statistics.

Outcomes and remedies

A social worker usually assesses the circumstances surrounding the offence and reports to the court. Conviction may lead to a fine or in some cases to a care or supervision order. If the young person is considered to be beyond parental control, the social services may assume parental rights and, in some cases, take the youngster into the care of the local authority. Otherwise the young person may be supervised by the social worker whilst living at home.

Since 1980, with the introduction of the 'short, sharp, shock', the young offender may be punished in detention and youth custody centres. However, this approach does not seem to have been effective in reducing the crime statistics.

Others argue for an alternative approach, calling for minimal intervention on the grounds that by punishing more heavily the young person is likely to be labelled a criminal and accelerated into a life of crime. The danger is that when young people are herded together in penal institutions they may have their anti-social values reinforced by the group. Some would see detention and youth custody centres as schools of crime.

The cautioning system is widely used in some areas as a preventive measure. Youngsters may be cautioned by the police, with no action taken if no further problems recur. Intermediate treatment or IT is another alternative treatment; programmes are set up by social workers for youngsters who are at risk. Various interesting and purposeful activities are run in the community to keep youngsters out of trouble and hopefully teach them pro-social attitudes.

Hoghughi (1980) argued that minimal intervention is not the answer to delinquency. He pointed out that despite many recommendations to the contrary (such as the Court, Warnock and Seebohm Reports) there is a fragmentation of support services and no consensus between professional groups about how best to deal with delinquents. Hoghughi believes part of the reason for this is the lack of any common classification of young peoples' problems, and our dealings with delinquents are often reactive and crisis-ridden. Intervention practices are seldom carefully worked out in terms of good practice and likelihood of a successful outcome. The emphasis, in his view, is often on care, control and stabilization, with insufficient problem clarification and planned intervention.

As far as prevention is concerned, Rutter and Madge (1975) were more hopeful about the possibility of change. Although they acknowledged that at present we know little about the factors which facilitate breaking out from the cycles of disadvantage, large-scale political and social change is sometimes invoked: 'we delude ourselves if we think that nothing short of massive social change can influence cycles of disadvantage'. But they also point out that disadvantage occurs at all levels in society, and inadequate living conditions do not necessarily imply disadvantage in other respects. Scottish children, for example, are better readers than their English counterparts, but twice as many homes are overcrowded. In their opinion, what needs to be researched is why some disadvantaged children manage to stay out of trouble. We need to know what positive factors can stop serious disruption. It is possible that if a child has one good relationship, he can be inoculated from trouble. In reality, we still have little knowledge about this.

Prognosis

It is interesting to enquire about the prognosis of delinquent behaviour, and wonder how pessimistic we need to be. Where petty crime is concerned, Wilmott (1966), and West and Farrington (1973), argued that many young people will pass through a phase of delinquency and eventually become law-abiding adults. In fact, most delinquents receive only one court appearance. However, of the 6 per cent of youngsters in Wilmott's study who were sent to borstal or detentions centres for some serious offence, half returned after committing further offences, and these youngsters tended to become hardened recidivists. Thus it must be said that serious criminal behaviour in youth has a poor prognosis. In West and Farrington's study, those who continued with delinquent activities tended to come from the more socially deprived backgrounds, had more criminals in the family, and committed more offences on their own. Those who gave up were more likely to report committing crime for enjoyment, and they had now ceased contact with their former delinquent peer group.

SCHOOL ATTENDANCE PROBLEMS

Ever since the earliest days when schooling was made compulsory, there have been some children who have failed to attend school regularly for other than health reasons. The present law is clear on this. Parents have a responsibility under the 1944 Education Act to ensure that their child attends school regularly. If the child is absent for no justifiable reason, they are breaking the law, and local authorities have a responsibility to take action.

Most local authorities will have their own procedures, and in some cases parents are first invited to an attendance panel to discuss the child and give reasons for their absence from school. Their responsibilities, as parents, will be pointed out. If problems persist, ultimately parents may be taken to the magistrates' court if they are deemed to be failing to ensure their child's school attendance either through wilful decision or apathy and it is believed that the effect of court action would encourage them to ensure attendance. A fine is the usual result of court action, although a short term of imprisonment can result.

Alternatively, the child may be taken to juvenile court, under the Children and Young Persons Act (1969), if they are thought to be beyond their parents' care and control and it is not thought that punishing the parents would effectively enable them to gain control or give them sufficient incentive to regain it. Supervision or care orders may result from such action.

Attendance figures

Surveys based on school attendance figures are notoriously unreliable, as there are considerable variations in attendance patterns according to the time of year, the day of week, as well as the age of pupils. The spring term, for example, tends to be particularly poor, and Mondays and Fridays are commonly low attendance days. The attendance rates in primary school tend to be higher than at the secondary stage, and the final year of compulsory schooling is generally particularly poor for attendance. There are also differences in school attendance figures between regions and even between schools within the same catchment area (Rutter *et al.*, 1979). What is more, it is well known that registers, although legal documents, are frequently unreliable indicators of attendance. Some children who are in school, are late for registration and so are marked absent. Others, who get their mark, later absent themselves from the school premises.

With these cautions in mind, the figures presented in a 1975 DES one-day survey are fairly typical. It was found that 9.9 per cent of children were absent, and of these, 2.2 per cent had no legitimate reason for this.

Definitions of truancy and absenteeism

Tyerman (1968) defined a truant as a child who is absent from school on his own initiative, without his parents' permission. Truancy was thus distinguished from parentally condoned absence and from school refusal or 'school phobia'. Most writers on the subject have separated those children who choose not to attend school, from those with an emotional problem who feel they cannot attend. The two groups are often regarded as having different personal characteristics and different family situations. Different courses of action to remedy the difficulties are usually advocated.

The term truancy, however, is probably unhelpful, as it tends to carry negative connotations, and places the problem within the child. Carroll (1977) preferred to use the term absenteeism, which is less emotive, and also focuses the problem more generally. Galloway *et al.* (1982) and Reid (1985) also pointed out that the majority of children miss school with parental knowledge, or at least with parental apathy, so attempting to distinguish truancy from parentally condoned absence is probably largely misguided. Reid thus adopts Carroll's term 'absentee' and defines the 'persistent absentee' operationally for his study, as 'any child who is absent from school for more that 40 per cent of the time'.

Personal and social characteristics

Research has shown (for example, Galloway *et al.*, 1982; Reid, 1985) that the large majority of truants or absentees are likely to come from socially disadvantaged homes. They tend to come from low-income families, where the father is un-employed, unskilled or semi-skilled. Housing conditions are frequently poor and overcrowded. There is a high incidence of one-parent families, divorce and separation, or else the father's employment frequently takes him away from home. These children tend to have low academic ability, and low self-esteem, and come from families with little interest in education. They are frequently shy, rather isolated children; and only the minority have the stereotypic happy-go-lucky personality.

Reid also found that persistent absentees tend to be rather solitary, unhappy children. They are frequently not very popular with their peers, and when in school they may well be disruptive and find school work difficult. They are often regarded with distrust as children who tell lies or steal.

There would also appear to be a strong relationship between absenteeism, poor home circumstances and delinquency (West and Farrington, 1973): 'to be concerned about delinquents means one must also be concerned about truants'. Thus absence from school can have severe social repercussions; when young people are unsupervised in the community with little money, they may well be open to temptation.

There is also a common link between poor attendance and low attainments (Fogelman, 1976). In many cases absentees come from low streams, and non-academic classes. By missing lessons they frequently create a self-fulfilling prophecy in terms of school achievement.

Reid suggested there are broadly four groups of children who persistently miss school:

(a) Traditional or typical absentees (Tyerman's truants). These children, as noted, characteristically come from adverse social circumstances, and their behaviour is conceived by Reid as a plea for help. They often feel guilty about their absence from school, and may fear ridicule or punishment were they to return.

(b)   Institutional absentees are those children who miss school for reasons broadly connected with the strictures of school as an institution. They tend to be popular, extravert children, who are alienated from school. When they do attend, they often confront teachers and disregard authority, and frequently dislike conforming to school rules.

(c)   Psychological absentees, sometimes called school phobics or school refusers, miss school for psychological reasons. They may have various fears and anxieties about school or home which may or may not have a rational basis. School anxieties may be associated with travelling to school, with peers, teachers, school work, or the school building. Others may have anxieties rooted in the home; for example, they may be concerned about the health or welfare of a parent, there may be jealousy about a sibling or worries about relationships within the family.

(d)   Generic absentees: some children have a mixture of the characteristics noted above.

Reasons given for absenteeism

In order to find out from young people themselves why they do not go to school, Reid (1985) interviewed a group of 128 persistent absentees from two large comprehensive schools in South Wales, and compared their views with groups of academic pupils in the same school, and a group of good attenders from the same class. Subjects were matched for sex, age and social class. Reid discovered the following reasons for absence:

Reasons for absence (Reid, 1985)

- 56 per cent gave school reasons (bullying, curriculum, teachers, rules);
- 16 per cent gave psychological reasons (illness, irrational fears etc.);
- 28 per cent gave social reasons (peer group, domestic pressure, employment etc.).

It is interesting that the majority of pupils explained their behaviour in terms of the failure of school as an institution, rather than connect it with their social situation or personal or family characteristics. School reasons included the feeling of boredom in class, falling behind with work and being unable to catch up, unsuitable curriculum, bullying (20 per cent gave this as a reason), extortion, and classroom strife, etc. Many also mentioned conflict with teachers, or feelings of unfairness (78 per cent had unfavourable opinions about teachers). Many pupils also felt unable to comply with school rules concerning uniform or punctuality. School was frequently unrewarding academically and socially for these pupils.

Although they rarely blamed parents, in many cases these pupils had poor parental support. 38 per cent said their parents were not interested in school work and 83 per cent said parents never visited school voluntarily. Although only 9 per cent said their parents approved of their absence from school, and 65 per cent claimed parents actively disapproved, only 15 per cent reported that their parents took action, although 50 per cent reported rows at home as a result.

According to Reid, the ages of 11, 13 and 15 are critical. 18 per cent of his persistent absentees started to truant in the primary school, 31 per cent in the first year of the comprehensive, and 25 per cent in the third year of the comprehensive school. The peak age was 15, but interestingly only 5 per cent started after the age of 14. Poor attendance would seem to be a habit which can start young, and if it is not thwarted early it tends to persist. Fogelman had a similiar finding: 60 per cent of those who started to truant by 11 years old continued to do so at 16.

When out of school, the young people were not necessarily having a good time. More than half claimed to spend time largely on their own, many stayed in bed late or wandered aimlessly around the locality or town. Many felt guilty and unhappy about their behaviour.

Ways of overcoming the problem

Reid suggested that there are various reasons for persistent absenteeism, and each group requires a different type of treatment and approach. In his opinion, the first group, who are absent largely through social adversity, require positive assistance and understanding. There is much that school could do to both prevent and overcome problems. Although 25 per cent of his persistent absentees felt no change in school could help their position, Reid suggests various approaches could have ameliorated the problem. Appropriate help may be changing a class or subject option; better pastoral care to prevent bullying or extortion; providing uniform for those with financial difficulties; or gaining more parental support and encouragement.

Reid suggested that there is a distinct group of pupils who require firm control rather than understanding as such. He sees their behaviour as one manifestation of more global antisocial behaviour. It is important that they attend school, as they are at high risk in the community.

Finally, the group of pupils with more deep-seated psychological fears and anxieties may need expert help from one of the support services.

Blagg (1987) identified some 'universal ingredients' in successful management in schools which he suggested could cut down on school attendance problems. These include: good relations between the school and the child's family; empathetic class teachers; a variety of management techniques judiciously applied; and carefully controlled enforced school attendance.

School characteristics

Some of the earlier school studies, which reveal differences between schools serving similar catchment areas, may well be illustrating the point that it is, to some extent, within the power of schools to affect the attendance rates of pupils. For example, Reynolds (1976) investigated nine secondary schools, and found differences between high and low truancy schools. They found that high attendance rates were associated with small school size, less rigorous enforcement of rules, close pupil–teacher relationships, and low institutional control. Schools with high truancy rates were more narrowly custodial and had a wide gulf between teachers, parents and children. He suggested the notion of a 'truce' existing in low truancy schools, where co-operation is traded with turning a blind eye when rules are broken.

Rutter *et al.* (1979) also found wide differences between schools from similar catchment areas. Absenteeism rates varied between 5 per cent and nearly 26 per cent. As discussed in Chapter 5, Rutter found that the differences were best explained in terms of the general notion of a positive school ethos; this included such factors as low staff absence and turnover, low levels of punishment, good teacher–pupil relationships, good care of buildings, emphasis on academic progress and high expectations of good behaviour.

Conclusions

Although there are many reasons for children failing to attend school, in all cases the problem should be investigated and taken seriously. Research has indicated that it is wrong to overgeneralize about all absentees, but nevertheless, the majority tend to come from unfavourable and unsupported home backgrounds and they may well have impoverished relationships at school and home. They frequently have learning difficulties and experience academic failure, as well as behavioural and psychological problems. They are likely to find it difficult adjusting to school rules, and in addition, they are at high risk of delinquency in the community. They may well constitute the core of the school's disaffected pupils.

Due to the fact that these children are missing from lessons, they are as a group frequently forgotten by schools. Where blame is attributed, the child, his family or social circumstances are frequently seen as the root problem. However, recent studies suggest that schools should be taking far more responsibility in providing for the needs of all of their pupils. It may be that the school's pastoral care could be improved, that bullying or intimidation needs curtailing, and that a personal interest should be invested in all pupils. There could be a greater effort to involve all parents in their children's education, a greater choice in option subjects or more help with learning difficulties, if required. There is no obvious panacea for school absenteeism, but early detection of problems would appear to be an important preventive measure, as well as checking on curriculum relevance, and ensuring that school is rewarding for all pupils.

SUBSTANCE ABUSE

The problem of substance abuse by young people should be set in context. Desforges (1983) noted that 'we live in a drug orientated society, where drugs are a widely accepted solution to a variety of medical and social problems, as well as an important method of relaxation'. Drugs are commonly used to alleviate pain and psychological distress. In 1981, for example, Kennedy found that about 10 per cent of prescriptions were for tranquillizers and antidepressants, and 11 per cent of those people questioned had taken drugs of this type in the previous two weeks.

In addition, drugs are frequently used for recreational purposes, and alcohol and cigarettes are widely used to induce relaxation and pleasurable states of mind. In other parts of the world, opium and marijuana are commonly used for the same effect.

Drug dependence or addiction refers to the compulsion to take a drug because of its desired effects, and this can be either a psychological or physical need. Most people are addicted to some substance, be it nicotine in cigarettes, or caffeine in coffee or tea. Obviously some addictions are more damaging to the individual and society at large than others. Most people would wish to distinguish between the socially acceptable use of drugs like alcohol, and alcohol abuse.

There is much public anxiety about the use of drugs by young people, this being bound up in issues to do with adolescents striving for independence and autonomy. There is, however, little substantial evidence about the number of youngsters who use different types of drugs, so it is difficult to know whether there is a growing problem, or whether there is a progression from soft to hard drugs, as many people fear. Surprisingly, little research has been conducted and valid statistics are difficult to obtain.

According to some recent Home Office statistics, there appears, if anything, to have been a downward trend in

Table 6.2 Persons found guilty or cautioned for drug offences

Age	1973	1980
Under 14	5	12
14–16	609	267
17–20	5,973	594

Source: 'Statistics of the misuse of drugs in UK 1980', *Home Office Statistical Bulletin*, 15/81.

convictions for drug offences in the adolescent group from 1973 to 1980, despite a two and a half times increase in adult users over this time. (Table 6.2).

Over 80 per cent of all offences involved cannabis; narcotics and other similar drugs accounted for 5 per cent; and amphetamines for 15 per cent.

In most surveys of secondary school pupils, 5–10 per cent admit the misuse of drugs (Dorn & Thompson, 1976). Amphetamines were commonly used in the 1960s, and narcotics and LSD seemed to increase in the late 1960s and early 1970s. Since this time, the abuse of solvents seems to be more popular.

Solvent abuse

Solvent abuse is not a new phenomenon; in the nineteenth century ether was sniffed by the middle classes at parties, presumably for its intoxicating effects. By the end of the 1970s, solvent abuse by young people was seen as a social problem requiring official intervention. Partly due to the media and various pressure groups, it was widely felt that 'something ought to be done'.

Solvent abuse is a term used for those who intentionally inhale solvents for their intoxicating effects. Solvents are volatile hydrocarbons which are used in a variety of household substances such as glues, adhesives, cleaning fluids, aerosols, lighter fuel and hair lacquer. Many abusers are young teenagers, between 11 and 17 years, who are unable to buy alcohol or hard drugs so find other more convenient substances to experiment with.

There is a lack of consensus about the dangers of solvent abuse, and what if anything should be done about it. Some see it as a harmful and preventable pastime and urge intervention by professionals. Others see it as a relatively harmless pastime and as minor antisocial behaviour associated with boredom and risk-taking, which characterize youth. This view advocates taking a low-key approach with intervention seen as generally undesirable.

As far as the law is concerned, solvent abuse is not illegal although it can be used as a sign that the youngster is in need of care and control.

Most people now agree that it is necessary to distinguish between the type of solvents used (whether glue, gas or aerosols) and between the experimental, regular and chronic user. The degree of harm will depend on what is sniffed, how often it is sniffed, and whether or not different substances are used together. What is also relevant is where and how it is sniffed, and with whom. There are various types of user, and it is important to distinguish between them and not overgeneralize. Some users employ more dangerous practices than others.

Many youngsters only experiment with solvents and other substances and may use them on a few occasions only. The vast majority cease after twelve months. Others may regularly sniff substances in social situations, possibly once a week with a group of friends. However, a few young people become chronic daily sniffers, often doing so as a solitary occupation. Psychological dependency on chemicals is most possible with this group, so they are probably most at risk.

There is no clear evidence that glues have a toxic effect. Other volatile substances are regarded as more dangerous; however, it remains unclear what long-term harm the effects of aerosols may have. The major risk seems to be that of accident whilst using solvents. Suffocation can result from placing a plastic bag over the head, and there is also the danger of inducing asthmatic attacks, particularly in those prone to asthma. Probably the greatest danger is that of accidents occurring whilst the youngster is inebriated or unconscious, and this can be a particular hazard when sniffing alone.

POSSIBLE SIGNS OF SOLVENT ABUSE

The following signs may indicate a youngster is possibly abusing solvents:

1 Drunken behaviour.
2 Loss of appetite, stomach pains, sickness.
3 Coughing, general debility, listlessness and tiredness.
4 Smell or traces of glue on clothings.
5 Rashes, boils or spots around the nose and mouth.
6 Behaviour change, aggression or moodiness, uninhibited behaviour or a tendency to isolate oneself.
7 Blank looks or a dreamy appearance.

EFFECTS

Sniffing solvents is a cheap and quick method of intoxication, and about half of those who sniff also experience hallucinations. It can, in the short term, give euphoria and exhilaration which lasts from 5–30 minutes. In cases of high concentration, it can result in drowsiness or even unconsciousness.

As far as after-effects are concerned, headache and depression are common. There is no evidence of long-term physical dependence, but psychological dependence on chemicals to change the state of mind is more common, and it has been found that solvent abuse in adolescence can be replaced by an over-reliance on alcohol in later years.

TREATMENT AND MANAGEMENT

At present there is little common understanding about solvent abuse, and no obvious source of 'expert' help. Because of the dearth of systematic or long-term research, professionals have varying views about appropriate forms of treatment. Teachers, social workers, education social workers, psychologists, doctors and the police all have various contributions to make, and the type of help offered is likely to reflect their professional orientation. In most cases the abuse is rarely seen as the problem *per se*, and the youngster's social, personal and environmental circumstances are likely to be investigated.

Since parents and teachers are likely to be the major source of help, they may need information about appropriate responses. Where regular users are concerned, the aim should be to reduce the possibility of accidents, or the more serious toxic effects. As far as non-users are concerned, many people feel it is best not to educate them about solvents, as it might encourage curiosity rather than prevent the problem.

The aim of education and counselling is to avoid judgement, confrontation and disapproval which might harden attitudes and set up further barriers between the peer group and adult world. Instead, an attempt should be made to build trusting relationships so that the risks can be openly discussed and evaluated, without hostility. The degree of risk should not be overexaggerated. In 1980, for example, thirteen youngsters died from solvent abuse, whilst 1,200 died as a result of motorbike accidents that year. It is important to be aware of the risks, whilst avoiding the creation of an attractive alternative youth culture. Other preventive approaches are possible, such as urging shopkeepers and parents to take greater responsibility, or structuring young people's leisure time so that there is less room for boredom.

CHILD SEXUAL ABUSE

Definitions

Michele Elliot (1985) defines child sexual abuse as 'the exploitation of a child under the age of 16 for the sexual gratification of an older person'. Children are naturally affectionate, but when the affection between children and adults turns to sexual stimulation or exploitation this becomes sexual abuse. It can involve a range of activities, such as obscene telephone calls, indecent exposure, the showing or taking of pornographic photos, touching, intercourse or rape. It might happen once, or recur over a number of years.

Incest is legally defined as sexual abuse taking place between particular blood relatives, however problems more commonly occur with stepfathers or boyfriends of the mother. About 98 per cent of reported cases involve abuse by men.

Incidence

The sexual abuse of children has always been known to occur, but recently it has received much media attention and is now generally acknowledged to have been a largely underestimated problem. Reliable figures have been difficult to establish as most research was done in America. Finkelhov (1979), in a survey of college students in America, found that 14 per cent claimed to have been sexually abused as children. Russell, (1983), in a survey of 930 people in San Francisco, found that 28 per cent of reported abuse had occurred before the age of 14, and 38 per cent by 18 years. It was unknown if these statistics could generalize to Britain. However, there has been a recent MORI survey conducted (Baker and Duncan, 1985), when over 2,000 men and women over the age of 15 years were questioned. The survey dispelled many myths about sexual abuse, as well as confirming much of the American research.

The incidence of 10 per cent corresponds closely with Finkelhov's research and shows that, contrary to popular opinion, both boys and girls can be subjected to sexual abuse, although girls tend to experience this for the first time at an earlier age, often before puberty. Most abuse is a single event, but about a quarter of the group were abused on several occasions, and there is a high incidence of abuse occurring within the family. Although half the experiences involved no physical contact, and much of this will include relatively less serious offences such as sexual exhibitionism, about 5–6 per cent of both boys and girls reported full sexual intercourse. About half the sample felt they had been damaged by the abusive experience, and only a minority had positive feelings about it. These were practically all adolescent boys who had had relationships with older women, who were not family members. As with the American research, the overwhelming majority of abusers were men. Baker and Duncan's findings are summarized in Table 6.3.

Effects

Studies of sexually abused women frequently report that they experience long-term problems with large numbers showing

Table 6.3 Alleged sexual abuse

Incidence	10% had been sexually abused before 16 years (12% women; 8% men)
Age	61% were 11 years or over when abuse occurred Girls were abused for the first time at younger ages
Relationship	49% abusers were known to the victims 14% of abuse took place within the family
Frequency	63% reported a single abusive event 23% were repeatedly abused by the same person 14% were subjected to abuse by several people
Type	51% of abuse involved no physical contact 44% had physical contact but no intercourse 11% (6% women; 5% men) had full sexual intercourse
Effects	51% felt they had been damaged by the experience 4% felt it had improved their quality of life Females reported damage more frequently

Source: Baker and Duncan, 1985.

delayed psychological disturbance. A common experience is misplaced feelings of guilt and responsibility for past events. Frequently they have been forced into secrecy, and there may be lingering feelings of shame and worthlessness, a negative self-image, mistrust of men and sexual dysfunction. Those who have had incestuous relationships may experience role confusion when they become parents, finding it difficult to draw appropriate boundaries between themselves as adults and their own children. With such distorted parental modelling, it is perhaps not surprising to find that many abusers were themselves victims as children. As far as physical problems are concerned, infection by sexually transmitted disease is fairly common, and occasionally pregnancy results. Violent abuse of the very young may lead to the damage of sexual organs.

Symptoms of possible abuse

There are various danger symptoms of possible abuse, but since they may also be common behavioural disturbances of childhood, they should be viewed with caution. Elliot noted characteristics such as a lack of concentration; sleep disturbance or tiredness; school performance suddenly dropping; isolated preoccupation; regressive behaviour such as thumb sucking; overt sexual behaviour; the onset of day or night enuresis; and fear of particular people. Medical symptoms include urinary infections, sexually transmitted disease, self mutilation and attempted suicide.

Treatment

Once the abuse has come to light, it is generally felt to be crucially important to help the victim understand that as a child they cannot be responsible, and that the fault lies with the adult concerned. Feelings of personal guilt can be crippling in the long term.

If the abuse occurs within the family, it is likely that family members may need to be separated initially and therapeutic work usually first centres on the child's feelings, and later on the child's relationship with the mother. The child often experiences guilt and anger. This may be directed against both the father who they feel they have betrayed, and the mother who may seem to have ignored their plight. The mother's feelings are also frequently ambivalent, and their role in the whole affair unclear. Sometimes they have had suspicions which were ignored to make life easier; for others, the news is unbelievable, bewildering and difficult to come to terms with. Some mothers find it easier to blame the child than her husband, and she must come to terms with her own feelings at having failed as a mother and as a wife. The relationship between mother and child may not be as close as that between the child and her father, thus family dynamics may need adjusting. The mother must also be encouraged to give the protection which has been lacking. Later, therapeutic work may involve the father apologizing to the child and accepting full responsibility. There is a fairly high risk of reoffence, so communication within the family must improve if the child is to be protected in future.

There are various self-help groups (Incest Survivors, Opus, etc.), which have been set up so that experiences can be shared.

Prevention

Because of the high incidence of sexual abuse of one type or another, the only effective means of prevention is probably education. Michele Elliot has pioneered work in this area, and has developed a practical guide for parents and teachers based on simple principles of 'good sense defence'. She points out that children are usually taught to obey adults, particularly their parents, without question. This means they are natural victims and make easy prey. Adults must learn to listen to children and believe them. Young people rarely lie about such matters, as the events would otherwise be outside their experience. Sometimes they may use the wrong vocabulary and so mislead, but only about 2 per cent are thought to make substantially false allegations. Adults also need to be taught that a child's need for love and affection is not sexual.

Elliot has advocated that children can be taught to protect themselves from abuse from their earliest days at school: 'This can be done by teaching children to recognise dangerous situations and appropriate touching, to say no when someone tries to do something which makes them frightened or confused, to refuse to keep secrets and to seek adult help.'

She has developed a teaching kit (Kidscape materials) using puppets, toys and adapted well-known stories. This includes discussing 'good' and 'bad' touching, and the right to say 'no', even to parents, if children feel uncomfortable. Similar concepts can be taught to older children, using more appropriate age-related materials and strategies.

7

Meeting special educational needs

OVERVIEW

This chapter and the next outline a variety of facilities and resources for meeting children's special educational needs. This chapter focuses on school facilities with emphasis on the curriculum, specialist teaching techniques and other special resources. A central theme is the way the learning process can be organized so that children's special needs can be better met. The next chapter takes a wider view and deals with provisions in terms of agencies and the general context of education.

INTRODUCTION

Although much of this book has been taken up discussing the conceptualization of special education and outlining a range of learning and behavioural difficulties, probably of central concern for teachers, parents and children is the way such difficulties can be overcome.

As we have discussed earlier, to say that a child has a learning difficulty is to say as much about the learning context as about the child. The type of special educational provision recommended for children with learning or adjustment difficulties should depend less on the personal characteristics of the child than on school factors, such as the curriculum, the way teaching groups are organized, the amount and quality of additional support available, and the philosophy and ethos of the ordinary school. Some pupils, for example, require more intensive teaching programmes, a more supportive setting or a higher teacher–pupil ratio than is usually provided in the ordinary school. All these aspects of school organization should now be taken into account when describing a child's educational needs. If the child's special educational needs cannot be met from within the ordinary school's resources, then alternative or additional provision must be made available by the LEA, either within the school, or on a part-time or full-time basis elsewhere.

Special needs are, by definition, unmet needs, so the learning situation requires adaptation if the child's needs are to be met. Although some schools may have just a few children with learning and behaviour difficulties, so that individualized programmes to meet their needs may be sufficient, others may have very large numbers, thus necessitating a more comprehensive adaptation of the curriculum and organization of the school.

Special needs and the curriculum

The Warnock Report proposed that about 20 per cent of pupils with learning difficulties require additional or alternative provision to meet their needs, in the form of a special curriculum, specialist teaching and special facilities and resources. Effective access to properly trained and specialist teachers and other professionals on a full- or part-time basis, and where needed, an educational and physical environment with special aids, equipment and resources, were regarded as the distinctive features of special educational provision.

The report stated that special educational needs are likely to take the form of a need for one or more of the following:

(i)   access to the curriculum through special equipment, facilities or resources, modification of the physical environment or specialist teaching techniques;
(ii) the provision of a special or modified curriculum;
(iii) attention to the emotional climate or social structure of the class or school.

The 1981 Act accepted Warnock's broad concept of special educational needs, but largely confined itself to protecting the needs of the small proportion of children with complex or severe learning difficulties. Special education was defined more narrowly as being 'additional to, or otherwise different from, the educational provision made generally for children of his age in schools maintained by the local authority concerned', and the child's difficulties must be 'significantly' greater than average. There is a change of emphasis, and according to Brennan (1985), 'gone is the precision of concentration on facilities and curriculum'. He maintained that Warnock's definition was largely written for educators, whereas the Act's was for administrators. The Act like most legislation, rather than being revolutionary, legitimized educational thinking which was already being practised and provided the legal framework necessary for enforcing certain priorities. Its main concern was with accountability and with a productive use of available resources.

Both the Act and the Warnock Report recognized that special educational needs can range from mild to severe, and can be short term or permanent. There is no simple relationship between the severity of a problem and its effect on learning. As noted earlier, severe physical handicaps may have little or no curricular consequence, for example, whereas some mild physical handicaps involving central nervous system dysfunction may have greater effects on learning.

Statements of special educational need

As noted in Chapter 1, the new draft circular which is intended to revise Circular 1/83, suggests that the statement should specify the child's educational needs by describing the child's functioning in terms of both his strengths and weaknesses, and detailing the educational and developmental objectives the child is expected to achieve. It is also proposed that the statement should specify in detail the special educational provision the LEA considers appropriate. This should include facilities and equipment, staffing arrangements, teaching and learning approaches, and the emotional climate and social regime required, and where relevant, access and transport provision. In addition, in accordance with Section 18 of the Education Reform Act (1988), the draft circular proposes that the statement should specify how the national curriculum needs to be either modified or disapplied for the child concerned. For example, where relevant, it will need to set out alternative programmes of study outside the national curriculum framework designed to meet the child's needs; or any necessary modifications to the attainment targets, programmes of study or testing and assessment arrangements. Without this being shown on the statement, the school is obliged to offer the child all the usual subjects of the national curriculum. The statement also names the school or other arrangements which the LEA determines will meet the child's needs. Finally, the statement notes additional non-educational provision which may be required, such as physiotherapy, speech therapy, or medical surveillance.

The purpose of a formal assessment is to identify the child's special educational needs and the resources required to meet them. Although the Act does not concern itself in the same detail about the larger group of children with learning difficulties, the LEA and school governors are given the responsibility of ensuring that their needs are also properly met in school. The Act makes it clear that, with certain exemptions, children should be educated in mainstream schools; and where they cannot be taught alongside their peers, teachers have a duty to ensure social integration as far as possible.

Instating the concept of need as a basis for educational planning and as a means of determining resources for children with learning difficulties, although well intentioned, is open to criticism. As will be discussed further in the final chapter, Booth (1985) pointed out that it presumes an unproblematic relationship between educational needs and their satisfaction. The content and organization of schooling is far more complex than this. There are all sorts of pressures, finance being a major one, to fit children into existing resources regardless of need, despite the fact that professionals are urged to give their advice without heed to these considerations.

MEETING THE NEEDS OF CHILDREN WITH LEARNING DIFFICULTIES

How then are the needs of children with learning difficulties to be met? Ainscow and Tweddle (1979) argued that teachers who have children with special needs within their class have an important role to play in providing structured learning experiences for the children. They advocated that 'the greater the learning handicap, the greater is the need for a carefully planned intervention by the teacher if the pupil is to learn successfully'. Since children who have fallen behind their peers are frequently slower at learning new skills, 'patience and understanding – despite their obvious desirability – are not enough'. Teachers need expertise in formulating, and implementing carefully designed programmes of work for children with learning difficulties. To prevent failure, the teacher must provide a stimulating setting to work and learn in, and their role is to provide learning opportunities which 'guide, prompt and encourage children to learn'.

The curriculum

It is first necessary to clarify what we mean by the term 'curriculum'. The DES (1975) defined the curriculum as 'a school's plan for facilitating a child's growth and for developing selected skills, ideas, attitudes and values'. Brennan (1985) made the point that the concept is now generally considered to refer more broadly to all the opportunities for learning provided by the school whether officially planned or not. This would include the formal programme of timetabled lessons, extracurricular activities such as those which go on outside normal school hours, and 'the hidden curriculum' – the emotional climate in the school, roles and relationships, attitudes, styles of behaviour – all of which make up the quality of life in the school community.

A curriculum is based, consciously or unconsciously, on the general aims of education. The Warnock Report maintains that the aims of education are the same for all children whether or not they have learning difficulties; these are conceived first in terms of enlarging the child's knowledge, experience, and imaginative understanding, moral values and capacity for enjoyment; and secondly, in enabling the child to enter the world after formal education as an active responsible participant in society, with as much independence as possible.

Most people maintain that the aims of special education must be consistent with the general aims of education. Teachers must decide to what extent children can be accommodated within the normal curriculum, and to what extent their special needs require the curriculum to be individualized.

What, then, is a 'special' curriculum? According to Wood and Shears (1986), 'the curriculum is special, i.e. different from mainstream curricula, as it lays out specific guidelines for the generation of aims, objectives and teaching methodology and therefore gives guidance as to what and how to teach and what passes for education; it produces precise, clear objectives so that teachers may know precisely what it is they are or should be teaching.'

The 'hidden curriculum' is frequently not consciously thought out by schools but nevertheless transmits important messages. Swann (1983) questioned what is learned via the hidden curriculum in special schools, when the child with learning difficulties is removed from ordinary children and surrounded by others with learning difficulties. He suggested that by being constantly in each others' company, disability may become an essential part of their self concept. They are segregated from the rest of the community and friendships rarely extend beyond the school day. Swann argued that the educational process keeps them in a weak and dependent position.

Clearly, the curriculum is ultimately a matter of values, since fundamental decisions about what education should comprise will be based on value judgements. None of the following approaches to curriculum planning will help sort out what is ultimately a moral decision.

TYPES OF CURRICULUM

The term 'modified curriculum' is sometimes used to describe the type of curriculum required for children with moderate learning difficulties. It refers to the fact that these children require modifications to the mainstream curriculum if their educational needs are to be met. In practice, this usually means, as noted in Chapter 2, that learning objectives are more carefully graded and broken down into smaller steps. Complex skills of reading for example, may be analysed into various component skills and taught accordingly, so that mastery can be achieved. A functional analysis of the desired task is often needed. If the child is to be taught to cook a meal, it may be sufficient to learn to heat frozen food in a microwave cooker, if the more traditional approach to cooking is too complex.

Frequently the term 'developmental curriculum' refers to the curriculum thought to be most appropriate for children with more severe learning difficulties, although it may well be suitable for younger children with milder difficulties. The curriculum is usually conceived in terms of the acquisition of developmental skills, such as fine and gross motor skills, language and communication, cognitive development, emotional and social development etc. In many cases, self-care and independence are seen as long-term goals, with normalization being the fundamental aim.

Swann (1983) questioned the creation of a special curriculum, however, arguing that it does not foster integration and detracts from the central task of curriculum development which is to make the mainstream curriculum available to a wider range of children. The danger is that a special curriculum can be too narrow and rigid so that children with learning difficulties are denied valuable aspects of the mainstream curriculum.

MODELS OF CURRICULUM PLANNING
The 1981 Act has given LEAs and governing bodies statutory responsibility for planning provision for children with special educational needs, and an outcome has been that they are now asking schools for more explicit educational aims. Aims are frequently written as general statements of teaching intentions, which are difficult to translate into detailed curricular plans. Thus teachers often plan their lessons without reference to the school's overall curricular aims as they seem to have little relevance. In fact Brennan's survey (1979) found that many primary, secondary and special schools lacked written curricula. Fewer still had clearly defined objectives-based curricula, even

in basic skill areas, although this was called for in both primary (DES, 1978d), and secondary schools (DES, 1979), as well as in special schools (Warnock Report, 1978).

Lister and Cameron (1986) stated that a written curriculum provides a shared language within the school which helps with communications between teachers and problem clarification with professionals visiting the school. It also improves curriculum planning and teaching, provides on-going teacher-based assessment, and evaluation of the curriculum and teaching methods.

They outlined various early curriculum models, including one by Tansley and Gulliford (1960), who proposed a curriculum in two main parts: a core of language and number, with creative abilities, practical interests and knowledge of the environment, taking up a peripheral part.

The objectives model developed in the 1970s, and described in further detail later in this chapter, has been found to be particularly useful for precisely defining learning and behavioural objectives. Brennan (1979) proposed a model based on learning and teaching objectives. He suggested that teachers should begin with general aims, refine these into general objectives, and then decide on curricular content and methods, followed by evaluation and feedback.

Ainscow and Tweddle (1979) offered a similar three-stage model of curricular planning, starting with a statement of curricular content areas, followed by teaching goals, and ending with statements of pupil objectives.

Gardner, Murphy and Crawford (1983), working with children with severe learning difficulties, proposed a more detailed skills analysis model where core developmental curricular areas, such as mobility or self-help, are subdivided into smaller sections, such as feeding and dressing. Objectives are written for each area and ordered sequentially; programmes are devised, taught and evaluated.

Cameron (1981) argued for a more flexible model of curriculum management, maintaining that different levels of planning are required for different teaching needs, and teachers can choose the degree of specificity they require. The most general level of planning can be used for planning class lessons, whereas a more detailed level would be required for some individual pupils in the class with special needs. General teacher objectives would be a minimum requirement once the curriculum content has been specified. Precise behavioural objectives in terms of what the pupil will be able to do, and detailed task analysis, are not usually appropriate for the majority of pupils who are making steady progress, although they might be needed for one or two pupils in the ordinary class, or all the pupils in a small special-needs class. Cameron's rule is that a more specific level of planning is required only when the child fails to learn at the more general one.

Cameron's levels of curriculum planning can be summarized as follows:

1 Teacher management objectives: that is, the teacher's intentions or objectives.
2 Pupil objectives: that is, what pupils will be able to do, in observable detail, as a result of the teaching.
3 Curriculum content: this may be considered in terms of the 'open' curriculum and 'closed' curriculum, objectives relating to optional and essential teaching, where mastery is essential.
4 Sequencing objectives: that is, planning a sequence which makes learning easier.
5 Task analysis (see below).
6 Behavioural objectives (see below).
7 Attribute analysis: the main features or attributes of a task are linked to specific teaching methods which can be used to generate teaching programmes (such as shaping, fading, errorless discrimination learning and training).

Brennan (1985) agreed with Cameron that there has been a tendency to over-elaborate behavioural objectives in curriculum planning and that the degree of precision should depend on the degree of difficulty. Nevertheless, he suggested a general model of curriculum planning, where the broad aims of education can be refined into general objectives for the school curriculum; in turn, these can be translated into specific learning objectives for the classroom.

INDIVIDUALIZING THE CURRICULUM

In recent years there has been a proliferation of the use of individualized programmes, and teachers have been encouraged to write and plan their own programmes for those children in their classes who do not learn by more usual teaching techniques. In addition there are many published schemes where the child uses workcards or workbooks. The benefits are obvious; the work is structured and made appropriate for the child's needs, and he can work at his own pace. At its best, individualized learning of this nature is probably one of the most effective methods of teaching. However, there are a number of objections to an individualized approach, the main one being the amount of work required to make the initial assessment and for planning work and monitoring. In larger classes it is more difficult to adopt an individualized approach, and it can be argued that individualized programmes fail to promote co-operative learning experiences and the stimulation of shared ideas.

However, there are misapprehensions over the term 'individualization'. Brennan (1985) maintained that individualized teaching does not mean that one pupil is taught by one teacher, but means that pupils learn what is most appropriate to their needs. This might mean that at various times they may learn on their own, receive individual tuition, work in a small group or work with the whole class. Thus although the teacher may have a general plan for the lesson, topics are organized to allow individualization within the class. Pupils are encouraged to learn at their own pace, and careful records will be required to check on progress and determine when skills are mastered. According to Brennan, 'individualised teaching means using the widest selection of available techniques – not just one-to-one situations – in a manner intimately related to the identified special educational needs of the pupils'.

In the same way, to derive an individualized curriculum, a selection is made from all the curricular resources in the school to meet the identified curricular needs of individual pupils. It does not mean that pupils must have a separate curriculum for themselves; they may share some activities with the class or with other pupils. Thus a child with mild learning difficulties may require individual timetabling of small group activities for some time each day, whereas a child with severe difficulties may require an individual timetable with arrangements for him to participate in social activities with his peers, and a totally different curriculum from the normal class at other times.

Teaching methods and approaches

Sometimes the terms curriculum and teaching are confused. Whereas the curriculum can be seen as course objectives or planned learning activities, teaching is the carrying out of these activities, the methods required to reach the goals. Teaching is said to be a purposeful activity, and can be contrasted with incidental learning, where no deliberate teaching takes place. Learning, of course, does not always result from intentional teaching.

Male and Thompson (1985) point out that many children with learning difficulties present the following problems:

a They may be unable to understand complex or abstract ideas.
b They may have difficulty remembering new information.
c They may finish their work more slowly and not complete tasks.
d They may find it difficult to generalize what they learn to other situations.

Clearly, these difficulties are not insurmountable, and the teacher must adapt the curriculum and teaching methods to meet the child's needs. In many cases 'special' teaching is no more than good teaching, and the implications might be:

a A lot of concrete examples are required to help the acquisition of new abstract concepts. Complex skills may have to be broken down into small steps and sequenced.
b The children may need longer time to practise new skills, and more opportunities for reviewing them. Daily practice may be helpful.
c They may need time extensions, or the task may need adapting and simplifying.
d They may need to be deliberately taught to transfer skills to

different situations. Planned cross-curricula links may be required.

As Faupel (1986) commented, there is a continuum of teaching approaches ranging from loosely structured informal classes, typical of many 'informal' primary classrooms, where the aims of teaching in terms of outcome are imprecise, through to highly structured 'individualized' teaching programmes. The more 'structured' the teaching, the more prescribed will be the aims of teaching. The skilled teacher will select the most appropriate teaching methods and strategies according to the various needs of the children in the class.

Behavioural approaches to teaching and curriculum planning

Many of the specialist teaching methods and approaches which have been developed for use with children with learning and behaviour difficulties have derived from the principles of behavioural psychology. This is particularly the case where children have severe difficulties, so that 'special educational approaches' have frequently been identified with behavioural methods.

Behavioural psychology stresses the external factors influencing learning and behaviour, rather than the child's personal characteristics. When difficulties are analysed, stress is placed on observable events – what the child actually does and what is happening in the environment at the time – rather than hypothesizing internal states within the child or interpreting behaviour in terms of past events or relationships. It is argued that we can only conjecture about the child's feelings, motives and mental states, whereas we can manipulate the external factors affecting the child's learning or behaviour. A behavioural approach usually suggests clearer strategies for change. It offers principles and practical techniques which can be employed to enable parents and teachers to meet the child's educational needs and overcome learning difficulties. A behavioural approach can be used for designing a curriculum or for teaching specific skills.

BEHAVIOURAL OBJECTIVES

An important landmark in the development of behavioural methods was Mager's distinction (1973) between 'fuzzies' (that is, imprecise, vague and ambiguous statements), and 'performances' which are clear, non-ambiguous, and operationally defined. He maintained that much of our educational language is fuzzy and lacks clear meaning, so that when we set out our teaching aims, it is frequently unclear what in fact we intend the child to do as a consequence of the learning process. He suggested using the 'Hey Dad' test as a strategy for determining a clear behavioural objective. 'Hey Dad, come and watch me' is inserted at the beginning of the objective, or a school alternative might be, 'Hey Sir', or 'Hey Miss'. For example, the fuzzy objective, 'to enable pupils to gain a greater awareness of their number bonds', would rapidly fail the 'Hey Sir' test. 'Hey Sir, come and watch me gaining a greater awareness of number bonds', is vague and we would not know what to look at. However, the operational objective, 'Hey sir, come and watch me adding up' is clearer. The basic principle is to use a verb in the objective which is observable ('state', 'write', 'add', 'count' for example), rather than one which is more abstract (such as 'appreciate', 'know', 'understand').

In order to gain more precision, it may be necessary to refine the objective further. Behavioural objectives can be written as precise descriptions of pupil behaviour as the result of learning, including the conditions under which the learning is expected to occur and the standard of performance (criterion or mastery level) required, if that objective has been mastered satisfactorily. An example of a precise behavioural objective might be: 'Chris will add five sums of two-column figures, with carrying, with no errors, on three successive days (for example, 24 + 37 = ?)'. If teaching objectives are written in this way, there should be no doubt what target behaviour is being aimed for.

OBJECTIONS TO THE BEHAVIOURAL APPROACH

There are, first, pragmatic arguments against a strictly behaviourist approach. Swann (1983) questioned the assumption that a special curriculum should be written with clearly defined objectives, pointing out that there is often a gap between intentions and realizations. For many class teachers, it is unrealistic and impractical to write precise objectives for large numbers of children in the class. To ask teachers to adopt a behavioural approach can therefore lead to a loss of confidence and feelings of inadequacy. The approach does not fit with the way most teachers think or organize their work, nor the time they have available for planning.

Moreover, Swann argued that there are 'many features of special school life that are beyond the control of individual teachers; they include aspects of the hidden curriculum such as other children in the school, the school's resources and location, its relationship with the parents and the wider community, perceptions of the school by the community and by mainstream schools'. Curriculum development should start from 'a detailed and sympathetic understanding of classroom life', and the behavioural objectives approach fails to appreciate this.

Others have pointed out that many important aspects of the curriculum, such as aesthetics, moral values, etc., are not easily translated into objectives and it is not always possible, nor necessarily desirable, to specify what the outcome of teaching will be. They emphasize the creative aspect of many worthwhile educative experiences which cannot be planned for. Process or holistic models stress the value of the educational process enriching the child's life in the here and now, rather than concentrating on what the child will become and the specific skills he will need.

Wood and Shears (1986) also questioned the underlying assumptions behind some behavioural approaches when applied to children with special needs. They maintained that the basic aim to normalize children with severe learning difficulties devalues them in terms of the people they are and 'creates handicap itself'. In their view behaviour modification techniques, which will be outlined later, treat children with severe learning difficulties as if they were objects. They are seen as 'malfunctioning systems' and are devalued by being compared to the norm. Wood and Shears acknowledged the utility of behavioural approaches for teaching basic skills. Nevertheless they rejected techniques which deal solely with extrinsic control, for example the use of food or 'time out' as reinforcers for appropriate behaviour. They believe that teachers should be teaching the child self-control, and be more concerned with the child's happiness and dignity now, rather than focusing on what they will become.

In their view, children with severe learning difficulties are discriminated against because of their lack of access to resources, facilities and activities in the community. They have limited opportunities and are conferred low status; a disability is seen as a negative attribute. What they require is a socially valued role in our society. In addition they maintain that the 1981 Act is merely a sop to children with severe learning difficulties since it gave no additional resources to enable proper access to mainstream schools. Without a massive input of resources, there is little chance of children with significant learning difficulties being taught alongside their normal peers. It is argued that without access to positive role models, handicap is created out of disability.

For these and other reasons, there has been a move away from a strict behavioural approach in special education. However, there is room for both holistic and behavioural methods to co-exist; both views can inform and enhance the other. Cameron's model, for example, allows flexibility and makes it clear that precise behavioural strategies are only advocated for those children who do not progress with normal class-teaching methods.

Some behavioural teaching techniques

TEACHING THROUGH ASSESSMENT

Assessment of relevant skills is usually seen as the first step in any remedial action, and it usually remains an intrinsic part of the teaching process. When setting up a specific teaching programme, not only is a criterion-based assessment required of what the child knows now, but continuous assessment is needed to check what the child achieves during the course of the programme. To do an initial screening of the pupil's skills, various published checklists and criterion-referenced tests are available particularly for reading and number work (see Pumphrey, 1985), or teachers may prefer to devise their own.

Once teaching objectives have been set, a teach–assess–reteach–

review cycle can be entered into. Progress should be carefully monitored and recorded, so that it is clear what the child knows, how quickly he is learning and what he needs to learn next (see Solity and Raybould, 1988).

TASK ANALYSIS

Children with learning difficulties frequently have difficulty in acquiring complex skills incidentally, and so may need to have them deliberately taught. This is often most successfully done by breaking them down into small component parts, and sequencing the steps to ensure mastery.

Clarke and Clarke (1974), demonstrated that it was possible to teach severely mentally handicapped adults complex tasks such as assembling a bicycle pump, if the process was broken down into very small steps which were then taught on a carefully monitored programme. What was highlighted was that everyone can learn, if the task is properly structured.

Children with severe learning difficulties respond particularly well to highly structured approaches to learning, and the Hester Adrian Centre has been influential in developing a behavioural approach for this group of children. Basic skills such as using a knife and fork or toilet routines are broken down into teaching objectives and ordered into incremental steps using a task analysis paradigm.

Steps in task analysis

Step 1 Specify clearly the long-term pupil objective.
Step 2 Assess the pupil's existing skills relating to the task.
Step 3 Agree on one target that the pupil could reach in a short period of time and formulate an appropriate behavioural objective.
Step 4 Analyse the target objective into several smaller objectives, or steps, and sequence to complete the gap between the short-term objective (c), and long-term objective (a).

The steps are tailored to meet the learning abilities and requirements of each child. It is important to consider the size of the step, as well as the way they are sequenced or ordered.

Some children are able to acquire the skill in one teaching session whilst others may need one session to learn the very first step and may need regular further practice. The teacher can evaluate the child's progress in terms of the objectives set, and adjust the programme accordingly.

This task-analysis model assumes that all learning is hierarchical and its structure can be discovered. It has been criticized on the grounds that the precise structure of complex skill acquisition is, in fact, hard to determine, and learning not only proceeds by the gradual acquisition of subskills but also by leaps of intuition. There is also concern that without careful planning the skills may not generalize to other situations.

However, task analysis has proved to be particularly successful for planning carefully structured learning programmes with severely handicapped children (see Raymond, 1984). It also promotes a more constructive attitude towards learning difficulties; traditional views of learning have tended to assume a deficiency within the child, and ignored the possibility of faulty instruction or inappropriate curriculum objectives.

Task analysis can therefore be used:

(a) to teach specific skills and plan what should be taught next;
(b) to monitor progress;
(c) to design a curriculum.

DIRECT INSTRUCTION
This approach, derived from the work of Bereiter and Engelmann (1966), assumes that all children can learn so long as teaching is well planned and carefully implemented. Children are taught to generalize new skills by showing them different examples of the same concept, and examples of how it differs from others. The method was used initially for enriching language skills with culturally disadvantaged children, but has been subsequently used to teach reading, arithmetic and spelling in a highly structured way. DATA PAC and Distar, mentioned later, are structured-teaching programmes incorporating direct instruction. In general, the teaching method is carefully prescribed to ensure successful learning, so that often teachers work through scripted lessons; 'correction procedures'

are incorporated into the scheme, so that teachers go through further teaching routines if the target skill had not been completely mastered.

PRECISION TEACHING

Precision teaching was developed in the 1960s and is particularly useful when teaching basic skills. Despite its name, precision teaching is not a teaching method but a criterion-referenced assessment device. It is a way of measuring children's progress when learning a task, in order to find out to what extent they have mastered it. Precision teaching does not constrain the teacher to any particular teaching method, but provides a means of evaluating the learning process. It also helps teachers to evaluate their own teaching, since they can measure precisely how much the child has learned each day. In particular, it provides a direct measure of learning by assessing the child daily using individually tailored tests called probes.

One of the main benefits of using precision teaching is that the probes usually take only a minute to administer. Secondly, they give teachers and pupils immediate feedback about the effectiveness of the teaching, so that the objectives set can be carefully monitored.

Solity and Bull (1987) suggested that when teaching basic literacy and numeracy skills, tasks can be categorized into three groups:

(a)   those which are governed by a rule and contain repeated examples, such as phonic and mathematical skills;
(b)   those which are governed by a rule and do not contain repeated examples, such as oral reading;
(c)   and those which are not governed by a rule, such as sight vocabulary.

Probes can be designed to reflect each of these different characteristics. They are a useful device to use when a child appears to be making very little progress, when it would be helpful to target one specific skill and teach it systematically until mastered. Children can be taught and tested daily using a probe, and records can be kept and progress charted. If progress is not satisfactory according to some predetermined criterion, then the programme or teaching strategies may need to be changed accordingly.

Steps for devising a precision teaching programme

Step 1   The task to be taught is first set out in behavioural objectives.

Step 2   A criterion for mastery is established; for example, the child may have to read aloud twenty sight words correctly in one minute.

Step 3   'Probes' are designed to test mastery of the skill. Usually two dimensions of skill acquisition can be assessed: fluency (speed), and accuracy.

Step 4   Progress is assessed, recorded and charted on a daily basis.

STRUCTURED TEACHING MATERIALS USING THESE TECHNIQUES

The Portage Project   A number of projects have been developed using structured learning techniques, including perhaps the most extensive which was designed in Portage, in the United States (Bluma *et al.*, 1976). The aim of the project was to develop a curriculum based on a developmental approach to teaching, incorporating devices for recording the child's existing skills as well as those acquired once the programme is in operation. It also aimed to include suggestions about how new skills could be taught.

The Portage Project was promoted in this country by Cameron, and has since been used extensively by special schools and pre-school services who work with families. The project makes use of an extensive checklist of behaviours which is organized in five developmental areas: language; self help; motor; socialization; cognitive skills; plus a section on infant stimulation. Each section is arranged in a developmental sequence where possible, so that a developmental profile can be extracted, revealing the child's strengths and weaknesses in various areas, and indicating skills which need to be learned or improved. Each skill is broken down into a series of teaching steps and the scheme includes checklists and activity charts so that parents can take a major role in continuing the teaching programme at home.

The EDY project The Education of the Developmentally Young Project (EDY) was funded by the DES, and was based at the Hester Adrian Centre in Manchester. The aim of the project was to develop a workshop which could be used to train staff working with children with severe learning difficulties in behavioural techniques; and also to train instructors from different parts of the country who could run workshops in their own LEAs, to ensure the materials were disseminated widely. The programme covers behavioural techniques such as operant behaviour, prompting, task analysis, time out, shaping etc. The training is very practical and involves video demon-strations, role play, and work with a child under the close supervision of an instructor. The next stage involves planning individual programmes for children.

The project has had considerable impact. It started in 1980, and by 1985 workshops had been run in well over 25 per cent of schools for children with severe learning difficulties (Farrell, 1985).

SNAP The Special Needs Action Programme (SNAP) (Ainscow and Muncey, 1981), is an in-service programme which was devised in Coventry for ordinary teachers who are responsible for the initial identification and assessment of children with special needs. The programme includes a basic skills checklist which can be used as a screening device to identify the child's strengths and weaknesses in basic curricular skills. The SNAP course also teaches how to devise learning programmes for individual children with learning difficulties, using task-analysis techniques. Priorities are determined, teach-ing objectives drawn up, and tasks analysed into small teaching steps. Records are kept to enable careful evaluation of progress. Ainscow and Munsey claim that the programme is geared towards prevention of learning difficulties so that teachers can identify problems at an early stage and intervene appropriately. As well as giving teachers valuable skills, it enables the school to consider its special needs policy.

In Coventry, SNAP was used to train teachers designated to

co-ordinate special-needs work in their schools. It has been used since in other LEAs as an in-service training course for all primary teachers, as one response to the 1981 Act.

DATA PAC DATA PAC (Tweddle, 1982) is another useful package which has been developed recently, with ideas based on many of the behavioural methods already mentioned: behavioural objectives, precision teaching, direct instruction, and task analysis.

Four areas of basic-skill teaching are covered; arithmetic, reading, spelling and handwriting. The child's present level of functioning is first assessed via a checklist, and he is placed on a carefully graded programme of learning targets. The programme is usually devised by an educational psychologist or specialist teacher, but administered by the class teacher. Short (about five minutes), individual teaching sessions are given to the child, usually on a daily basis. Records are kept, and the programme evaluated, usually after six weeks. The programme relies on consistent structured teaching over a period of time, to enable progress to take place. Usually a clear contract is set up at the start of the programme so that roles are assigned and commitment is made by all concerned.

MORE GENERAL METHODS FOR TEACHING BASIC SKILLS
A general principle for teaching children with learning difficulties is to make the process as enjoyable and stimulating as possible. The effective teacher will spend time preparing materials which are interesting and attractive, and planning activities which enhance the child's attention and motivation.

Reading and spelling Good systematic teaching can do much to remediate learning difficulties. If children do not pick up reading skills through experiential methods, mentioned in Chapter 2, they may need structured learning programmes where, for example, after assessing where the difficulties lie (which skills have been acquired and which need to be learned next), skills are carefully and consistently taught. There are various helpful books available with skills checklists and ideas for teaching activities (for example, Dean and Nichols, 1974; Reason and Boote, 1986).

A careful analysis is also useful when a child has a spelling problem. Spellings can be analysed and the nature of the difficulty discerned from the pattern of errors. Some children misapply phonic rules, and overgeneralize, ('cud' for 'could', for example). Others rely too strongly on visual cues, producing words with a visual resemblance to the correct spelling but are incorrect (such as 'verg' for 'very'). An analysis of misspellings is the first step in a remediation programme (see Peters, 1970).

When literacy failure extends into the secondary years, the approach to remediation may change since it is likely that by this stage the child is resistant, defeated and unlikely to respond. The emphasis is usually placed on the literacy skills needed for adult life such as filling in forms, answering official letters, reading recipes, and using a telephone directory and dictionary.

PAIRED READING   One approach to remediating literacy difficulties derives from the recognition that teachers are frequently hard-pressed to find time to listen to children read, and parents have a vital educative function with their child. Paired reading has also drawn upon behavioural learning theory, and tries to improve reading skills directly, rather than improve supposed underlying skills. The technique involves simultaneous reading and reinforced individual reading. In simultaneous reading, the parent and child read together in close synchrony. The child is encouraged to signal when he wishes to continue reading independently, and the child does this with minimum correction of errors by the parent.

The essence of paired reading is to provide the child with a sense of fluency and enjoyment. Various paired reading schemes have been developed; all have involved some initial training of parents/tutors. (Bush, 1983; Topping and McKnight, 1984). A simpler version of this technique is called 'shared reading'. Emphasis is placed on parent and child participating together, with pleasure (Greening and Spenceley, 1984).

Evaluations of the effect of parental involvement with reading have been very encouraging (see, for example, Tizard, Schofield and Hewison, 1982).

LOOK–COVER–WRITE–CHECK METHOD (Peters, 1970) Peters advocated a particular approach to spelling remediation where poor spellers are encouraged to look carefully at the word they are learning, cover it, write it down, and check if they are correct. The process should be repeated if learning is not mastered.

SIMULTANEOUS ORAL SPELLING, METHOD (Bradley, 1981) Bradley proposed another method. The word in question is written for the child, he is told the word, is asked to say it aloud and copy it simultaneously. This ensures good concentration and the use of several sensory modalities.

FERNALD'S WHOLE WORD METHOD (1943) This method attempts to engage all the child's senses, in an attempt to master the spelling pattern. The child is asked to trace over the letters with his finger, pronouncing each syllable as he traces. He then writes it from memory. If this is done correctly it is repeated once. If incorrect, the pattern is traced again.

MULTISENSORY APPROACH Children with specific difficulties may need to combine the above approaches. The idea is to incorporate as many sensory channels as possible to help the child to memorize the spelling pattern.

Mathematics There are many conventional published schemes for children with learning difficulties; these are reviewed by Duncan (1978).

Teaching mathematics to children with learning difficulties usually needs to be individualized; the teacher will first need make a careful assessment of the child's present abilities, decide what skills should to be learned next, and devise an appropriate programme. The pupil will need to work at his own pace, and progress will have to be monitored carefully to ensure that learning has a firm foundation. A well planned progression is essential with exercises to ensure consolidation of each step. The mathematics component of DATA PAC provides an example of a scheme that meets all these criteria.

Another interesting approach to mathematics teaching evolved from a project in the United States (Lomans, 1976). It recommended that mathematics problems should:

(a)   have immediate practical relevance to pupils' lives;
(b)   have no 'right' solution;
(c)   require pupils to generate a number of possible solutions;
(d)   be capable of being solved within the pupils' existing skills.

The Cockcroft Report, (DES, 1982) researched the mathematical demands of adult life and employment, and emphasized a practical approach to mathematics teaching. Gulliford (1985) summarized the report's major conclusions as follows.

Children need to acquire 'the ability to read numbers and count; to tell the time; to pay for purchases; to weigh and measure; to understand timetables, graphs and charts; to carry out any necessary calculations . . . to make sensible estimations and approximations'.

The curriculum for children with learning difficulties should be aimed at achieving at least some of the needs of adult life, rather than attempt to enter the more esoteric realms of maths. The emphasis must be on the practical and concrete aspects of number.

MEETING THE NEEDS OF CHILDREN WITH MOBILITY PROBLEMS

Children with mobility problems need only attend special school when it is considered that it would be detrimental to their health or educational development to go to ordinary school.

One of the main aims of an educational programme for such children will be to achieve a degree of mobility and self reliance. Medical specialists such as physiotherapists and occupational therapists have a considerable role in achieving these aims. In addition to specialist personnel there is a wide range of equipment available to the physically handicapped child including special lifts, pulleys and wheelchairs through to hydrotherapy pools. In recent years computers have come to have a special role with such children because they are a flexible teaching aid and because a great deal can be accomplished with the minimum of mobility.

Many children with mobility problems have learning difficulties which relate to restricted motor perceptual development. For this reason a multi-sensory approach to the acquisition of reading and numeracy skills is usually taken. Touching felt letters and tracing over letters allows the child to learn about letter shapes through a medium other than vision. Many of the usual remedial techniques discussed earlier are used with these children.

Where the child has an added difficulty with speech, an alternative communicaton system can be taught.

Conductive education

In recent years there has been considerable interest in an educational system for children with mobility problems which originated in Hungary and was founded by Andras Peto. The aim of conductive education is to achieve what is termed as 'orthofunction': this is the ability to function independently in the world despite the underlying motor disorder. The orthofunctional child can get about without the need of a wheelchair or special apparatus and needs no modifications to the ordinary environment. The Peto Institute in Budapest works principally with children with cerebral palsy and spina bifida. The younger the child the better the prognosis, and the system also works best with co-operative children who are not also severely cognitively impaired.

Conductive education is provided by specially trained staff known as 'conductors'. All the conductors at the Peto Institute in Budapest are specialist teachers whose training involved an understanding of motor disorders and a great deal of practical experience working with children and adults with motor disabilities. The approach taken involves intensive exercising, training and relearning movements but the guiding force of the system is the belief in achieving independence rather than the acceptance of dependence and the reliance on aids that is the accepted practice elsewhere.

The first institute for conductive education in this country opened in Birmingham in 1987, and teachers are currently being trained at the Peto Institute in Budapest.

Perceptual motor programmes

There are a few perceptual motor development schemes available, for children with poor fine motor co-ordination, in particular one developed by Frostig (1964) in the United States. The problem with such schemes is that there is little evidence that the skills generalize, so that the child may become adept at the activities on the programme but remain incompetent at other related activities.

A controversial approach to severe learning difficulties has been taken by Dolman and Delacato in the USA. They maintain that motoric patterning in the pathways of the brain are prerequisite for learning and their approach is to retrain children in basic early motor activities such as crawling. Apart from objections to their underlying theoretical position, the amount of time needed for their programmes is often inordinate.

MEETING THE NEEDS OF CHILDREN WITH SPEECH, LANGUAGE AND COMMUNICATION DIFFICULTIES

Approaches to assessment

There are various approaches to the assessment and remediation of speech and language difficulties.

Tough (1975) adopted a functional approach. She identified seven areas of language function and a child's competence is assessed in relation to these:

(a) self-maintaining and guarding one's own interests;
(b) directing self and others' activities;
(c) reporting on present and past experiences;
(d) using reason and logic;
(e) predicting and anticipating events;

(f)   projecting into the experience of others; and
(g)   using fantasy and imagination.

Tough's work is aimed at socially disadvantaged children rather than those with a clinical disorder, and she gives a useful remedial scheme to accompany assessment of problems.

In contrast, Crystal (1976, 1985) approached language problems from a structural basis. He identified at least three levels of language production:

(a)   the level of speech sounds or phonological level;
(b)   the level of sentence organization and grammar or the morphological level;
(c)   the level of meaning and understanding or the semantic level.

Problems can occur at any of these levels, for example, articulation disorders are usually confined to the phonological level, 'Ja n Ji nt up d ill'. Morphological problems occur with dysphasia; an example might be 'Jack and Jill up the hill went'. And semantic disorders occur with conditions such as autism, and result in mistakes such as 'Jack and Jill went up the well'.

Traditionally, standardized tests of language development have been used to assess speech and language, the two most widely used being the Illinois Test of Psycholinguistic Abilities (ITPA) and Reynell's Language Development Scale. ITPA attempts to assess some of the underlying skills thought to be prerequisites for normal language development such as memory, sequencing, recall, etc., and the Reynell test looks explicitly at the child's language acquisition in comparison with other children of the same age.

Traditional testing is currently being superseded by detailed observation and assessment of children's use of language, often with the help of checklists using models such as Tough's and Crystal's. More recently, assessment has been more closely associated with remediation linked packages (see below, p. 208).

The assessment and provision of remedial help with language problems will clearly depend on their type and severity. Children with speech and language difficulties are referred to a speech therapist for specialist help and they will frequently work via teachers and parents who have a major role to play.

The remediation of moderate and severe language difficulties

Language remediation is regarded as of primary importance in the curriculum for children with severe learning difficulties. Most of the available programmes attempt to mirror normal language development. Usually a vocabulary of single words is first taught followed by the introducion of action words and an attempt to promote combinations. All the available programmes, such as the Peabody Language Development Programme, 'Jim's People' and the Portage Project, are highly structured. Portage now draws attention to the importance of the development of prelinguistic skills which are part of the wider communication process, such as establishing eye contact, playing co-operatively, etc.

One of the most highly structured programmes, the Distar programme, involves the child learning responses to routine prompts which the teacher shapes through repetition. One common problem, however, is that while the individual child may perform well on the programme, the language he learns does not always generalize to other situations.

The Derbyshire Language Scheme (Masidlover, 1982), is designed to improve language skills in children who have delayed language development. It was originally designed for children with severe learning difficulties, but can be used with any child with a specific language problem. It is used by teachers and speech therapists to assess the child's ability, and then design appropriate learning programmes. Children are encouraged to become actively involved in enjoyable learning experiences, so there is a stress on two-way communication. The scheme focuses on grammatical aspects of language rather than vocabulary, as it is assumed that only during structured language sessions would sentence construction be emphasized. The aim is to teach a child to use and understand, in a social context, a range of different types of sentence which become progressively longer and more complex.

Other language schemes are also available. Gillham (1983) researched the basic vocabulary acquisition of severely handicapped children and produced a scheme for teaching and extending vocabulary.

Children with very severe dysphasia are rare but they need a great deal of specialist help and there are a few special residential schools which cater for such children. The dilemma is that the child forgoes family life, and is necessarily excluded from good language models by mixing with an ordinary peer group. The trend has been towards smaller units which can offer specialist help on a daily basis whilst offering opportunities for integration with normal children.

The remediation of mild language difficulties

Apart from children with severe problems, there are many more whose language problems are relatively mild and transitory, but this may well adversely affect educational attainment.

Language remediation projects began in the USA under the impetus of Project Headstart, and have been transported across the Atlantic (see, for example, Bereiter and Engelmann, 1966; Karnes, 1970). By comparison with the USA, compensatory education in Britain has been far less extensive. Results from American studies indicate that preschool intervention has beneficial effects on the language acquisition of socially disadvantaged children. Studies in this country such as the West Riding Project (1975), and initiatives undertaken by the Schools' Council (Tough, 1975), have confirmed that very early intervention is more beneficial. Projects that have involved teaching mothers how to extend their child's use of language have also proved successful. Examples of published schemes available to teachers include 'Goal' and 'Concept 7–9', as well as Tough's materials.

The Bullock Report (DES, 1975) evaluated reading and literacy standards in schools and called for a concerted assault on language skills in schools. It was recommended that a language consultant who would specialize in language remediation should be given special responsibility in each school. The report did much to highlight the importance of the child's level of language competence across the school curriculum and all teachers were urged to accept responsibility for promoting language skills. It also emphasized the crucial role of language in learning and the importance of linguistically stimulating experiences in school. Although the stress was on general linguistic enrichment, the report also pointed out that some children need precise learning objectives, and the provision of a more carefully planned language experience, than was currently available in most nursery and infant schools at the time.

Since then various language–experience approaches to reading have been advocated (see, for example, Gillham, 1974). A published version of this approach, *Breakthrough to Literacy*, (Mackay, Thompson and Schaub, 1970) encourages children to build up their own working vocabulary of words they wish to use, and construct their own sentences, rather than reading from published reading books.

Crystal (1976, 1985) gave important general principles for language remediation and stressed the need for an individualized approach:

> In the first place, any person undertaking language remediation must have a thorough understanding of normal language development. Any language development programme must be graded to provide a clear and precise statement of teaching goals. However, it is comparatively easy to know which structures the child already has but much more difficult to deduce which ones he has not yet gained. Balance in a teaching programme is also very important since if particular language skills are over-learned they may dominate and intrude when new skills are introduced.

Crystal emphasized that language remediation must always aim to be appropriate to the child's needs and experiences and in harmony with his natural expectations of language. For those planning language remediation programmes he stressed:

(a) the importance of maintaining conversation directed to the young child;
(b) the need to link language to purposeful action wherever possible;
(c) the need to avoid talking for the child and giving him enough time to work out a reply for himself;

(d) the need to be aware of normal and expected errors or the immature grammar of an earlier stage, and the need to avoid explicit correction;

(e) finding ways of expanding and extending normal speech patterns.

Nelson (1973) also advocated that language development can be promoted by the acceptance of the child's attempts at communication and the avoidance of a dominant correcting role by the teacher or parent. Studies of normal children find that less control (fewer questions and commands) from the adult tends to increase the frequency and length of the child's utterances (see Wood and Wood, 1983). Wells (1979) also emphasized the importance of language in the context of shared social activities (such as doing housework together).

Alternative communication systems

Makaton is a system of about 200 gestures indicating basic needs and providing a child with a very limited vocabulary. It is usually used with children with very limited intellectual ability but it can be used as an introduction to more complex systems.

Paget Gorman is a more complex and flexible communication system which uses an extensive vocabulary of gestures and hand signals, where sentences with grammar and tense can be expressed. This is particularly useful for many children with severe hearing impairment.

The child with limited speech and limited mobility in the arms can be taught the Bliss symbolic system. The Bliss system makes use of a board with a matrix of simple visual symbols. The child can indicate basic needs and build simple sentences by pointing to the symbols. Symbols can be invented and added to the board according to their relevance for the child.

Provision

Children with specific speech and language difficulties may require speech therapy; some may need to attend special language classes and units if they need more extensive help.

Where possible, children with speech and language difficulties are best taught with their normal peers where they can be exposed to normal speech patterns.

MEETING THE NEEDS OF THE HEARING IMPAIRED CHILD

There has been a long controversy over whether the profoundly deaf should be trained to communicate orally only or manually through a signing system, sometimes known as the total communication approach.

Auditory training and speech or lip reading are associated with the oral approach, and some schools adopting this method prohibit the manual approach. The manual approach includes using sign languages and/or finger spelling. Traditionally the latter method was the most popular method but this has waned. The schools which adopt the oral approach argue that signing can make the deaf child more isolated from his hearing peers and that signing discourages the development of residual hearing. Furthermore, it may prohibit the development of abstract thinking because all signing systems are necessarily limited in comparison to normal language. Finally, the underlying thrust of the oral method is to 'normalize' the deaf child as much as possible. However surveys have shown that about half of the profoundly deaf have recognizable speech and it is argued that deaf people will use the natural medium of communication if at all possible; but for those where it is impossible, it is wrong to deny them an alternative. It is also pointed out that some children can have a much wider vocabulary with signing techniques than they can acquire orally, and signing can be used as a medium for introducing new speech words (Gregory, 1986).

Many schools and units manage a compromise between the two approaches and try to meet individual needs although, in the case of deaf children, the individual's means of communication is affected by the way others communicate around him. The most appropriate method to teach the child depends also on the child's abilities, and whether the hearing impairment occurred before or after some language had been acquired.

Auditory training is recommended for most deaf children to improve any hearing ability they may possess. Children are first made aware of sounds, particularly speech sounds, and are then trained to make gross discriminations between sounds, listening to their difference and extracting as much information as they can. Auditory training, even without an aid, should begin as soon as a diagnosis is made, and parents are encouraged to give their child listening practice as early as possible.

Lip reading or speech reading involves teaching children with a hearing loss to use visual information to aid their comprehension of speech. This may involve teaching situational cues which accompany speech, and the normal non-verbal communication used by everyone as an accompaniment to speech.

Manual methods of communication include Makaton and Paget Gorman, as previously described, and the British Sign Language. Finger spelling, in contrast to signing general ideas, is a method of signing words using the alphabet letter by letter. It has one advantage in that it is easy for the hearing person to learn, but it is extremely slow and limiting for the deaf person to use.

Cued speech is another method which enhances information given or received orally. Here hand signals in the vicinity of the mouth may provide phonetic information such as vowel sounds, and this is combined with clear speech for lip reading.

Unfortunately, deaf children do tend to fall behind their in academic achievement. All disorders of hearing are handicapping since speech and language are such a vital part of life, and are fundamental to the acquisition of many skills. The average intellectual ability of profoundly deaf children is significantly below the norm, although this may be misleading because the comparison is usually made on tests designed for the hearing. Furth (1961) maintained that the cognitive abilities of deaf children are not necessarily impaired, with the exception of concepts which rely heavily on language. However, such a view may be optimistic due to the close relationship between language and the development of complex, abstract thought.

Hearing impaired children may also display behaviour

problems due to the frustration resulting from their communication difficulties. Another frequent response is withdrawal.

MEETING THE NEEDS OF THE
VISUALLY IMPAIRED CHILD

A great difficulty with blind babies and young children is that there are marked delays in motor development. Vision appears to be necessary to trigger the child's exploratory instincts and many blind babies never crawl and only 50 per cent walk independently by 24 months. Some blind babies find resource in internal stimulation by rocking, finger flicking or head banging; such activities have to be gently discouraged and every effort made to encourage mobility and external stimulation. Perceptual development can be promoted through auditory and tactile experiences although those who become blind after birth, although advantaged in some understanding of visual concepts, are disadvantaged in terms of the adjustment they have to make to blindness.

Learning to read braille is far more complex than learning to read print and suitable reading material is relatively difficult to obtain. Visually impaired children are encouraged to use their residual vision as much as possible; studies suggest it can be improved through systematic training (Ashcroft, Halliday and Barragan, 1965).

Children learning to use braille tend to learn much more slowly than children learning to read print. The DES survey of braille reading (1970) found that 36 per cent of visually handicapped children had not mastered the mechanics of reading by 11 years of age. A comparison of matched groups of normal and visually impaired older children found that although their comprehension skills were similar, the sighted read at twice the speed. Time allowance for examinations is usually necessary, and blind children are frequently allowed to record their answers orally, using a tape recorder.

School provision

There are only 3,500 registered blind children in Britain, thinly distributed over the country so that special schools on a county-wide basis are impractical. Most of the special schools for the blind are residential. The majority are run by the Royal National Institute for the Blind (RNIB), a voluntary organization which also runs the Sunshine Homes and an advisory service for parents, and is a major publisher of braille books. Most of the schools for the partially sighted are run by LEAs and these are mainly day schools. Only one-third of partially sighted children need residential schooling. Alternative provision such as peripatetic support services and integrated units in ordinary schools have become more popular in recent years. There are three establishments for the higher education and further training for these children.

Unfortunately, residential schooling is necessary for some blind children from an early age, although the Vernon Report (DES 1972b) recommended that children should not board away from home under 5 years of age, unless the circumstances were exceptional. The report also stressed the importance of early education for the visually handicapped. Nursery schooling is often commenced at 2 years so that the child learns both intellectual and social skills from an early age.

MEETING THE NEEDS OF CHILDREN WITH EMOTIONAL AND BEHAVIOUR DIFFICULTIES

There are three major approaches to helping children with adjustment difficulties, each relying on different theoretical perspectives:

(1) Individual-centred therapies which see the problem as either lying within the child or as the child being the best recipient for therapy.

(2) Family-centred therapies which look at the child within the context of the dynamic family unit, and assume that treatment must involve the unit as a whole rather than any individual within it.

(3) Systems approaches, which regard the child as a product of the circumstances that surround him, rather than the instigator of his own difficulties. Change would focus on manipulating the factors which maintain the behaviour.

Individual-centred approaches

COUNSELLING AND PSYCHOTHERAPY
Various counselling techniques may be used, with the aim of establishing a therapeutic relationship, within which the pupil can explore his own difficulties with the aim of promoting insight and enabling change to occur.

Some psychotherapeutic approaches are derived from psychoanalytical traditions. Here the therapist explores with the young person his early fears and memories, in an attempt to elucidate present behaviour in the light of past experiences and actions. The aim is to resolve deep-seated emotional problems though the interpretation of past events.

Most counselling and psychotherapeutic techniques are based on humanistic principles which owe much to Carl Rogers (1951), where the fundamental aim is to improve the individual's self-regard and sense of self-worth. Many children have very low self-esteem, as discussed in Chapter 5, because of the social and physical disadvantages they incur. A skilful counsellor can facilitate personal growth in young people by enabling them to explore and clarify unresolved thoughts and feelings.

Bogler (1986), for example, has proposed an interesting three-stage a–c–b model (affective–cognitive–behavioural), which draws on various sources. It includes Carl Rogers' client-centred therapy, psychoanalytic theory, rational-emotive and other cognitive approaches and behavioural techniques. He maintains that counselling should be progressive, developing through stages as the counsellor increases his understanding of the pupil's difficulties. Because the model combines a variety of approaches to counselling, it will be described in more detail.

Stage 1　The affective stage　A relationship is initially established which is client-centred, and characterized by Rogers' 'unconditional positive regard'. The counsellor aims to be non-judgemental, completely accepting the young person as he is, conveying concern, warmth and respect. The counsellor listens at this stage, and seeks to understand the young person's feelings with 'primary accurate empathy' (Egan, 1975). The youngster is enabled to ventilate and clarify thoughts and feelings through this process of self-exploration.

Stage 2   The cognitive stage   At this stage, if the young person is ready to move forward, the counsellor enters Egan's phase of 'advanced accurate empathy'. He will draw attention to what is implied as well as what is said, to contradictions and anomalies, to recurring themes, and to what is being denied as well as what is asserted. Youngsters are encouraged to examine the basic life positions which they adopt, and what they are saying about themeselves, verbally and non-verbally. According to Bogler, 'understanding the nature of self-talk is an important step towards client self-control'.

The skilled counsellor can effect, he believes, a process called 'cognitive restructuring' (Ellis, 1962). Ellis pointed out the link between reason and emotion, and that the ways we interpret what is happening in our lives affects the feelings which we attribute to events. At this stage, the young person is helped to reach a realistic and objective understanding which will help him to make constructive plans. Self-understanding, and an understanding about the root of difficulties, should move on to a wish for change. It is important that the youngster comes to want change for himself, and that this is not just the wish of parents or teachers. At this stage Bogler advocated drawing up an explicit behavioural contract, spelling out the behaviour that the pupil wishes to change, and what he and others concerned will do to ensure this takes place. Even if goals are kept informal, he stressed the importance of making them overt rather than remaining in the counsellor's mind.

At this stage, then, issues are clarified, plans discussed, and a commitment to change established.

Stage 3   The behavioural stage   At this stage various action plans are worked out together, in an attempt to change behaviour. Bogler described four phases:

a learn – methods are taught, demonstrated and practised;
b practice – the homework phase, when new skills are tried out;
c monitor – the pupil reports back, is encouraged, praised or consoled;
d evaluate – the assessment of progress and setting of new goals.

The counsellor has a choice of methods, and is not restricted to a passive role. Bogler summarizes these as follows:

1 Life skills: that is, identify and practise new skills such as remedial, social or study skills.
2 Reinforcement: that is, find out what rewards/incentives work for the pupil.
3 Cognitive restructuring: that is, help the pupil to think more positively and stop negative thoughts.
4 Self-monitoring: that is, diaries, checklists etc. can be used to help the pupil understand his behaviour.
5 Relaxation training.
6 Desensitization: that is, teach the pupil to adjust gradually to his anxieties.
7 Social drama: that is, role play to rehearse and practise skills.
8 Behaviour contracts: that is, formal plans for a programme of change.
9 Tender loving care: supportive counselling.

BEHAVIOURAL METHODS
Behaviour modification has developed over the last twenty years as a technique for controlling and changing behaviour. In order to work out a successful programme, the teacher must first identify the target behaviour she wishes to change and define it in precise objective terms (shouting out in lessons, for example). Next, in order to measure behavioural change, it is necessary to establish a baseline by recording the incidence of the behaviour which is to be changed. A system of reinforcement is then worked out, using rewards that are powerful for the child concerned. These might be social rewards such as praise or special privileges, or more concrete items such as sweets or

merit marks. Alternatively, normal routines can be arranged so that activities that the child enjoys are made consequential on completing the target behaviour. The incidence of the behaviours are measured after the instigation of the programme, and change in behaviour is monitored (see Leach and Raybould, 1977; Poteet, 1973).

Many interesting studies have shown how behaviour can change with systematic reinforcement. It has been used particularly in special school settings, both with behavioural problems (O'Leary and O'Leary, 1976), and with severe learning difficulties (Kiernan, 1978; Raymond, 1984). It has also been shown to be useful in the ordinary classroom in managing disruptive children as well as motivating children to work harder and achieve better results (Becker *et al.*, 1974; Ulrich, Stachnik and Madry, 1970). Teachers and parents are likely to use a system of reinforcement consciously or unconsciously; the behavioural teacher applies these principles methodically and consistently.

As well as changing behaviour, it is possible to change fears and phobias using the same behavioural techniques.

A FUNCTIONAL APPROACH

Westmacott and Cameron (1981) offered a system for dealing directly with problem behaviour, which they termed a functional approach. The key idea is that if you want to change behaviour you must be clear about what you wish to change, and analyse all the influences exerted by the events which occurred before, during and after the problem behaviour. There is little evidence that behaviour changes as a result of insight, but most behaviour results from learning to behave in a certain way, or not being taught to behave differently.

Westmacott and Cameron proposed that behaviour should first be analysed using an A–B–C approach:

ANTECEDENTS – BEHAVIOUR – CONSEQUENCES

A   B   C

'The trick about changing behaviour is to (a) first isolate the behaviour, (b) find the various factors which allow it to occur (or prevent it from occurring) in the first place, (c) establish what makes it possible for it to continue or decrease in the future.' Children's difficulties are thus understood by making a precise analysis of the context or 'setting events', and the events that precede and follow it. A fundamental principle of behavioural psychology is that learning depends on the context in which it takes place. Emphasis is placed on the here and now, rather than dwelling on the child's history.

Behaviour, using this model, is understood to be maintained by a balance between A, B and C. By changing one of these elements behaviour also can change. For example, for a child who is constantly interfering with the work of others, temptation can be removed, seats can be changed, early warnings can be given, or attention can be given to good behaviour, etc.

In order to change behaviour a clear plan of attack is usually helpful, using a problem-solving framework (see below). In addition, Westmacott and Cameron (1981) noted that to implement a successful plan good teaching is required. This can be simply conceptualized as involving the four Ps:

a   Preparation
b   Planning
c   Performing
d   Post-mortem

It is important to plan how the new behaviour will be taught, success rewarded, and progress recorded. The child must never be put in a situation where he is likely to fail. Careful monitoring and evaluation are also required.

Westmacott and Cameron's problem-solving framework can be summarized as follows:

Step 1.   List the child's strengths or assets.
Step 2.   Make a clear statement of the problems – without speculating about inner causes.
Step 3.   Decide on priorities – i.e. which problem to tackle first.
Step 4.   State the desired outcome, or target behaviour.
Step 5.   Plan a course of action to reach the target

behaviour. If the goal is too distant, task analysis
may be required to break it into smaller steps.

Step 6.   Implement the programme and monitor.

Step 7.   If successful, choose another problem.
           If unsuccessful, reconsider 4, revise 5 or change 6.

Family-centred approaches

Family-centred approaches offer the whole family the opportunity to explore their relationships and dynamics with a
trained therapist. Problem behaviour may be seen as the
consequence of the role imposed on an individual by his family
members. The therapist will try to understand how the family
functions; how members have come to adopt certain roles and
habits of response and whether these dynamics are successful or
damaging to all or some members. It may be possible to
change roles and family dynamics to the benefit of everyone or
to shift the focus of the problem.

The interpretations that the therapist will make about the
clients and their interactions will depend on the training of the
therapist. However, the basic methods are very similar,
although interpretations may differ. Usually the whole family
attend a number of contracted sessions and two therapists may
work with the family, one taking an active role in facilitating
discussion about family functioning, and the other acting as an
observer. The two therapists may retire from the room to
exchange observations and plan interventions. At the end of
each session the family may be given insight into its dynamics
and tasks may be set to start the process of change.

Problems arising from inconsistent parenting, issues over
parental responsibilities and control and the scapegoating of
individual family members, can be successfully addressed using
this approach.

Systems approaches

In systems approaches it is argued that the child's behaviour
can only be understood by reference to all the circumstances
that surround him. Frequently an upset child is reacting to
circumstances over which he has very little control. A systems

approach views the child in relation to those circumstances and attempts to help the child by changing his situation. For example, a child with learning difficulties may be regularly offensive and aggressive to his teacher. He may also come from difficult home circumstances so the family as a system may need to be investigated. However, it might be decided that it is easier to change the school system in which he interacts than to change dynamics in the family system or alleviate social disadvantage.

Thus one way forward might be to change the child's curriculum as a means of changing his aggressive behaviour. It might also be worth considering the way classes are organized, looking at the low status conferred by being a member of the bottom set. Or it may be that the relationship between the child and his year tutor needs enhancing. Alternatively, if the staff were better supported, they might avoid escalating conflicts, and feel able to tolerate the child's difficulties more easily.

Focus is frequently placed on the school organization and on teachers' skills, since it is these aspects of the child's life which may be most amenable to change. A fundamental assumption behind this approach is that it is better to seek change with those factors we can control, than try to intervene with those where we have less influence.

It is also important to consider, as discussed in Chapter 5, that the school organization may well have a part in creating problems. McGuiness and Craggs (1986) put this quite starkly: 'if a group of psychologists, expert in attitude formation, were invited to devise a situation and create a series of experiences specifically to provoke young people into disruptive, hostile or aggressive behaviour, they could well come up with something uncomfortably close to what is experienced by large numbers of pupils in many British secondary schools'. In their view the education system stunts potential and makes many young people frustrated, resentful and hostile.

At the same time it should be noted that the system extracts its toll from teachers. There is evidence that teacher stress is very high (Kyriacou and Sutcliffe, 1977) due to pupil misbehaviour, poor working conditions, time pressures and poor school ethos. Dunham (1977, 1986) also found that stress resulted from organizational and curricula change, role conflict, role ambiguity, difficult working conditions, and children's behaviour and attitudes. It seems likely that there is an interaction between disruptive pupil behaviour and teacher stress, and that this is a two-way process.

IN-SERVICE TEACHING MATERIALS

Various materials have been developed to enhance teachers' skills based on a systems approach, such as *Preventive Approaches to Disruption (PAD)* (Tweddle 1987). *PAD* is based on five hypotheses:

(a) Disruptive children are not disruptive all the time.
(b) Disruptive children only disrupt with certain teachers.
(c) Prevention of problems is much better than cure.
(d) Techniques of control and management can be made explicit and can be easily learned.
(e) Internal initiatives are likely to be more successful than external experts intervening.

A course is constructed from the materials, based on the interests of the school staff. This may include ways of observing and describing behaviour; effective patterns of communication in school; key aspects of lesson organization; teaching skills and ways of managing pupils and avoiding conflict situations.

A similar in-service course which looks at ways of preventing disruptive behaviour in school was devised by Grunsell (1981). Again, teachers are encouraged to share ideas about problem behaviour and look at their own management skills.

Another course, devised by the SNAP team in Coventry (Ainscow and Muncey, 1981), aims to improve teacher's skills with difficult children. This course is based on the A–B–C approach popularized by Westmacott and Cameron, mentioned above, and also includes a consideration of staff/pupil relationships, the importance of the child's self-concept, ways of reviewing class and school policies, etc.

These and other courses allow teachers to focus on their own teaching skills, and on various aspects of school organization such as the curriculum, assessment, rewards and sanctions, the school management structure, and factors related to the general 'school ethos'. As noted in earlier chapters, children's behaviour is thought to be significantly affected by these school factors.

In addition to these published materials, there are now many useful books available summarizing research into effective classroom management skills (for example, Laslett and Smith, 1984; Robertson, 1981). Classroom management in this context is defined by Kounin (1970) as teaching 'producing a high rate of work involvement with a low rate of deviancy in academic settings'.

TEACHER SUPPORT GROUPS
Clearly, the number of children who present problems for teachers is large; too large for them all to be referred to outside agencies. Teachers must therefore frequently find their own solutions to the problem of dealing with children's emotional and behavioural difficulties. As noted above, teaching is a highly stressful job, not least because teachers tend to be isolated, and support is not always readily available, nor is it necessarily of a helpful nature.

Hanko (1985) advocated school-based staff support groups where teachers can share experiences and explore problems together in a collaborative way. The aim is to discuss particular issues in a supportive setting; usually particular children form the focus of the discussion, and any member of the group is free to bring up a problem they would like to share. The role of group leaders (educational psychologists, specialist teachers, etc.) is to facilitate the group process, rather than give advice; the problem remains the responsibility of the teacher who raised it, but the sharing of views often helps to resolve feelings, clarify problems, establish priorities and help decision-making. The aim is to establish mutual staff support and the sharing of difficulties.

PROVISION FOR CHILDREN WITH ADJUSTMENT DIFFICULTIES
As we have previously discussed, the incidence of emotional and behavioural difficulties is hard to determine but it has been estimated that between 10 and 20 per cent of children exhibit troubled behaviour at some time during their school careers

(Rutter, Tizard and Whitmore, 1970). It may be that we need to question our assumption that one adult can provide a stimulating educational environment for thirty or more children of diverse needs. Conflict and stress may in fact be inevitable.

The number of children whose behaviour is so difficult to manage that they require some form of special education, however, is much lower than these figures. Lunzer (1960) found that many pupils improve without receiving additional help, and noted a 'spontaneous remission' rate of about two-thirds with children in secondary schools. This was confirmed in Topping's (1983) review, where he commented that research comes up with this figure with 'stunning regularity'. This might be explained in various ways, one being that many children seem to go through a phase of bad behaviour from which most emerge. It would be unfortunate if this remission is made less likely by the process of labelling a child as problematic.

Topping's Cascade Model (1983) A range of provision options are available for children who present persistent disruption problems. These are reviewed by Topping who produced a 'cascade', or resource continuum of alternative provisions. The cascade represents a hierarchy of interventions which are evaluated in terms of their cost and effectiveness in bringing about adjustment.

There are various types of provision available, within the school and off-site. On-site resources include: routine sanctions reorganization, curriculum reorganization; parent training; pupil training, teacher training; consultants; itinerant support teachers; crisis rooms; time-out rooms; and special classes. Off-site provision includes: suspension centres; alternative schools; off-site units; day special schools; and residential special schools.

Interestingly, Topping's research revealed that the most expensive resources are not in fact the most effective. He concluded that off-site provisions are extremely costly, particularly residential schools, and the evidence of improved adjustment is unimpressive. Very few children returned to ordinary school in the short term, and only about two-thirds achieved a longer term adjustment and were regarded as 'stable' in adult life.

Topping concluded that the following were the most cost-effective and successful interventions: routine sanction change; curriculum reorganization; parent training (home–school liaison); pupil training (self-recording); teacher training; consultants; and support teachers. In contrast, separate day and residential units were found to be strictly a 'luxury'.

8

Meeting special educational needs – the wider context

OVERVIEW

This chapter and Chapter 7 outline the variety of facilities and resources for meeting children's special educational needs. The previous chapter dealt in the main with the way special needs can be met via the curriculum and special teaching methods, whereas this one will consider the wider context of provisions and resources. The chapter begins with a discussion of various educational settings for meeting special educational needs. The statutory agencies are then outlined, and finally, pre- and post-school provisions are briefly described and discussed.

EDUCATIONAL SETTINGS

As we have noted earlier, under the terms of the 1981 Education Act the LEA is responsible for meeting children's special educational needs. The Warnock Report had previously described integration as 'the central contemporary issue' in special education, and the Act, adopting this principle, made it explicit that children should, with certain provisos, be educated in ordinary schools.

Since the implementation of the Act, LEAs have responded in different ways. Some have made minor adjustments in their provisions and resources whilst others have seized the opportunity to radically overhaul the basic structure of their provision. One might have expected a wholesale move towards integration and a commensurate shrinking of segregated special school places, but, so far, government statistics show a continuing rise in special school places. This could be due to delays in responding to the Act, and we may start to see a decline in numbers transferring into segregated provision. It could also be argued that a continuing growth merely reflects the previous scarcity of provision. However, it is likely that a major reason is the fact that the 1981 Act made no financial provision for children with special needs, and without a strong impetus for change, the status quo remains. As Topping (1983) commented, 'it may be that some authorities will have heavy capital (and, in some cases, emotional) investment tied up in long-established physical resources which cannot be dismantled without political embarrassment. This clearly constitutes a managerial problem concerning effective reallocation of resources'.

There is also a danger in promoting integrationist policies without proper financing. The NUT (1988) noted the dangers of 'unplanned and under-resourced integration, operated on a piecemeal basis', and argued for additional funding.

Dessent (1983) saw the question of responsibility being a major block to integration occurring. By assigning children to segregated provision, the responsibility for these children is removed from the normal class teacher. The teacher feels absolved of responsibility for the child's failure to learn, and the problem disappears. Moreover, whilst children remain integrated in mainstream schooling, educational psychologists also feel they are held responsible for every facet of the child's development. Integration is arguably not in their interests either. Dessent asserts that to overcome these difficulties, the advantages of the special school must be diverted into integrated provision. Responsibility for children must be shared, and the good resources and teacher–pupil ratios of special schools maintained in the ordinary school.

Dessent also proposed that it is a myth that different groups of children need different forms of teaching. In his view, rather than having separate special facilities for children with learning difficulties and behaviour problems in ordinary schools, one

Table 8.1 Comparison between costs and staffing in various types of school provision

	per capita	pupil/staff ratio
Cost of special school place	£1,978	7:4
Cost of secondary school place	£ 629	16:1
Cost of primary school place	£ 436	22:1

Source: Lukes (1981).

special-needs department could cope with both.

Swann (1983) also asked how the special school curriculum can be preserved once children are transferred to mainstream. At present special schools receive some measure of positive discrimination, and these benefits of 'equipment, expertise and attention' should not be lost. He agreed with Dessent that most special education is in fact ordinary, although the costs are higher, largely due to staffing ratios. Costs and staffing in various types of school are compared in Table 8.1.

Between 1985 and 1987, nearly one-quarter of school-age children on statements attended mainstream school; however, there are wide variations between local authorities; for example, 74 per cent attended ordinary schools in Cornwall, compared to just 1 per cent in Oxfordshire.

The national picture is therefore a confusing one and it is more meaningful for professionals, parents and children to consider provisions on a local basis whilst bearing in mind the ideals of the 1981 Act.

The range of provision available on a country-wide basis can be summarized as follows:

1 Special schools: residential (weekly boarding, termly boarding or full-time).
2 Special schools: day.
3 Special units: segregated from ordinary school.
4 Special units: attached to an ordinary school.
5 Special classes: segregated.
6 Special classes: with part-time integration.

7   Withdrawal groups: using outside peripatetic teaching staff.
8   Withdrawal groups: using internal staff.
9   Child supported entirely within the ordinary class either by his own teacher or with the help of an additional resource (ancillary worker or support teacher).

Provision may be part-time or full-time, and it should be kept constantly under review in keeping with the changing needs of children. Links are being created between special schools and units and mainstream schools, with opportunities being developed for social interaction as well as curricular integration of pupils for particular subjects.

It may be unrealistic at present to expect all the range of alternatives to exist in any one LEA, although a variety of options should be available so that there is a continuum of provision, as Warnock proposed. Provision should reflect the diversity of children's needs; thus we should move away from rigid thinking about the location of education. The teachers' own commitment to new ideas and willingness to adapt working patterns are likely to be key features of change. It is to be hoped that in time the range of alternatives will widen.

THE STATUTORY AGENCIES

In Britain the child with special needs and his parents may receive help and support from a large number of agencies and, in some cases, many professionals may be involved. The three main government departments which provide essential services and care are:

1   The local education authority;
2   The health service;
3   The social services department.

In addition, there is a wide range of voluntary and charitable organizations for the handicapped. In this chapter only the three statutory agencies are briefly outlined, but a list of the major voluntary agencies working with children is provided in the Appendix.

One important point to be made initially is the position of
position of parents and children in relation to the law. As
instanced by the 1981 Act, it is a legal right that parents must
be consulted and should be in agreement with any change in
the education or health care of their child. It is hoped that
parents and statutory agencies will work in partnership, as
advocated by the Warnock Report. However, the government,
through legislation, also has some legal rights and responsibilities
for the child; most importantly, education is compulsory, and
the physical, emotional and moral wellbeing of the child is the
concern of society at large. Parents occasionally forfeit their
rights over the care of their child if it can be shown in a court
of law that the child's wellbeing is seriously jeopardized.
Parents are the natural caretakers of their children and their's is
the lifetime commitment, but society too shares a responsibility
for all its members.

The local education authority

As discussed in Chapter 1, the current structure of the
educational system of England and Wales was established by
the Education Act, 1944, although there have been many
changes and modifications since. The 1944 Act had a section on
the education of handicapped children and the fundamental
structure of special education remained relatively unaltered
until the 1981 Act. A major change occurred in 1971, when the
LEAs assumed responsibility for the education of severely
mentally retarded children. Another change affecting special
education was the compulsory introduction of comprehensive
schools (Education Act, 1976); the general movement towards
comprehensivization has the principle of non-segregation as an
integral part of its policy. Although we now have new
legislation and a different framework for special education, we
are still working with a structure laid down in 1944, and it will
undoubtedly take many years for the changes to have their full
impact. Also, as will be discussed in the next chapter, there are
now radical proposals for a restructuring of the whole of the
educational system which will have major consequences for
special education; so at present special education is in a stage of
change and uncertainty.

SPECIAL EDUCATION TEACHERS

The 1944 Education Act did not consider the training of teachers of the handicapped, although special training was at this stage already given to teachers of the blind and deaf. The report of the National Advisory Council on the Training and Supply of Teachers (DES, 1954) was devoted entirely to the training of teachers of handicapped pupils, and it was recommended that all teachers intending to work with handicapped children should, after a period in ordinary schools and some preliminary experience with handicapped children, take a full-time course of additional training. Although the recommendation was accepted it proved to be a 'straw man' and up to 1980 only 5 per cent of teachers in special schools had any additional training. The Warnock Report considered the issue and sensibly recommended that, since integration was a cornerstone of the report and teachers in ordinary schools might regularly expect to encounter children with special needs, then there should be a special education component in all initial training. In addition they recommended that every teacher should receive some in-service training to prepare them for teaching children with special needs. These recommendations have undoubtedly had an impact, but they were not embodied in the 1981 Act and statistics on the number of people now being given additional training in special education are difficult to obtain.

Most LEAs now provide a support service to ordinary schools, with a team of special teachers. The services are known by various titles such as learning support, education support, or special needs support service. As discussed in Chapter 2, these teachers work in various ways according to the size and philosophy of the service. Some withdraw children for individual help, others advise teachers and adopt a whole-school approach rather than teaching individual pupils. Their experience and specialisms vary across authorities.

Many LEAs also have peripatetic specialist teachers for children requiring specialist teaching help, such as preschool children, and those with hearing or visual impairment or language disorders. Sometimes these teachers work in separate units, or they may visit children and teachers in ordinary schools.

EDUCATION WELFARE OFFICERS, OR EDUCATION SOCIAL WORKERS

Education welfare officers used to be employed by the education welfare service as school attendance officers. Their main duty was to ensure regular school attendance. Their role has extended to more general education social work, although the EWO is still empowered to bring children and parents before the courts for non-attendance at school. In addition many have the duty of advising families about the extra provisions that the state makes available through the LEA, such as free school meals, free transport, clothing allowances, etc. Inc. easingly EWOs are qualified social workers, but some with relevant experience (NSPCC, police liaison, etc.) are employed.

EDUCATIONAL PSYCHOLOGISTS

Educational psychologists are employed by the LEA to work with schools, children and their families, to maximize efficient learning and promote the emotional wellbeing of children. As well as working informally advising, consulting with teachers, and doing direct casework with children, their advice on children's special educational needs is sought by the LEA as part of the formal assessment under the 1981 Education Act. They are also frequently involved in the in-service training of teachers and may undertake various projects for the LEA. An educational psychologist must have taken a degree in psychology, be qualified as a teacher, and have at least two years' teaching experience. He or she will also have taken a postgraduate training course in educational psychology lasting one or two years.

EDUCATIONAL ADVISORS AND INSPECTORS

Advisors and inspectors are employed by the LEA to monitor the quality of education in schools and provide generic or specialist advice about curriculum, legislation, staffing and other matters. Some authorities have an advisor for special needs, who works with special and mainstream schools advising about work related to children with learning difficulties.

The health service

The national health service was set up in 1948 following on the Beveridge Report, establishing the 'welfare state'. Ultimate responsibility for the service devolved to the minister of health. The service was divided into three autonomous sections:

(a) hospital and specialist health services, provided on a regional basis;
(b) personal and family practitioner services, set up and administered through local councils; these services included dental, ophthalmic and pharmaceutical services;
(c) a cluster of services, now designated community services, provided on a local basis, including school health, family planning and maternity care and the ambulance service; these services are often provided in health clinics.

The 1946 National Health Service Act attempted to cover all aspects of health care. The tripartite division has proved to be useful but it should be noted that the whole of the administrative structure of the NHS was reorganized in 1974 and further modifications made in 1982. The administration of policy is now organized at a regional and a district level. The functions at regional level include the determination of spending priorities, allocation of resources to district health authorities, provision of major building projects and the appointment of senior staff. There are 201 district health authorities in England and Wales which are responsible for assessing and organizing local health needs. However, as far as the general public experience the NHS, the tripartite division of services remains the important one.

The child with handicapping conditions may come into contact with all three complementary branches of the NHS. He will certainly be known to his GP and he may have needed some form of hospital treatment. Also a wide range of services is provided as community based services. Preschool assessment and treatment are available to children including speech therapy, physiotherapy, and medical supervision of health needs, and are usually based at a local clinic. The more general child health services, such as school medical checks, immunizations, and assessments under the 1981 Act, are undertaken by clinical medical officers who are usually attached to a clinic and are employed by the district health authority.

In the last decade a number of governmental reports have advocated that handicapped and mentally ill people should be reintegrated into their communities rather than remain as long-stay patients in hospitals. It is interesting to note that this policy echoes similar moves to integrate children with handicaps in ordinary schools. As a result of the Local Authority Social Services Act, 1970, the social services departments became involved with the health departments in establishing a community-based approach to mental illness and handicap and many handicapped people have been moved out of hospitals and accommodated in hostels and approved lodgings.

The Court Report (DHSS, 1976) advocated a shift in medicine from curing to caring and prevention. There is now more emphasis on community medicine and the effects on health of stress.

GENERAL PRACTITIONERS
General practitioners are responsible for the health of all the patients in their practice. They have had extensive training in all aspects of medicine at graduate and postgraduate level. The GP is supported by the hospital and community services and he can refer his patients for specialist help to these services where necessary. Where the family has been in the community for years, the GP is often in the unique position of having known the child soon after conception, and he is often the first person parents approach with any worries and fears about their child's development.

HEALTH VISITORS AND COMMUNITY NURSES
The health visitor and community nurse work for the community health section of the NHS. The health visitors' duty is to help and advise on all aspects of health in the home, especially at times when a member of the household is particularly vulnerable: in babyhood, old age or after an operation. As health visitors are involved in the welfare and proper development of babies, they are frequently involved in

the early detection of handicaps and support for parents with children with severe learning difficulties. Community nurses also frequently visit parents at home, and advise about medication and specific problems arising in children with severe learning difficulties such as epilepsy, incontinence, eating and feeding difficulties. All community nurses and health visitors are qualified nurses and some have had a further training to specialize in their area of work.

CONSULTANTS IN THE HOSPITAL SERVICE

If a child has complex or severe difficulties, he is likely to be referred by his GP to a consultant. Consultants are employed by the hospital service and specialize in one particular aspect of health: paediatricians specialize in child health, psychiatrists in mental disorders, orthopediatricians in disorders of the feet and legs, etc. A consultant has studied medicine at graduate and postgraduate level and has further specialized in his chosen field. His training is a long one of at least eight years.

CLINICAL MEDICAL OFFICERS

The district health services employ a number of doctors other than those involved in general practice or hospital work. The clinical medical officer is generally responsible for advising the LEA about the health of all the children in a particular area, and thereby ensures that all children who are at risk, or whose parents do not visit their GP, are regularly medically examined. Clinical medical officers have been trained in medicine at graduate and post-graduate level and some have had further training in various aspects of child health, including psychometric assessment. Their advice is sought as a statutory requirement by LEAs for formal assessments under the 1981 Act.

The NHS also employs a range of paramedical staff who specialize in one particular aspect of handicap.

SPEECH THERAPISTS

Speech therapists work with children who have difficulties with speech, language and communication. They are usually based in a community health clinic but can also provide a service in hospitals, schools and sometimes in the patient's home, depending on needs. Most patients are treated individually although there is a trend towards working with groups of children, and advising and training carers such as teachers and parents. Speech therapists often provide language programmes for teachers and parents to implement. They are increasingly involved in facilitating the communication of preschool children through play, or they may sometimes advise about specialist eating problems through their knowledge of the mouth, lips, palate and tongue. Speech therapists have trained for at least three years and it is becoming increasingly a graduate profession.

PHYSIOTHERAPISTS

Physiotherapists seek to rehabilitate the body using exercises, electrotherapy, massage and ultraviolet light to treat the injured, the sick and the handicapped. Patients are usually only referred via a medical practitioner. The vast majority work in the hospital service but sessions may be held in clinics, special schools and in the patient's home. As well as individual treatment they will advise about the management of children with sitting, standing and general mobility problems. Physiotherapists are trained for three years full time.

OCCUPATIONAL THERAPISTS

Occupational therapists treat children with physical or intellectual difficulties by giving them practical training which can help them to be self-supporting or provide them with useful skills. They are frequently involved with rehabilitation following an accident. Occupational therapists have three years' training with about one year spent in a practical placement.

CLINICAL PSYCHOLOGISTS

Clinical psychologists usually work in collaboration with psychiatrists and neurologists in hospitals and clinics or in the community. Children are usually referred to them by general practitioners or others within the health service. Their role often involves the assessment, treatment and management of children with psychiatric disturbances or severe learning and behavioural problems in the home setting. Clinical psychologists have at minimum, a degree in psychology followed by postgraduate training for one or two years at higher degree level.

The social services department

The history of social welfare in Britain is long and chequered. Modern legislation has its roots in the Poor Law Act of 1832, and came of age in the Beveridge plan and the National Assistance Acts of 1948. Social services departments were set up on a local basis following these Acts. They were concerned with people who, for various reasons, experience problems such as poverty, poor housing, sickness, injury, old age, infirmity and physical and mental handicaps; in other words, all those people who have need of help and support from the general community. The legislation relating to children is vast and complex and we can only give a brief description here.

Officially, a 'child' is aged up to 14 years; a 'young person' is aged between 14 and 17 years and a 'juvenile' is aged up to 17 years. Traditionally, the social care services for children were divided into three areas: those for children deprived of normal home life; those for young offenders; and those for ill-treated children. It is useful to review services and legislation under these three headings. However, before doing so, it is necessary to understand some basic child-care provisions which can be applied in all of the three areas given above.

THE PROCEDURES RELATING TO THE PROTECTION AND CONTROL OF CHILDREN

There are occasions when a court may make an order for securing the 'care and control' of a child or young person. The order may be temporary or last until the young person reaches the age of 18. A child in need of 'care and control' is defined as one who is:

(a) beyond the control of his parent or guardian;
(b) exposed to moral danger;
(c) of compulsory school age and is not receiving efficient or suitable education;

(d) guilty of an offence;
(e) whose proper development is being avoidably prevented or neglected.

Any local authority, police or NSPCC officer may bring a child whom they have reason to believe is in need of care and control, and his parents, before a juvenile court. If the court is satisfied that the child is in need of care and control it may:

(a) issue a care order under which the child is committed to the care of the local authority;
(b) order the parent or guardian to enter into a recognizance to exercise proper care and control;
(c) make a supervision order;
(d) issue a hospital order under the Mental Health Act, 1959, where a child is seriously mentally ill and parents are resisting help.

A care order usually results in a child being brought into a community home run by the local authority. A supervision order involves a supervisor, usually a social worker, befriending and advising the youngster.

CARE OF CHILDREN DEPRIVED OF NORMAL HOME LIFE

The Child Care Act, 1980, states that the local authority has a duty to provide for children under the age of 17 when:

(a) they have lost both parents or been otherwise abandoned;
(b) that the parents are prevented by reason of mental or bodily disease or infirmity or incapacity to bring up their children;

A high proportion of children come into care under this provision on a voluntary basis and they can be taken home again at will. Community homes are used but fostering arrangements are preferred. Social service departments are frequently faced with parents made temporarily homeless, marriages in crisis, or mothers who are too ill to look after their children, for example, and the legislation is designed to provide for children in such circumstances.

TREATMENT OF OFFENDERS

The Children and Young Persons Act, 1969, changed the responsibility for children who had committed an offence to the control of the social services department. Previously, a delinquent youngster was dealt with solely through the legal system. The Act was designed to bring about a major change in the function of the juvenile courts and the relationship between the police, social worker and the offending youth. The Act was devised to promote the social, emotional and moral development of the child and to prevent the delinquent from becoming the prison recidivist of tomorrow, by emphasizing the role of support rather than punishment.

The social services department was empowered to be responsible for children in trouble with the police, and as a result no police officer may bring a youngster before the juvenile courts without consulting the social services department. The Act also attempted to provide an extensive range of alternatives to custody; this includes ordering payment of compensation to the injured party, attendance at a centre for rehabilitation, or regular attendance for intermediate treatment, or issuing a care or supervision order. Detention centres and youth custody centres are reserved for the older, more persistent juvenile offender.

A child under 10 years is not criminally liable for any offence. Between the ages of 10 and 14 years a child is liable for criminal charges if it is felt that he is responsible for his actions; otherwise he is dealt with through civil proceedings (that is, care proceedings). In fact, the distinction is without consequence because they are both heard in a juvenile court and subsequent decisions are substantially the same. Juveniles over 14, but under 17, are fully responsible for their criminal acts but they are dealt with under the juvenile court.

OFFENCES AGAINST CHILDREN

The Children and Young Persons Act, 1933, is the main statute for England and Wales designed to protect children from harm. It is an offence punishable by fine or imprisonment for any person over the age of 16 who has the custody, care or charge of any child under the age of 16 to, 'assault, ill-treat, neglect, abandon him or expose him to harm'.

Other offences include:

(a)   causing or allowing children to be used for begging;
(b)   giving intoxicants to children under 5;
(c)   preventing children from receiving education.

Sexual offences are prosecuted under the Sexual Offences Act, 1956. Children who are thought to be at risk are protected by the care and control procedures already described. If imperative, a child can be removed on a place of safety order secured from a magistrate.

Apart from the provisions made for children in crisis situations described above the social services department is expected to have some commitment to all children with special needs, especially those who will require support in adult life. A specialist social worker is usually appointed within each area team to liaise with the parents of physically and mentally handicapped children under the provisions of the Chronically Sick and Disabled Persons Act, 1970.

SOCIAL WORKERS

Social workers basically help individuals or families who require professional help with their problems. An important change in the organization of social work departments took place in the early 1970s when the separate specialisms of child care, medical, psychiatric, blind and deaf social work were integrated into one social work profession. Social workers are now generically trained in general social work; that is, they are trained to deal with any problem and with clients of all ages. Most social workers are er ployed by the social services departments and are organized in area teams.

To qualify as a social worker a certificate of qualified social work is required. Several different types of courses lead to this qualification, depending on the candidate's academic qualifications. The course for a CQSW is usually of at least two years' duration. Some candidates who are graduates with a relevant degree can qualify after a period of supervised practical work.

Social workers attached to other agencies   Some social workers are attached to agencies other than social services departments, such as hospitals, community health clinics, child guidance clinics or to the LEA. There are also social workers (residential child care officers) attached to residential children's homes, and others (probation officers) attached to the courts. These specialist social workers may have taken additional training, but not necessarily so.

MULTIPROFESSIONAL ASSESSMENTS

Due largely to the fact that the various support services have different management systems, and possibly due to rivalries between professional groups, the various professional workers often work independently of one another. However, there has been a growing awareness of the overlap of skills, and the need to share expertise, plan and work collaboratively as a team. This is particularly the case when children are multihandicapped, and many professionals may be approached to offer support to the family or school.

In many areas of the country, community teams are being established, where the various professionals liaise closely and make joint decisions about the most appropriate form of help. Following an initial assessment the team can offer expertise as necessary. In Newcastle-upon-Tyne, for example, a 'mental handicap management partnership' has been set up between the health authority, the social services department of the local authority, parents and voluntary organizations, the main aim being to improve services by providing a co-ordinated response to families with handicapped children. Parents are also involved in the joint planning and management of services (Newcastle City Council and Newcastle Area Health Authority, 1981).

The Warnock Report noted a need for a multiprofessional assessment when determining children's special educational needs, but under the provisions of the 1981 Act this takes the form of the separate professionals giving independent advice to the LEA, which means in effect that they are encouraged to make their individual contributions without conferring or pooling ideas.

POST-SCHOOL PROVISION

In Britain, preschool provision has developed piecemeal. Education under 5 years is not, of course, compulsory and there is likewise no obligation on the LEA to provide it, although its value has long been recognized.

In the 1970s nursery education was given prominence by the findings of Project Headstart in the USA which suggested that culturally deprived children benefited from early intervention. Educational priority areas were set up in this country and nursery schooling was seen as an integral part of a general compensatory education programme.

Halsey (1981) reported four lasting beneficial effects of preschooling:

(a) the beneficiaries are less likely to be assigned later to special or remedial classes;
(b) early education appears to protect its recipients from later educational failure;
(c) achievements in mathematics at age 10 are significantly improved by preschooling;
(d) children from poor families who had preschool education scored higher IQs than matched controls for up to three years after the experience.

Halsey concluded that preschool education can be beneficial and economical in ameliorating scholastic failure.

The Warnock Committee called for an expansion of nursery provision and recommended the importance of the early identification and amelioration of handicaps. In the government White Paper preceding the 1981 Act the desirability of the expansion of nursery provision was recognized and it was anticipated that LEAs and social services departments would liaise to develop further resources. However, the paper noted that 'the present economic situation precludes any large scale expansion'.

The 1981 Act made no comment on the provision of preschool resources and simply assumed that the health authority would be responsible for bringing children with special needs to the attention of the LEA. However, the principle of early identification was recognized in so far as notification to the LEA can be made from the age of 2½ years.

Problems have arisen in the length of time taken to statement a preschool child and over the fact that, at this stage, development is very rapid and needs are constantly changing. Almost invariably the child's needs will have changed by the time the statement is issued. Of even greater concern is the lack of resources once needs have been identified. Those LEAs without good preschool resources are likely to delay statementing young children. Only 10 per cent of children under 5 are currently in receipt of preschool education in Britain. Some LEAs have responded to the responsibilities imposed by the statementing of preschoolers by using support teachers on a peripatetic basis in the children's homes, sometimes working on the Portage Project, discussed in the previous chapter. Again, the select committee report on the implementation of the 1981 Act highlighted the gulf between the widely acknowledged need and the paucity of resources.

However, some educationists have pointed out the dangers of early identification, in that children can be labelled at a very young age, and this can have a detrimental effect in some cases. Swann (1985) pointed out a marked increase in the numbers of young children referred to ESN(m) schools between 1978 and 1982, suggesting this might be due to the increase in home visiting schemes over this period. Galloway *et al.* (1982) referred to the 'myth of early intervention', casting doubt on the assumption that problems are necessarily prevented by professionals becoming involved at an early stage. This is particularly argued with behaviour difficulties.

POST-SCHOOL PROVISION

Further education and employment for children with special needs

The post-school provision for the training, care and employment of youngsters and young adults with special needs is generally meagre. The fact that no one government department is responsible for post-school provision may contribute to this situation. It is also a sad fact that people with handicaps and disabilities tend to be overlooked in an increasingly competitive job market, although they are a group who are particularly vulnerable to isolation, loneliness and social neglect, so that employment is especially important for them. A handicapped person can register as a disabled person, although registration is entirely voluntary. Registration was intended to make it easier for a handicapped person to find a job, since firms employing over 100 staff have a statutory duty to employ a proportion of registered disabled people. However, in a survey conducted in 1970 by the National Children's Bureau, it was found that 19.1 per cent of their sample of handicapped young people were 'unemployed and seeking work', as compared with 4.4 per cent in a matched control group (Tuckey, Parfitt and Tuckey, 1973). So the outlook for employment for children with special needs is not encouraging and this is a frequently voiced concern of parents.

It has regularly been noted that youngsters with special needs are expected to manage the adult world, including employment, at a time when they may be especially vulnerable. These youngsters are often immature socially, emotionally or intellectually: adolescent adjustment difficulties may well be occurring around the transition between school and employment. Special schools are therefore usually far more flexible about the leaving age of their pupils, and the LEA has a duty to provide education up to the age of 19, if it is in the youngsters' interests. Also, as Gulliford (1985) points out, it is no longer accepted that intellectual and educational abilities reach a ceiling in early adolescence; young people continue to develop and acquire skills.

The Warnock Report identified provision for young people over 16 with special needs as a priority. Under the 1981 Act, the child's needs are reassessed at 13+ with vocational and post-school needs in mind, and most LEAs will employ a specialist careers officer for vocational guidance and advice. Vocational employment is one of the main goals of the educational process, but during the last decade this goal has been difficult to achieve for both disabled and able-bodied youngsters. A positive consequence of this has been the improvement in further education initiatives.

FURTHER EDUCATION PROVISION

As the Warnock Report highlights, most special schools and units are responsive to the needs of their pupils, and run leavers programmes in the final years of schooling. In mainstream schools, an alternative curriculum to the academic one has been evolving with impetus from the growing disaffection amongst low achievers. In 1978 the DES established the Further Education Curriculum Review and Development Unit, which produced a report entitled, *A Basis for Choice*. This advocated a curriculum of vocational preparation emphasizing the importance of social skills for low achievers. Another publication from the unit, *Skills for Living*, describes the development of an alternative curriculum for children with learning difficulties.

Teachers in special schools and units have also often been instrumental in encouraging initiatives in the local community, and in many areas youngsters attend bridging courses, link courses or undertake work experience. Further education and technical colleges are also rising to the challenge of arranging such courses.

In 1973 the Manpower Services Commission was set up to improve industrial and commercial training. In 1978 the commission set up the Youth Opportunities Programme (YOPs) to provide work-preparation courses in special centres and colleges for 20 per cent of the time and in employment for 80 per cent. Many children with special needs were able to avail themselves of this opportunity but the scheme also met with criticism. In particular, staff were recruited from industry and often had very little training in the needs of special children.

In addition to locally based initiatives, there are a number of residential colleges offering an opportunity to extend independence and self-sufficiency, as well as offering vocational training away from home, for one or two years. These are often run by charitable institutions such as the RNIB or the National Autistic Society, and training is usually specialized and aimed at a particular disability. Some of these residential establishments offer long-term care in residential communities such as the Camphill projects and the Home Farm Trust. Placements post-19 years may be funded by the Departments of Health or Social Services, although these departments are increasingly providing their own long-term care facilities.

POST SCHOOL

Under the Disabled Persons Act, 1986, the LEA must be informed if children on statements are disabled, before they leave school. This is so that the information can be passed on to the appropriate agencies once the Department of Education no longer has a responsibility for meeting their needs.

Unfortunately, a proportion of young people with special needs do not find work easily and remain unemployed. The Social Services Department has a duty to support all handicapped people in adult life and they will be involved in the continuing search for employment. Adolescent school leavers with severe learning difficulties can usually find employment in adult training centres or day care centres. Sheltered employment is provided in workshops for disabled people run by Remploy, social services departments and voluntary organizations.

After leaving school further vocational training is the responsibility of two government agencies: the Manpower Services Commission and the Industrial Training Boards. The latter runs the Training Opportunities Scheme (TOPS), which is intended to help adults to retrain for a new occupation. The Manpower Services Commission has two departments concerned with the handicapped person: the Training Services Agency (TSA) and the Employment Service Agency (ESA). TSA provides financial help for the training of disabled people of any age. It runs four residential colleges and caters for 800 disabled people per year. ESA maintains twenty-six employment rehabilitation centres, providing training and rehabilitation for adults following injury, illness or prolonged unemployment. It also provides a vocational assessment service for all handicapped people.

In conclusion, it is important to acknowledge that we have dwelt on the less able handicapped person in this section, perhaps because this is where employment prospects are most difficult, but handicapped people vary in their abilities and determination. Some pursue an academic curriculum, go on to university and then on to professional employment. Sussex University, for example, provides special facilities for deaf and physically handicapped students.

9
Conclusions:
future trends

OVERVIEW

In this final chapter the 1981 Education Act is reviewed in the light of several years' implementation. Criticisms of the Act and some of its basic concepts are now emerging and these are aired. The book concludes with a consideration of the implications of the recent 1988 Education Act for the education of children with special needs.

INTRODUCTION

We are now in the first decade of the 1981 Act and throughout this book we have attempted to reflect the way in which our thinking has been changing in special education as a result of this new legislation. This book follows quickly in the aftermath of a major revolution in procedures and concepts in special education and undoubtedly reflects the inevitable confusions and adjustments that are part of radical change.

Teachers, other professionals and parents have had several years to assess the impact and workings of the 1981 Education Act, data is accumulating and critical reviews are beginning to appear. The euphoria and enthusiasm that greeted the new legislation, and particularly the Warnock Report, has subsided into a more critical and circumspect phase as the problems of the new practices have emerged, although there would be few

248

educationists who would deny that the 1981 Education Act marks a major advance in the education of children with special needs. In particular, the Act has set out a legislative framework requiring that all pupils with special needs should be educated in ordinary schools, subject to certain exclusion principles. Not only should they attend, but they should participate in the normal activities of the school to the greatest extent possible.

Problems with the Act have been raised at several levels and by different groups. Teachers and their representatives have stressed the problem of inadequate resources to implement the changes envisaged by the Act. Parents have highlighted problems of communication as well as resources. Educationists have been critical of the bureaucratic procedures and cast a closer critical eye at the underlying assumptions and philosophies of the Act. In this chapter we propose to review the present status of the 1981 Act. We have already described in Chapter 1 the main findings of the government select committee report and further comments will be included here as it indicates where future changes might occur in the implementation of the Act. We will commence with some criticisms of the basic underlying assumptions made in the 1981 Act before proceeding to review the more pragmatic and procedural difficulties.

Conceptual problems

Booth (1985) argued that there are contradictory elements in the 1981 Act and in the Warnock Report that require some probing. He took a sociological and political perspective and asked whether the 1981 Act actually does further the interests of handicapped and disadvantaged children: this being the yardstick for measuring its success in his view. Dessent (1987) took a similar perspective, reviewing special education in the wider social, political and economic context. Both writers pointed out that, against humanitarian claims for special education, has been the hidden agenda of disposing of misfits in the interests of efficiency. Both would question whether the 1981 Act does ensure positive discrimination in favour of the child with disabilities.

One of the major reservations of the 1987 select committee report, outlined earlier, was that although the Warnock Report had identified 20 per cent of children as having special educational needs, only those children with a statement receive additional help as a right under the provisions of the 1981 Act. Booth and others have extended this reservation by pointing out that all children are 'special' and all have needs which should be met by the educational process. Moreover, by focusing on one group as special and different, teachers in ordinary schools may well feel that that group should not be their responsibility.

Booth also questioned the relationship between needs and their satisfaction. He suggested that a naive assumption is made that the relationship is simple and unproblematic. The concept of need is in reality tied to what provisions are available, or at best to what provisions are affordable. Professionals can delude themselves that they are now doing a better job by identifying needs, when the outcome in terms of resources is no better than it ever was. The notion of needs as a basis for planning resources is no more helpful than previous categories of handicap. He went further, claiming that categorization on the basis of disability has merely been replaced by categorization on the basis of special educational needs. Booth's view could be prematurely pessimistic since we have yet to assess the full impact of the concept of need, and at least it relocates the problem with resources rather than within the child. But Booth would argue that as long as one group of children are seen as 'special', in whatever terms, then certain consequences inevitably follow; and against all the benefits that a distinction might bestow in terms of additional resources, one must weigh the negatives of being perceived as different. As we discussed in Chapter 7, 'special resources', even when they are expensive and well planned, do not guarantee better outcomes; in fact, the evidence is to the contrary. Children appear to do as well and sometimes better if they can avoid special provisions (Topping, 1983). The damage to self-image as well as to others' perceptions by being labelled as special clearly can have a profound effect. In a celebrated article, Dunn (1968) reviewed special education in the United States and concluded that the stigmatizing effects outweighed the benefits.

Booth also echoed the disquiet raised in the select committee's report, that the identification of 'learning difficulty' and 'special educational need' is entirely relative and depends on a school's ability to cope with the children in their care. The school that makes systematic provision and has a good remedial department, for instance, will not need to identify as many children as having special needs as the school that makes little provision. Thus, paradoxically, schools are penalized that make available facilities for children with learning difficulties from within their own capitation and resources since they will have fewer children who need statements, and fewer external resources will be allocated. It could be argued, with some justification, that schools which provide little for their less able pupils, are unjustly 'rewarded' with additional help.

Relativity has always existed, however, and a decision to refer a child for special education has rarely rested on objective and standardized data but has always depended on the facilities within the school, the headteacher's sympathies and the teacher's competence and tolerance. There is no clear consensus about the target population for whom formal assessment is to be made and there remain no guarantees that a statement will give a child a better deal.

Tomlinson (1982) pointed out that the Warnock Report and the subsequent legislation hoped to further special education on the basis of an individual's needs, rather than on an analysis of the overall structure of provisions. The result is piecemeal provision at best, and incoherent and disproportional provision at worse. Tomlinson showed that an individualistic philosophy will tend to obscure rather than clarify objectives for the further development of special education. She said, 'it is only by moving from individualistic to structural analysis that it becomes possible to ask broader questions about the aims, forms, ideologies and changes in special education'.

An overriding problem for special education has always been that, however we attempt to dress up the terminology and however radical and reforming are the concepts within special education, the fact remains that learning difficulties and handicapping conditions are disadvantageous. Dessent argued that any analysis of special educational need must begin 'within the context of what education as a whole is seen to be about'. Our society rewards its members differentially and has a hierarchical structure, and the educational process is one of the main means by which our young are equipped for a role in society. Assignment to special education carries with it a public acknowledgement that the child will not be able to compete advantageously with his peers in the stakes for status and economic and financial advantage. However much we attempt to compensate the child through educational means, the fact remains that he will not be valued in these real terms as highly as his able and successful peers. Real changes in special education can only be accomplished alongside fundamental changes in the way in which people are valued and rewarded in society at large. Success in school is almost exclusively measured in terms of academic achievement, and Dessent pointed out that other factors, such as the level of attendance, the suitability of the curriculum, etc., which could be indices of success in terms of the children's wellbeing, are ignored.

A further problem is the fact that concepts and terminology within special education are deeply rooted in the history of normative assessment and selection. Indeed, it could be said that since all societies are hierarchical, this inevitably leads to selectivity at some stage. In British society, even with the extension of comprehensive schooling, selectivity arises through rigid streaming, private education and especially at the stage of further education. Assessments under the 1981 Education Act are supposed to be on the basis of needs, but comparison remains at the root. What is viewed as normal and what constitutes a special need, as pointed out in earlier chapters, depends partly on how children of the same age are progressing. Needs are not only related to resources but also to normative notions. Again, as long as there is a 'special education' which must involve assessment and selectivity, comparison along some criteria will be inevitable and a model of normal child development must dominate educational practice.

An allied objection to the statementing process is that the focus of assessment remains on the child rather than on the curriculum or the school. Dessent commented that there is 'a mistaken notion that educational failure, of itself, requires psychological and medical investigation'. Any child-based assessment as opposed to a systems-based assessment carries with it the assumption that the problem lies within the child, and the covert but powerful corollary is frequently rejection and alternative placement.

It is hard to envisage an alternative to some form of selectivity, especially if we see education as merely about fitting our young for work and the 'correct niche' in society. Booth advocated an educational system concerned with the development and realization of a wide range of skills, irrespective of potential, where everyone is valued and rewarded equally. Such egalitarianism is unfashionable at the moment, but it is salutary to turn our gaze from the market place to the horizon in considering what education should be about.

In Booth's view, 'special education' need not exist if we had excellent resources and excellent teachers where all children could be taught at their own pace. He regards learning difficulties as a mismatch between the pupil and the curriculum and implicit in his writings is the belief that we would achieve more in terms of valuing individuals equally if no distinction were made between normal and special education.

The problem is that schools do not have sufficient flexibility because of the limitations of resources. When teachers are faced with classes of thirty or more children, teaching to 'the average child', irrespective of individual variance and needs, becomes almost inevitable. It could be argued that special education is the result of the limitations imposed by limited resources in our schools. Dessent took this view, suggesting that mainstream education is, arguably, 'a system of positive discrimination for the most able pupils in our schools'. He did not envisage the wholesale dismantling of special education but he argued for positive discrimination for children with special needs within a mainstream system. His view occupies a 'halfway house' between the traditional notions of special education and the reforming views of Booth and his Open University colleagues.

Bookbinder (1983) took a similar stance and made a plea for realism in the debate over special education: 'if schools are failing to provide for the majority who attend them, how can they be expected to meet the educational needs of the least able and the handicapped who will require additional resources and staff for which finance in unavailable?' In his view, the fact that educational needs are not met in one setting does not entitle us to transfer a child to another where some important social or emotional needs are frustrated. The priority is to find out what matters most to the families and decide only in the light of their views. Bookbinder foresaw 'that we will go on pretending that we can identify and provide for special needs and continue to emphasize the child's defects rather than defects in the education system'.

As far as the views of parents are concerned, recent research by Sandow, Stafford and Stafford (1987) suggested that it is a misapprehension to suppose that parents necessarily want integration for their children, as the Act assumes. Their study found that parents wish to be treated with respect, but not necessarily as equal partners in the multiprofessional assessment. Above all they want their children to be treated as individuals and for professionals to keep regular contact with them. There is a suggestion that at present parents and professionals do not share an understanding about their respective roles.

A number of commentators have noted that the principle of integration is proving difficult to implement and, until recently, the number of children in segregated provision was still rising. Swann has drawn attention to the rise in segregated provision for young children which is presumably a result of the new early identification procedures. The 1981 Act envisaged a retraction of segregated provisions but gave LEAs very little guidance as to how this was to be achieved. Dessent (1987) saw this call for integration as a 'hollow gesture' since there are numerous provisos and let-out clauses contained in the Act. The statement that children 'should wherever possible be educated in the normal school' appears to be contradicted by the guidelines in circulars which followed the Act that only 2 per cent of children will require statements: that is, those in segregated special schools and units and only those with 'severe and complex learning difficulties'. Dessent argued that these contradictory statements and compromises reflect a lack of genuine commitment to 'normalization'. Swann (1985) also regarded integration and normalization as an absolute necessity and the first step in any egalitarian prospect for special education. Dessent invoked Warnock's continuum of needs, suggesting that where no real distinction can be made between children with or without special needs no distinctly different provisions should exist. He objected to the term 'integration' on the grounds that the image invoked is one of an outsider, and he suggested that a more positive approach could be engendered if the term 'non-segregration' were adopted.

Procedural problems

Pragmatic problems have been aired in the press and in journals in relation to the 1981 Act. Many of these were mentioned earlier in the discussion of the select committee's report but the various professional groups have their own particular concerns.

The National Union of Teachers' response to the new legislation was very cautious and its main concern was that ordinary class teachers would be expected to take on further duties in dealing with children who would previously have attended segregated special schools, without additional assistance or extra resources. The union was also concerned about the career prospects of those teachers who worked in segregated special schools, and initially stated its opposition to the policy of integration. It would have to be said that the NUT's caution was justified in so far as the government select committee's major reservation about the implementation of the Act was that the venture was under-resourced.

Meade, O'Hagan and Swanson (1987) have reviewed the workings of the 1981 Act from the standpoint of the educational psychologist. They raised many of the conceptual issues discussed previously. In addition they drew attention to the oppositional role that psychologists may find themselves in, between teachers, parents and the LEA. The problem is that educational psychologists who are asked to identify children's needs are employed by the LEA. Parents and teachers may feel that educational psychologists are constrained to recommend what is convenient for the LEA to provide, and their viewpoints are not entirely objective. Meade, O'Hagan and Swanson conclude 'the 1981 Act exposes the [educational psychology] services to an uncontrollable expansion of casework, to the criticism of professional peers, and to the resentment and frustrations generated in schools, in the eyes of parents and of our colleagues in associated services'.

Another generally voiced problem with the Act is the complaint that the procedures take time to complete and are unwieldy. In many cases there is likely to be no disagreement or problem about the child's needs or how they will be met, but the whole procedure of statementing takes many months to complete. This means that sometimes the real issues concerning why the child was referred for assessment become distorted or obscured in the course of the long procedural battles.

The 1981 Act has brought about a growth in the numbers of educational psychologists employed by LEAs, but many feel that their role has become hidebound by the bureaucracy entailed by statementing, and as schools have gradually become aware that statementing may bring increased resources, referrals have risen. Dessent lamented the irony that, although resources are badly needed for children with special needs, the Act has largely produced a growth in personnel to deal with the increased bureaucracy. He feared that the 1981 Act might become abused: 'LEAs can intentionally utilise statements as a method of restricting access to limited resources . . . statements may become the only method whereby schools can register their special needs'. Potts (1983) had the same concern, and suggested that rather than spending resources on setting up multiprofessional assessments to identify needs, measures could be taken such as 'examining curricula, groupings, timetabling, teaching styles and the present use of existing people, buildings and equipment'.

Hargreaves (1984) feared that professionals involved with assessment may become too tied to individual-based casework. He described this role graphically as 'the fixers of aberrant pupils; sweepers-up on the margins of the educational system'. As we have discussed, the danger with this role is that a focus on the individual child detracts from the wider context. Scrutinizing the organization of schools and curriculum development, and contributing to in-service training, may well be more efficient and effective ways of helping individual children.

Finally, there is growing disquiet about the Act's provisions for preschool children. This concern is not only about the length of time it takes to produce a statement for a child whose age entails rapid changes in needs, but also about the undesirability of labelling at a very early stage in the child's life. The government select committee expressed particular concern on this issue, suggesting a radical overhaul of procedures for statementing preschool children.

THE 1988 EDUCATION ACT AND CHILDREN WITH SPECIAL NEEDS

At the time of writing, we are faced with the prospect of still more changes in the education of children, including those with special needs. The 1988 Education Act will bring about many changes in the basic structure of education, and a number of the proposals will have a direct bearing on the education of children with special needs. The Minister of Education has also proposed a swift implementation for these changes (by 1989, in some instances), and it is likely that they will have been implemented before this book goes to press. It is therefore important to review some of the proposals, especially those that may affect special education, and to anticipate some of the consequences and possible problems that may result.

There are four major changes in the Act which will have consequences for children with special needs:

1 The establishment of a national curriculum with a core curriculum of specified subjects for all primary and secondary schools.
2 Every child will be assessed on national criteria at the ages of 7, 11, 14 and 16.
3 Schools can opt out of LEA control on a majority of parents voting and choose to be funded centrally.
4 Restrictions will be lifted on the number of pupils schools are allowed to admit.

What might these changes mean for the child with special needs? A number of commentators have expressed some disquiet. Mittler (1988) writing in *The Times*, stated that the proposals in what was then the Bill seemed to overlook the interests of children with special educational needs and were inconsistent with the policies and aims of the 1981 Act. There are several related worries. By definition children on statements are likely to do badly on the new tests; and as they have already been thoroughly assessed, and their progress is regularly monitored, further testing would be irrelevant, and likely to damage children whose self-esteem is already low. Similarly the notion of a national curriculum with subjects that all children must follow runs counter to the developments in special education where the need for a modified curriculum for children with learning difficulties has evolved. As mentioned in Chapters 1 and 7, the DES intends issuing guidelines in a circular due out in 1990, which will enable children on statements to be exempt from certain subjects or parts of subjects in the national curriculum, or to have their programmes of study, the attainment targets or testing and assessment arrangements modified. However, this is potentially stigmatizing for children and runs counter to the concept of integration. There are also many practical problems for the professionals who must implement this proposal fairly.

Apart from these obvious concerns there are others which are potentially more serious. Mittler asked the pertinent questions: 'How will children with special needs fare when schools are judged by the extent to which their pupils reach acceptable levels of performance in the national curriculum? When schools have greater control over resources, what priority will be given to children who need additional staffing and materials?'

The present government is devoted to the operation of free market forces. By being able to opt out of LEA control, and having no bar to the numbers taken in, it is likely that schools will become far more competitive with one another. The fear is that they will show a greater reluctance to accept children with special needs and will refer more children for formal assessment, in the hope that alternative segregated provisions can be arranged. Similarly, if academic success is to be the sole criterion for judging a school, and it will almost certainly be the one most parents will use, there will be even less incentive to use resources to raise the standards of children whose attainments are below average. It was an avowed feature of the proposed reforms that schools should become more competitive on the basis of the academic attainments of their pupils, and it is precisely in this area that children with special needs fail. Schools may feel deterred from accepting or retaining such children and this is in direct opposition to the major concept of integration embodied in the 1981 Act. Many professionals who have worked hard to help schools to integrate children with special needs view the new changes with alarm and despondency, not just over the issue of integration but because of a seeming return to a system of values in education that views children and the educational process narrowly and selectively. In fact, in 1982 Tomlinson predicted a new tripartite educational system made up of independent, comprehensive and special schools, which would function 'to preserve the social, economic and cultural status quo'.

However, if resources were to be tied to assessment results so that additional teaching support and smaller classes could be given to improve standards in some schools, this could have positive implications for children with special needs.

As we have discussed throughout the book, the nature of special education is always changing, but we are living through particularly interesting and confusing times. We have recently undergone what Thomas Kuhn (1962) termed 'a paradigm shift', where our previous concepts and practices have been turned on their head. Whatever happens in the next decade with all the new changes in the 1988 Education Act, it will be difficult to lose sight of the principles embodied in the Warnock Report, because they have captured minds and imaginations. We may not always have the resources or the will, but we have, at least, a better sense of purpose and idea of what is right for the education of children with special needs.

Appendix

Voluntary agencies involved with children with special needs:

Association for All Speech Impaired Children (AFASIC).
347 Central Markets, London EC1. Tel. 01-236 6487
Founded to promote the early diagnosis and assessment of speech and
language disorders in children.

Association for Spina Bifida and Hydrocephalus
Tavistock House North, Tavistock Square, London WC1H 9HJ. Tel.
01-388 1382
The Association is concerned with the welfare of persons suffering
from spina bifida and/or hydrocephalus. It promotes research in the
field and provides advice for families.

Dr Barnardo's
Tanner's Lane, Barkingside, Ilford, Essex 1G6 1QG. Tel. 01-550 8822
This famous organization, founded in 1866, provides care and
treatment, both residential and non-residential, for children in need
and those who are orphaned or homeless. There are 100 homes in the
British Isles. There is also a fostering and adoption service.

Breakthrough Trust (Deaf-Hearing Group)
Frank Barnes School, Central Street, London EC1. Tel. 01-691 6229
The aim of this organization is to bring deaf and hearing people into
continuous contact with each other through the development of local
groups, courses and workshops.

British Association for Early Childhood Education
Montgomery Hall, Kennington Oval, London SE11 5SW. Tel. 01-582
8744
Its aim is to promote the establishment of nursery schools and classes
in all parts of the country. They offer advice to all those involved in
nursery education.

260

The British Council for the Rehabilitation of the Disabled (REHAB)
25 Mortimer Street, London W1N 8AB. Tel. 01-637 5400
The council is involved in all aspects of problems affecting the disabled. This includes research, educational courses and advice and information for the disabled, their families and professionals.

The British Deaf Association
38 Victoria Place, Carlisle, Cumbria CA1 1HU. Tel. 022-85 20188
An organization concerned with the problems and needs of all deaf people.

British Diabetic Association
3–6 Alfred Place, London WC1E 7EE. Tel. 01-323 1531
Founded to provide information and advice to diabetics and the parents of diabetic children.

British Epilepsy Association
New Wokingham Road, Wokingham, Berks RG11 3AY. Tel. 034-46 3122
Their object is to inform the public about the facts of epilepsy and its social effects. They offer skilled advice and will attempt to solve individual problems.

British Youth Council
57 Chalton Street, London NW1 1HU. Tel. 01-387 7559
The council is unique in Britain in that it links together the traditional and voluntary organizations with national student movements. The council organizes contacts for various youth groups.

Camphill Village Trust, Ltd (Registered Charity)
Delrow House, Aldenham, Watford, Herts WD2 8DJ. Tel. 01-779 6006
Based on Rudolph Steiner principles, the trust offers mentally handicapped adults residential care and education designed to lead the individuals towards independence. Children in Rudolph Steiner schools may proceed on to the trust.

Child Poverty Action Group
1 Macklin Street, London WC2. Tel. 01-232 9149
Its aim is to promote action for the relief of poverty among children and families with children. It publishes a periodical, *Poverty*, and conducts research into the nature and extent of poverty.

Children's Country Holidays Fund
1 York Street, London W1H 1PZ. Tel. 01-935 8373
This organization provides two weeks summer holiday for approximately 3,500 disadvantaged London children every year.The fund is entirely supported by voluntary contributions.

Compassionate Friends
50 Woodways, Watford, Herts
This is an international organization of bereaved parents who offer advice, support and comfort, where needed, for parents who lose a child.

Cystic Fibrosis Research Trust
5 Blyth Road, Bromley, Kent. Tel. 01-464 7211
Its main concern is to finance research to find a cure and to improve on current methods of treatment. Groups have been established throughout the UK for the purpose of helping and advising parents with the problems of caring for CF children.

Dyslexia Institute
133 Gresham Road, Staines TW18 2AJ. Tel. 81-59498
Founded in 1974 to provide informed advice for parents and teachers on the problems of dyslexia.

Handicapped Adventure Playground (HAPA)
Fulham Palace, Bishops Park, London SW6. Tel. 01-736 4443
Helps to make provision for adventurous play for children and young people with mental, physical or emotional handicaps.

Institute for the Study and Treatment of Delinquency
34 Surrey Street, Croydon, Surrey. Tel. 01-680 2068
The objects are to promote scientific research into the causes and prevention of crime as well as to provide educational facilities into the study of delinquency.

Invalid Children's Aid Association
126 Buckingham Palace Road, London SW1W 9SB. Tel. 01-730 9891
This organization provides free help and advice for the parents of handicapped children. It also runs five residential schools; two for severely asthmatic boys and three for children with speech and language disorders.

Lady Hoare Trust For Physically Disabled Children
7 North Street, Midhurst, Sussex GU9 9DJ. Tel. 0730-81 3696
The general aim is to attend to the welfare of physically disabled children. To this end, the trust runs a comprehensive welfare service employing twenty-five professional social workers who look after the families under the care of the trust.

MIND (National Association for Mental Health)
22 Harley Street, London W1N 2ED. Tel. 01-637 0471
Its object is to promote mental health and help the mentally disordered and to press for improvements in the statutory mental health services. The association promotes research and arranges conferences and short courses on a wide range of mental health issues.

Muscular Dystrophy Group of Great Britain
Nattrass House, 35 Macaulay Road, London SW4 OQP. Tel. 01-7720 8055
It was founded in 1959 to raise funds for research into the cause and cure of muscular dystrophy and allied diseases.

National Association for Maternal and Child Welfare
1 South Audley Street, London W1Y 6JS. Tel. 01-491 2772
The association is concerned with the furtherance of education in matters connected with maternal and child welfare. The Education Department provides an advisory service.

National Association for the Welfare of Children in Hospital
Exton House, 7 Exton Street, London SE1 8VE. Tel. 01-261 1728
It was founded in 1961 to promote the welfare of sick children in general and to make the special needs of children in hospital more widely known. Sixty branches in the UK give services locally, setting up play programmes, providing toys and equipment, etc.

National Children's Bureau
8 Wakely Street, Islington, London EC1 7QE. Tel. 01-278 9441
The bureau is a national, interdisciplinary organization concerned with children's needs in the family, school and society. Its comprehensive concern for children includes preschool work and intermediate treatment.

National Council for One Parent Families
255 Kentish Town, London NW5 2LX. Tel. 01-267 1361
The council is concerned to ensure that one-parent families are

recognized as real families, respected and integrated into society. It offers a wide range of help and advice.

National Deaf Children's Society
31 Gloucester Place, London W1H 4EA. Tel. 01-486 3251
The objects are to obtain for deaf children the maximum benefits in education and welfare and to give support to all parents of deaf children.

National Library for the Blind
35 Great Smith Street, Westminster, London SW1P 3BU. Tel. 01-222 1767
The aim is to provide a library for the blind and partially sighted.

National Listening Library (Talking Books for the Handicapped)
49 Great Cumberland Place, London W1H 7LH Tel. 01-402 8380
This organization provides a postal lending library service for the benefit of physically and perceptually handicapped adults and children. A medical certificate is necessary.

National Society for Autistic Children
1a Golders Green Road, London NW11 8EA. Tel. 01-458 4375
This society provides day and residential centres for the care and education of autistic children. It helps parents by arranging meetings and providing an advisory information service. The society runs five schools.

National Society for Epileptics
Chalfont Centre for Epilepsy, Chalfont St Peter, Bucks SA9 0RJ. Tel. 02407 3991
The society was founded in 1892 to provide residential care and assessment on a long and short term basis, and in general to promote the welfare of people with epilepsy. The centre can accommodate up to 500 men and women from the age of 16.

National Society for Mentally Handicapped Children
117 Golden Lane, London EC1. Tel. 01-253 9433
This is the only national organization exclusively concerned with the mentally handicapped and their families. It has about 35,000 members in over 400 local societies. It offers help and support for parents of mentally handicapped children throughout its network of local societies.

National Society for the Prevention of Cruelty to Children
1 Riding House Street, London W1P 8AA. Tel. 01-580 8812
The objects are to safeguard the welfare of children in their own families and to help the material needs of families faced with a sudden crisis.

Partially Sighted Society
40 Wordsworth Street, Hove, East Sussex BN3 5BH. Tel. 0273 736053
The society's aim is to promote research in education and employment for the benefit of partially sighted and visually handicapped persons.

Pre-school Playgroups Association
Alford House, Aveline Street, London SE11 5DH. Tel. 01-582 8871
The aim of the association is to provide information and assistance to those who wish to form playgroups for children under 5.

Royal National Institute for the Blind
224–8 Great Portland Street, London W1N 6AA. Tel. 01388 1266
The institute wishes to promote the better education, training, employment and welfare of the blind, and generally to watch over and protect the interests of the blind and to further the prevention of blindness. Among their activities are the production of braille books, the organization of Sunshine Homes, nursery schools for blind babies and young children and special schools for the blind.

Royal National Institute for the Deaf
105 Gower Street, London WC1E 6AH. Tel. 01-387 8033
The institute promotes and encourages the prevention and mitigation of deafness and the better treatment, education, training, employment and welfare of the deaf. The institute has six homes for the deaf.

Shelter (National Campaign for the Homeless)
157 Waterloo Road, London SE1. Tel. 01-633 9377
The aim is to raise money to fund projects in the housing field and to act as a pressure group on behalf of the homeless and inadequately housed. It works through 300 voluntary groups throughout the country.

Spastics Society
12 Park Crescent, London W1N 4EQ. Tel. 01-636 5020
This society is the world's leading organization for the care, treatment, training and welfare of spastics. It has established schools, education

centres, residential homes and workshops throughout England and Wales.

Spinal Injuries Association
5 Crowndale Road, London NW1. Tel. 01-388 6840
The association was formed by paraplegics and tetraplegics in order to provide information on all aspects of their disability. Two bulletins and a regular newsletter are published and a book, *So You're Paralysed*, which advises people on how to cope from the beginning.

Toy Libraries Association
Seabrook House, Wyllyotts Manor, Darkes Lane, Potters Bar, Herts EN6 2HL. Tel. 77 44571
The best (and sometimes specially adapted toys) are available to handicapped children. They constitute what is often the only really local meeting place for parents and children. They also provide an opportunity for a close informal partnership between parents and local professional people.

Bibliography

Acts of Parliament (London: HMSO):
  1933 The Children and Young Persons Act.
  1944 Education Act.
  1948 National Assistance Act.
  1959 Mental Health Act.
  1959 The Handicapped Pupil and Special School Regulations.
  1962 Amending Regulations to the Handicapped Pupil and Special
    School Regulations.
  1969 Children and Young Persons Act.
  1973 The National Health Service Act.
  1980 Health Services Act.
  1980 The Child Care Act.
  1981 Education Act.
  1988 The Education Reform Act

Advisory Centre for Education (1980), *Disruptive Units, Where*, No.
  158, pp. 6–7.
Ainscow, M., and Muncey, J. (1981), *Tutor's Guide: SNAP* (Coventry:
  LEA Publications).
Ainscow, M., and Tweddle, D. (1979), *Preventing Classroom Failure*
  (New York: Wiley).
Andrews, G., and Harris, M. (1964), *The Syndrome of Stuttering*
  (London: Spastics Society Medical and Educational Information
  Unit).
Ashcroft, J., Halliday, C., and Barragan, N. (1965), *Study 2: Effects of
  Experimental Teaching on the Visual Behaviour of Children Educated as if
  They Had No Vision* (Washington, DC: US Office of Education).
Atkinson, E., and Gains, C. (1985), *The New A–Z List of Reading
  Books* (London: Heinemann).
Baker, W., and Duncan, S. (1985), 'Child sexual abuse: a study of
  prevalence in Great Britain', *Child Abuse and Neglect*, vol. 9, pp.
  475–87.
Baldwin, J. (1972), 'Delinquent schools in Tower Hamlets', *British
  Journal of Criminology*, vol. 12, pp. 399–401.
Baller, W., Charles, D., and Miller. E. (1966), *Mid-Life Attainment of
  the Mentally Retarded – A Longitudinal Study* (Lincoln: University of
  Nebraska Press).
Bax, M. (1964), 'Terminology and classification of cerebral palsy',

Developmental Medicine and Child Neurology, vol. 6, pp. 295–7.

Becker, H. (1977), *Sociological Work – Method and Substance* (New Brunswick: Transaction Books).

Becker, W., Madison, C., Arnold, C., and Thomas, D. (1974), 'The contingent use of teacher attention and praise in reducing behaviour problems', in P. Williams (ed.), *Behaviour Problems in Schooi* (London: London University Press) pp. 201–26.

Bee, H. (1974), *Social Issues in Developmental Psychology* (New York: Harper & Row).

Belson, W. (1975), *Juvenile Theft – The Causal Factors* (London: Harper & Row).

Bereiter, C., and Engelmann, S., (1966), *Teaching Disadvantaged Children in the Pre-school* (Englewood Cliffs, NJ: Prentice-Hall).

Bernstein, B. (1971), *Class, Codes and Control* (London: Routledge & Kegan Paul).

Binet, A., and Simon, T. (1905), 'Méthode nouvelles pour le diagnostic de niveau intellectual des anormaux', *Année Psychologique*, vol. II: pp. 191–244.

Bird, C. (1984), 'The disaffected pupil: a suitable case for treatment', in C. Lloyd Smith (ed.), *Disrupted Schooling* op. cit., pp. 15–27.

Bishop, J., and Gregory S. ch. 4, pp. 29–48, in W. Gillham (ed.) (1986), *Handicapping Conditions in Children* (London: Croom Helm).

Blagg, N. (1987), 'School phobia; the best way to treat it', *Education*, 14, vol. 170, no. 7, p. 133.

Bluma, S., Sheirer, M., Frohman, A., and Hilliard, J. (1976), *Portage Guide to Early Education* (Portage, Wis.: Corporative Educational Service Agency, 12).

Bogler, A. (1986), 'Counselling in the treatment of disruptive pupils', in D. Tattum (ed.), *Management of Disruptive Pupil Behavior* (New York: Wiley).

Bookbinder, G. (1983), 'The 1981 Education Act; a discordant view', unpublished, quoted in T. Booth and P. Potts (1983).

Booth, T. (1983), 'Integrating special education', in Booth and Potts, op. cit., pp. 1–27.

Booth, T. (1985), 'Inservice training at the Open University', in J. Sayer and N. Jones (eds), *Teacher Training and Special Educational Needs* (London: Croom Helm).

Booth, T., and Potts, P. (eds) (1983), *Integrating Special Education* (London: Croom Helm).

Bowlby, J. (1952), *Child Care and the Growth of Love* (Harmondsworth: Penguin).

Bradley, L. (1981), 'The organisation of motor patterns for spelling; an effective remedial strategy for backward readers', *Developmental Medicine and Child Neurology*, vol. 73, pp. 83–91.

Brennan, W. (1979), *The Curriculum Needs of Slow Learners* (London: Evans).

Brennan, W. (1985), *Curriculum for Special Needs* (Milton Keynes: Open University Press).

Brophy, J., and Good, T. (1974), *Teacher Pupil Relationships – Causes and Consequences* (New York: Holt).

Brown, R., and Bellugi, U. (1964), *New Directions in the Study of Language*, ed. E. Lenneberg (Cambridge, Mass.: MIT Press).

Bryant, P., and Bradley, L. (1985), *Children's Reading Problems; Psychology and Education* (Oxford: Blackwell).

Burt, C. (1909), 'Experimental tests of general intelligence', *British Journal of Psychology*, vol. 3, pp. 94–177.

Burt, C. (1937), *The Backward Child* (London: University of London Press).

Bush, A. (1983), 'Can reading be improved by involving parents?' *Remedial Education*, vol. 18, no. 4, pp. 167–70.

Calnan, M., and Richardson, K. (1976), 'Speech problems in a national survey: assessments and prevalence', *Child Care Health and Development*, vol. 2, pp. 181–220.

Cameron, R. (1981), 'Curriculum development: clarifying and planning curriculum objectives', *Journal of Remedial Education*, vol. 16, no. 4, pp. 163–70.

Cameron, R., Owen, A., and Tee, G. (1986), 'Curriculum management: assessment and education', *Educational Psychology in Practice*, vol. 2, no 3, pp. 3–9.

Caplan, G. (1970), *The Theory and Practice of Mental Health Consultation* (Oxford: Blackwell).

Carroll, H. (1977), *Absenteeism in South Wales; Studies of Pupils, their Homes and their Secondary Schools* (Swansea: Faculty of Education, University of Wales).

Chazan, M. (1973), *Compensatory Education* (London: Butterworth).

Chazan, M., Laing, A., and Jackson, (1971), *Just Before School* (Oxford: Blackwell).

Chazan, M., Laing, A., Jones, J., Harper, G., and Bolton, J. (1983), *Helping Young Children with Behaviour Difficulties* (London: Croom Helm).

Clark, M. (1976), *Young Fluent Readers: what can they teach us?* (London: Heinemann).

Clarke, A. M., and Clarke, A.D.B. (1974), *Mental Deficiency, the Changing Outlook*, 3rd edn. (London: Methuen).

Clay, M. (1979), *The Early Detection of Reading Difficulties* (London: Heinemann).

Clegg, A., and Megson, B. (1968), *Children in Distress* (Harmondsworth: Penguin).

Clunies-Ross, L. (1984), 'Supporting the mainstream teacher', *Special Education*, vol. 11, no. 3, pp. 9–11.

Coffield, F. (1986), *Growing up at the Margins* (Milton Keynes: Open University Press).

Cohen, A. K. (1955), *Delinquent Boys* (Glencoe, NY: Free Press of Glencoe).

Cohen, S. (1971), *Images of Deviance* (Harmondsworth: Penguin).

Coleman, J. (1966), *Equality of Educational Opportunity* (Washington, DC: US Printing Office).

Collins, J. (1961), *The Effects of Remedial Education*, Monograph no. 4, (Birmingham: Birmingham University Institute of Education).

Coulby. D. (1984), 'The creation of the disruptive pupil', in Lloyd-Smith, op. cit., pp. 98–119.

Coulby, D., and Harper, T. (1985), *Preventing Classroom Disruption* (London: Croom Helm).

Craft, M., Bicknall, B., and Hollins, S. (1985) (eds), *A Multidisciplinary Approach to Mental Handicap* (London: Tindal).

Creak, M. (1961), 'Schizophrenic syndrome in childhood: progress report of a working party', *Cerebral Palsy Bulletin*, vol. 3, pp. 501–4.

Critchley, M. (1970), *The Dyslexic Child* (London: Heinemann).

Crystal, D. (1976), *Child Language, Learning and Linguistics* (London: Edward Arnold).

Crystal, D. (1985), *Introduction to Language Pathology* (London: Edward Arnold).

Crystal, D., Fletcher, P., and Garman, M. (1976), *The Grammatical Analysis of Language Disability: a Procedure for Assessment and Remediation* (London: Edward Arnold).

Cummins, J. (1984), *Bilingualism and Special Education: Issues in Assessment and Pedagogy* (Clevedon: Multilingual Matters).

Davie, R., Butler, N., and Goldstein, H. (1972), *From Birth to Seven – A Report of the National Child Development Study* (London: Longman).

Davies, L. (1980), 'The Social Construction of Low Achievement', in Raybould, Roberts and Wedell, op. cit., pp. 18–28.

Davies, S., and Stewart, A. (1987), *Nutritional Medicine* (London: Pan).

Dean, J., and Nichols, R. (1974), *Framework for Reading* (London: Evans).

DES (1954), *National Advisory Council on the Training and Supply of Teachers* (London: HMSO).

DES (1955), *Report of the Committee on Maladjusted Children* (Underwood Report) (London: HMSO).

DES (1967), *Units for Partially Hearing Children* No. 4. (London: HMSO).

DES (1968a), *The Education of Deaf Children* (London: HMSO).

DES (1968b), *Blind and Partially Sighted Children*, Education Survey 4 (London: HMSO).

DES (1972a), *Children with Specific Reading Difficulties* (Tizard Report) (London: HMSO).

DES (1972b), *The Education of the Visually Handicapped* (Vernon Report) (London: HMSO).

DES (1973), Circular 2/75, *The Discovery of Children Requiring Special Education and the Assessment of their Needs* (London: HMSO).

DES (1975), *A Language for Life* (Bullock Report) (London: HMSO).

DES (1978a), *Special Educational Needs. Report of the Committee of Enquiry into the Education of Handicapped Young People* (Warnock Report) (London: HMSO).

DES (1978b), *Behavioural Units: A Survey of Special Units for Pupils with Behavioural Problems* (London: HMSO).

DES (1978c), *Truancy and Behavioural Problems in Some Urban Schools* (London: HMSO).

DES (1978d), *Primary Education in England* (London: HMSO).

DES (1979), *Aspects of Secondary Education* (London: HMSO).

DES (1981), *West Indian Children in our Schools* (Rampton Report) (London: HMSO).

DES (1981), Circular 8/81, *The Discovery of Children Requiring Special Education* (London: HMSO).

DES (1982), *Mathematics Counts* (Cockcroft Report) (London: HMSO).

DES (1983), Circular 1/83, *Assessments and Statements of Special Educational Needs* (London: HMSO).

DES (1985), *Education for All; the Education of Children from Ethnic Minority Groups* (Swann Report) (London: HMSO).

Desforges, M. (1983), 'Drugs, adolescents and adults', in G. Lindsey (ed.), *Problems of Adolescence in the Secondary School* (London: Croom Helm), pp. 161–81.

Dessent, A. (1983), 'Who is responsible for children with special needs?' in Booth and Potts, op. cit., pp. 90–9.

Dessent, A., (1987), *Making the Ordinary School Special* (Brighton: Falmer).

DHSS (1976) Committee on Child Health Services, *Fit for the Future?* (Court Report).

DHSS (1980) *Inequaliities in Health* (Black Report) (London: HMSO).

Dorn, N., and Thompson, A. (1976), 'Decision-making skills: a possible goal for drug education', *Health Service Journal*, vol. 35, pp. 248–57.

Douglas, J., Ross, J., and Simpson, H. (1964), *The Home and the School* (London: MacGibbon & Kee).

Douglas, J., Ross, J., and Simpson, H. (1968), *All our Future* (London: MacGibbon & Kee).

Dowling, E., and Osborne, E. (eds) (1985), *The Family and the School: A Joint Systems Approach to Problems with Children* (London: Routledge & Kegan Paul).

Downing, J. (1969), 'I.T.A. and slow learners; a reappraisal', *Educational Research*, vol. 11, no. 3. pp. 229–31.

Duncan, D. (1978), *Teaching Mathematics to Slow Learners* (London: Ward Lock).

Dunham, J. (1977), 'The effects of disruptive behaviour on teachers', *Education Review*, vol. 29, pp. 181–7.

Dunham, J. (1986) *Stress in Teaching* (Beckenham: Croom Helm).

Dunn, L. (1968), 'Special education for the mildly retarded – is much of it justifiable?', *Exceptional Children*, vol. 35, pp. 5–22.

Egan, G. (1975), *The Skilled Helper* (New York: Brooks Cole).

Elliot, M. (1985), *Preventing Child Sexual Assault* (London: Bedford Square Press).

Elliott, D., Jackson, J. and Graves, J. (1981), 'Oxfordshire mental handicap register', *British Medical Journal* 282: 789.

Ellis, A. (1962), *Reason and Emotion in Psychotherapy* (Edinburgh: Lyle Stuart).

Farrell, P. (1985), *EDY: its Impact on Staff Training in Mental Handicap* (Manchester: Manchester University Press).

Farrington, D. (1978), 'Family backgrounds of aggressive youths', in L. Hersov and M. Berger (eds), *Aggression and Anti-social Behaviour in Childhood and Adolescence* (Oxford: Pergamon).

Farrington, D., and West, D. (1971), 'A comparison between early delinquents and young aggressives', *British Journal of Criminology*, vol. 11, pp. 341–58.

Faupel, A. (1986), 'Curriculum management (Part 2)', *Educational Psychology in Practice*, vol. 2, no. 2, pp. 4–15.

Fernald, G. (1943), *Remedial Techniques in the Basic School Subjects* (New York: McGraw Hill).

Ferri, E. (1984), *Stepchildren* (Slough: NFER/Nelson).

Feuerstein, R. (1980), *Instrumental Enrichment* (Baltimore, Md: University Park Press).

Finkelhov, D. (1979), *Sexually Disadvantaged Children* (New York, Free Press).

Finlayson, D., and Loughran, J. (1976) 'Pupils' perceptions of high and low delinquency schools' *Educational Research*, vol. 18, pp. 130–45.

Fish, J. (1985), *Special Education: The Way Ahead* (Milton Keynes: Open University Press.)

Fogelman, K. (1976), *Britain's Sixteen Year Olds* (London: National Children's Bureau).

Forfar, J., and Arneil, G. (1984), *The Textbook of Paediatrics*, 3rd edn. (Edinburgh: Churchill Livingstone).

Frazer, G., and Friedman, A. (1968), *The Causes of Blindness in Childhood* (Baltimore, Md: Johns Hopkins University Press).

Frostig, M. (1964), *The Frostig Programme for the Development of Visual Perception* (Chicago: Follett).

Furth, H. (1961), 'Influence of language on the development of concept formation in deaf children, *Journal of Abnormal and Social Psychology*, vol. 63, pp. 386–9.

Galloway, D. (1981), 'Institutional change or individual change?' in Gillham op. cit., pp. 168–83).

Galloway, D. (1985), *Schools, Pupils and Special Educational Needs* (London: Croom Helm).

Galloway, D., and Goodwin, C. (1979), *Educating Slow Learning and Maladjusted Children* (London: Longman).

Galloway, D., and Goodwin, C. (1987), *The Education of Disturbing Children* (London: Longman).

Galloway, D., Ball, T., Bloomfield, D., Seyd, R. (1982), *Schools and Disruptive Pupils* (London: Longman).

Galway, J. (1970), 'Classroom discipline', *Comprehensive Education*, vol. 4, pp. 24–6.

Gardner, J., Murphy, J., and Crawford, J. (1983), 'The skills analysis model; an effective curriculum for children with severe learning difficulties' (Kidderminster: British Institute of Mental Handicap Publications).

Garman, M., (1988), 'Using LARSP in assessment and remediation', in F. Jones (ed.), *Language Disability in Children* (London: MTP Press).

Garnett, J. (1988) 'Support teaching – taking a closer look', *British Journal of Special Education*, vol. 15, no. 1, pp. 15–18.

Gillham, W. (1974), *Teaching the Child to Read* (London: University of London Press).

Gillham, W. (1979), *The First Word, Language Programme* (London: Allen and Unwin/Beaconsfield Press).

Gillham, W. (1981), *Problem Behaviour in the Secondary School* (London: Croom Helm).

Gillham, W. (1983) *Two Words Together* (London: Allen & Unwin).

Gillham, W. (ed.) (1986), *Handicapping Conditions in Children* (London: Croom Helm).

Gipps, C., Gross, H., and Goldstein, H. (1987), *Warnock's Eighteen Percent* (Brighton: Falmer).

Glynn, E. (1980), 'Parent child interaction in remedial reading at home', in M. Clark and E. Glynn (eds), *Reading and Writing for the Child with Difficulties* (Birmingham: University of Birmingham Press Occasional Publications, no. 8).

Good, T., and Brophy, J. (1972), 'Behavioural expression of teacher attitudes' *Journal of Educational Psychology*, vol. 63, pp. 617–24.

Good, J., and Brophy, J. (1978), *Looking in Classrooms*, 2nd edn (New York: Harper & Row).

Greening, M., and Spenceley, J. (1984), 'Shared reading: a review of the Cleveland project', *Psychology*, vol. 11, no. 2, pp. 10–13.

Gregory, S. (1976), *The Deaf Child and his Family* (London: Allen & Unwin).

Gronlund, N. (1970), *Stating Behavioural Objectives for Classroom Instruction* (New York: Collier Macmillan).

Grunsell, R. (1981), *Finding Answers to Disruption* (London: Longman).

Gulliford, R. (1960), *The Education of Slow Learning Children* (London: Routledge & Kegan Paul).

Gulliford, R. (1985), *Teaching Children with Learning Difficulties* (Slough: NFER/Nelson).

Halsey, A. (1981) 'Education can compensate', in W. Swann (ed.), *The Practice of Special Education* (Oxford: Blackwell).

Halsey, A., Heath, A., and Ridge, J. (1980), *Origins and Destinations:*

Family, Class and Education in Modern Britain (Oxford: Oxford University Press).

Hamblin, D. (1974), *The Teacher and Counselling* (Oxford: Blackwell).

Hamblin, D. (1978), *The Teacher and Pastoral Care* (Oxford: Blackwell).

Hanko, G. (1985), *Special Needs in Ordinary Classrooms* (Oxford: Blackwell).

Harding, L. (1986), *Learning Disabilities in the Primary Classroom* (London: Croom Helm).

Hargreaves, D. (1967), *Social Relations in a Secondary School* (London: Routledge & Kegan Paul).

Hargreaves, D. (1972), *Interpersonal Relations and Education* (London: Routledge & Kegan Paul).

Hargreaves, D. (1975), *Deviance in Classrooms* (London: Routledge & Kegan Paul).

Hargreaves, D. (1984), *Improving Secondary Schools* (London: Routledge & Kegan Paul).

Haring, N., Lovitt, T., Eaton, M., and Hansen, C. (1978), *The Fourth R: Research in the Classroom* (London: Merrill).

Harré, R., and Rosser, F. (1975), 'The rules of disorder', *Times Educational Supplement*, 25 July 1975.

Haskell, S., and Paull, J. (1973), *Training in Basic Cognitive Skills* (Harlow: ESA).

Haskell, S., and Paull, J. (1973), *Training in Basic Motor Skills* (Harlow: ESA).

Hegarty, S. (1985), 'Integration and teaching: some lessons from practice', *Educational Research*, vol. 21, no. 1, pp. 9–18.

Hegarty, S. (1988), 'Supporting the ordinary school', *British Journal of Special Education*, vol. 15, no. 2 pp. 50–3.

Hegarty, S., and Pocklington, K. (1981), *Educating Pupils with Special Needs in the Ordinary School* (Slough: NFER/Nelson).

Herbert, M. (1978), *Conduct Disorders in Childhood and Adolescence* (New York: Wiley).

Hinshelwood, J. (1917), *Congenital Word Blindness* (London: H. K. Lewis).

Hoghughi, M. (1980), *Assessing Problem Children* (London: Burnett Books).

Holt, J. (1969), *How Children Fail* (Harmondsworth: Penguin).

Hough, M., and Mayhew, P. (1983), *The British Crime Survey: First Report* (London: HMSO).

Ingram, D. (1976), *Phonological Disability in Children* (London: Edward Arnold).

Inner London Education Authority (1985), *Educational Opportunity For All* (The Fish Report) (London: ILEA).

Jencks, C. (1972), *Inequality; a Reassessment of the Effect of Family and Schooling in America* (New York: Basic Books).

Jensen, A. (1973), *Educability and Group Differences* (London: Methuen).

Jones, N. (1985), 'Attitudes to disability; a training objective', in J. Sayer and N. Jones (eds), *Teacher Training and Special Educational Needs* (London: Croom Helm).

Kamin, L. (1977), *The Science and Politics of I.Q.* (Harmondsworth: Penguin).

Kanner, L. (1943), 'Autistic disturbances of affective contact'. *Nervous Child*, vol. 2, pp. 217–50.

Karnes, M. (1970) 'Educational intervention at home by mothers of disadvantaged children', *Child Development*, vol. 31, no. 4, pp. 925–35.

Kelmer-Pringle, M., Butler, N., and Davie, R. (1966), *11,000 Seven Year Olds* (London: Longman).

Kelmer-Pringle, M., Butler, N., and Davie, R. (1971), *Born Illegitimate* (Slough: NFER).

Kempe, C. (1978), *Child Abuse* (London: Open Books).

Kennedy, I. (1981), *The Unmasking of Medicine* (London: Allen & Unwin).

Kidscape, *The Kidscape Primary Kit*, 82 Brook Street, London W1.

Kiernan, C. (1978), *Starting Off* (London: Souvenir).

Kirk, S., McCarthy, J., and Kirk, W. (1968), *Illinois Test of Psycholinguistic Abilities* (Urbana, Ill.: University of Illinois Press).

Klaus, R., and Gray, S. (1968), *The Early Training Programme for Disadvantaged Children*, Monographs of the Society for Research in Child Development, vol. 33, no. 4, serial no. 120 (Chicago, Ill.: University of Chicago Press).

Kolvin, I. (1971), 'Psychosis in childhood: a comparative study' in M. Rutter (ed.) *Infantile Autism: Concepts, Characteristics and Treatment* (Edinburgh: Churchill, Livingstone), pp. 7–26.

Kolvin, I., Garside, R., Nichol, A., *et al.* (1982), *Help Starts Here* (London: Tavistock).

Kounin, J. (1970), *Disciplines and Group Management in Classrooms* (New York: Holt, Rinehart & Winston).

Kuhn, T. (1962), *The Nature of Scientific Revolutions* (Chicago: University of Chicago Press).

Kyrincou, C., and Sutcliffe, J. (1977), 'Teacher stress – a review', *Educational Review*, vol. 29, no. 4, pp. 299–304.

Labov, W. (1970), 'The logic of non-standard English', in F. Williams (ed.), *Language and Poverty* (Chicago: Markham).

Lacey, C. (1970), *The School as a Social System* (Manchester: Manchester University Press).

Laskier, M. (1985), 'The changing role of the remedial teacher', in C. Smith (ed.), *New Directions in Remedial Education* (Brighton: Falmer).

Laslett, R. (1977), *Educating Maladjusted Children* (London: Staples, Crosby, Lockwood).

Laslett, R. (1983), *Changing Perceptions of Maladjusted Children* Association for Maladjusted Children Monograph no. 2, (Portishead: Association for Maladjusted Children).

Laslett, R., and Smith, C. (1984), *Effective Classroom Management* (London: Croom Helm).

Lawrence, D., (1973), *Improved Reading Through Counselling* (London: Ward Lock Educational).

Lawrence, J., Steed, D., and Young, P. (1984), *Disruptive Pupils? Disruptive Schools?* (London: Croom Helm).

Leach, D., and Raybould, E. (1977), *Learning and Behaviour Difficulties in School* (London: Open Books).

Lindsey, C. (1985), 'Some aspects of consultation to primary schools' in E. Dowling and E. Osborne (eds), *The Family and The School* (London: Routledge & Kegan Paul).

Lister, J. and Cameron, R. (1986), 'Curriculum management', *Educational Psychology in Practice*, vol. 2, no. 1, pp. 6–14.

Lloyd-Smith, M. (ed.) (1984), *Disrupted Schooling* (Edinburgh: Murray).

Lomans, E. (1976), *The USMES Guide* (Boston, Mass.: Educational Development Centre).

Long, M. (1988), 'Goodbye, behaviour units, hello support services: home-school support for pupils with behaviour difficulties in mainstream schools', *Educational Psychology in Practice*, vol. 4, no. 1, pp. 17–23.

Lukes, J. (1981), 'Finance and policy making in special education', in Swann, op. cit., pp. 314–34.

Lunzer, E. (1960), 'Aggressive and withdrawn children in the normal school', *British Journal of Educational Psychology*, vol. 30, pp. 1–10.

McGuiness, J., and Craggs, D. (1986), 'Disruption as a school generated problem', in D. Tattum (ed.), *Management of Disruptive Pupil Behaviour in Schools* (New York: Wiley).

MacKay, D., Thompson, B., and Schaub, P. (1970), *Breakthrough to Literacy* (London: Longman).

McNamara, E. (1979), 'The use of self recording in behaviour modification in a secondary school', *Behavioural Psychotherapy*, vol. 7, no. 3, pp. 57–66.

Mager, R. (1973), *Goal Analysis* (New York: Feardon Press).

Male, J., and Thompson, C. (1985), *The Educational Implications of Disability; a Guide For Teachers*, (London: Royal Association for Disability and Rehabilitation).

Marland, M. (1977), 'The Study and treatment of delinquency', *Psychology Today*, vol. 3, no. 4.

Marland, M. (1975), *The Craft of the Classroom: a Survival Guide* (London: Heinemann).

Marsh, P. (1978), *The Rules of Disorder* (London: Routledge & Kegan Paul).

Marra, M. (1981), 'The incidence and nature of secondary handicaps among children in day ESN schools', *Remedial Education*, vol. 16, no. 2, pp. 89–94.

Masidlover, D. (1982), *The Derbyshire Language Programme* (Ripley: Education Department, Derbyshire County Council).

Matza, D. (1964), *Delinquency and Drift* (New York: Wiley).

Meade, L., O'Hagan, F., and Swanson, W. (1987), 'Educational psychology; new pressures, new solutions', *European Journal of Special Needs in Education*, vol. 2, no. 2, pp. 111–16.

Meighan, R. (1981), *A Sociology of Educating* (New York: Holt, Rinehart and Winston).

Merton, R. (1957), *Social Theory and Social Structure* (London: Free Press).

Midwinter, E. (1977), 'Teaching in the urban environment', in J. Raynor and E. Harris (eds), *Schooling in the City* (London: Ward Lock).

Mittler, P. (1970), 'Language development', in L. Carmichael (ed.), *A Manual of Child Development*, 3rd edn (New York: Wiley).

Mittler, P. (1974), 'Language and communication', in Clarke and Clarke, op. cit.

Morris, M. (1966), *Standards and Progress in Reading* (Slough: NFER).

Moses, D., Hegarty, S., and Jowett, (1987), 'Meeting special educational needs; support for the ordinary school', *Educational Research*, vol. 29, no. 2, pp. 108–15.

Naidoo, S., and Kelmer-Pringle, M. (1975), *Early Child Care in Britain* (London: Gordon).

Nash, R. (1973), *Classrooms Observed* (London: Routledge & Kegan Paul).

Nash, R. (1976), *Teacher Expectation and Pupil Learning* (London: Routledge & Kegan Paul).

National Union of Teachers (1976), *Discipline in Schools* (London: NUT).

National Union of Teachers (1988), *Guidelines on Negotations for Special Needs* (Leicester: NUT).

Nelson, J. (1973), *Structure and Strategy in Learning to Talk*, Monographs of the Society for Research in Child Development, serial no. 149, vol. 37, no. 3 (Chicago, Ill.: University of Chicago Press).

Newcastle City Council and Newcastle Area Health Authority (1981), *Mentally Handicapped People and their Families; a Blueprint for a Local Service* (Newcastle: Area Health Authority).

Newson, J., and Newson, E. (1963), *Patterns of Infant Care in an Urban Community* (London: Allen & Unwin).

Newson, J., and Newson, E. (1977), *Perspectives on School at Seven Years Old* (London: Allen & Unwin).

Nirje, B. (1976), 'The Normalization Principle', in *Changing Patterns in Residential Services for the Mentally Retarded* (ed. R. Kugel and A. Shearer). Washington, DC: President's Commission on Mental Retardation, pp. 231–40.

Norris, N., Spaulding, P., and Brodie, F. (1957), *Blindness in Children* (Chicago: University of Chicago Press).

O'Brien, J., and Tyre, A. (1981), *The Principle of Normalization: foundation for effective services*, IMU/CM Hera.

O'Leary, S., and O'Leary, K. (1976), 'Behaviour modification in the school', in H. Leitenberg (ed.), *Handbook of Behaviour Modification* (Englewood Cliffs, NJ: Prentice-Hall).

Ornitz, E., and Ritvo, E. (1976), 'The syndrome of autism', *American Journal of Psychiatry*, vol. 133, pp. 609–21.

Ouston, J. (1984), 'Delinquency, family background and educational attainment', *British Journal of Criminology*, vol. 24, no. 1, pp. 2–26.

Patterson, G., Littman, R., and Bricker, W. (1967), *Assertive Behaviour in Children*, Monographs of the Society for Research in Child Development, serial no. 113, vol. 32, no. 5 (Chicago, Ill.: University of Chicago Press).

Pearson, L., and Lindsay, G. (1986), *Special Needs in the Primary School: Identification and Intervention* (Slough: NFER/Nelson).

Peters, M. (1970), *Success in Spelling* (Cambridge: Cambridge Institute of Education).

Peters, M. (1975), *Diagnostic Spelling* (London: Macmillan).

Philips, C., and White, R. (1974), 'The prediction of educational progress among cerebral palsied children', *Developmental Medical Child Neurology*, vol. 6, pp. 167–74.

Pidgeon, D. (1970), *Expectation and Pupil Performance* (Slough: NFER).

Pilling, D., and Kellmer-Pringle, M. (1978), *Controversial Issues in Child Development* (London: Elek).

Poteet, J. (1973), *Behaviour Modification; a Practical Guide* (London: Hodder & Stoughton).

Potts. P. (1983), 'Summary and prospects', in Booth and Potts, op. cit., pp. 195–214.

Power, D., and Quigley, S. (1973), 'Deaf children's acquisition of the passive voice', *Journal of Speech and Hearing Research*, vol. 16, pp. 5–11.

Power, M., Alderson, M., Phillipson, C., Schoenberg, E., and Morris, J. (1967), 'Delinquent schools?', *New Society*, 19 October.

Power, M., Benn, R., and Morris, J. (1972), 'Neighbourhood, school and juveniles before the courts', *British Journal of Criminology*, vol. 12, pp. 111–32.

Pringle, K., Butler, N., and Davie, R. (1966), *11,000 Seven Year Olds: Studies in Child Development* (London: Longman).

Pugh, G., (ed.) (1981), *Parents as Partners* (London: National Children's Bureau).

Pumphrey, P., (1985), *Reading: Tests and Assessment Techniques* (London: Hodder & Stoughton).

Quicke, J. (1985), 'Charting a course for personal and social education', *Pastoral Care in Education*, vol. 3, no. 2.

Raybould, E., Roberts, B., and Wedell, K. (1980), *Helping Low Achievers in the Secondary School*, Educational Review Occasional Publications, no. 7 (Birmingham: University of Birmingham).

Raymond, J. (1984), *Teaching the Child with Special Needs* (London: Ward Lock).

Reason, R., and Boote, R. (1986), *Learning Difficulties in Reading and Writing: a Teachers' Manual* (Slough: NFER/Nelson).

Reid, K. (1985), *Truancy and School Absenteeism* (London: Hodder & Stoughton).

Reynolds. D. (1976), 'When pupils and teachers refuse a truce'. in G. Mungham and G. Pearson (eds), *Working Class Youth Culture* (London: Routledge & Kegan Paul), pp. 124–37.

Reynolds, D., and Murgatroyd, D. (1977), 'The sociology of schooling and the absent pupil: the school as a factor in the generation of truancy', in H. Carroll (ed.), *Absenteeism in South Wales* (Swansea: Faculty of Education, University of Swansea).

Reynolds, D., Sullivan, M., and Murgatroyd, S. (1987), *The Comprehensive Experiment* (Brighton: Falmer).

Rimland, B., and Larson, G. (1983), 'Hair mineral analysis and behaviour: an analysis of fifty-one studies', *Journal of Learning Disabilities*, vol. 16, no. 5.

Robertson, J. (1981), *Effective Classroom Control* (London: Hodder & Stoughton).

Rogers, C. (1951), *Child-Centered Therapy* (New York: Houghton Mifflin).

Russell, D. (1983), 'The incidence and prevalence of intrafamilial and extrafamilial sexual abuse of female children', *Child Abuse and Neglect*, vol. 7, pp. 147–54.

Rutter, M. (1967), 'A children's behaviour questionnaire for completion by teachers: preliminary findings', *Journal of Child Psychology and Psychiatry*, vol. 8, pp. 1–11.

Rutter, M. (1971), 'The description and classification of infantile autism', in D. Churchill (ed.), *Infantile Autism* (Springfield, Ill.: Charles Thomas).

Rutter, M. (1972), *Maternal Deprivation Reassessed* (Harmondsworth: Penguin).

Rutter, M. (1973), 'Why are London children so disturbed?', *Proceedings of the Royal Society of Medicine*, vol. 66, pp. 1221–5.

Rutter, M. (1977), 'Brain damage syndromes in childhood; symptoms and findings', *Journal of Child Psychology and Psychiatry*, vol. 18, pp. 1–21.

Rutter, M. (1978), 'Family, area and school influences', in L. Hersov and D. Shaffer (eds), *Aggression and Anti-social Behaviour in Childhood and Adolescence* (Oxford: Pergamon), pp. 95–114.

Rutter, M. (1980), *Changing Youth in a Changing World* (London: Nuffield Hospital Trust).

Rutter, M., and Graham, P. (1966), 'Psychiatric disorders in 10–11-year-old children', *Proceedings of the Royal Society of Medicine*, vol. 59, pp. 382–7.

Rutter, M., Tizard, J., and Whitmore, K. (1970), *Education, Health and Behaviour* (London: Longman).

Rutter, M., Cox, A., Tupling, C., Berger, M., and Yule, W. (1975),

'Attainment and adjustment in two geographical areas', *British Journal of Psychiatry*, vol. 126, pp. 493–509.

Rutter, M., and Madge, N. (1976), *Cycles of Disadvantage* (London: Heinemann).

Rutter, M., and Quinton, D. (1977), 'Psychiatric disorder – ecological factors and concepts of causality', in H. McGurk (ed.), *Ecological Factors in Human Development* (Amsterdam: Holland).

Rutter, M., and Schopler, E. (eds), (1978), *Autism* (New York: Plenum).

Rutter, M., Maughan, B., Mortimer, P., and Ousten, J. (1979), *Fifteen Thousand Hours: Secondary Schools and their Effects on Children* (London: Open Books).

Sampson, O. (1969), 'A real need for researching', *Special Education*, vol. 58, no. 1, pp. 6–9.

Sandow, S., Stafford, D., and Stafford, D. (1987), *An Agreed Understanding*, (Slough: NFER/Nelson).

Schauss, A. (1980). *Diet, Crime and Behaviour* (Hemel Hempstead: Prentice Hall).

Scottish Education Department (1968), *Ascertainment of Children with Visual Handicaps* (London: HMSO).

Scottish Education Department (1978), *The Education of Children with Learning Difficulties in Scotland* (London: HMSO).

Selfe, L. (1983), *Normal and Anomalous Representational Drawing in Children* (London: Academic Press).

Selfe, P. (1987), *Sociology* (London: Pan).

Sennett, R., and Cobb, J. (1977), *The Hidden Injuries of Social Class* (Cambridge: Cambridge University Press).

Sewell, G. (1982), *Reshaping Remedial Education* (London: Croom Helm).

Shaw, C., and McKay, H. (1942), *Juvenile Delinquency and Urban Areas* (Chicago: University of Chicago Press).

Shearer, E. (1977), 'A survey of ESN(M) children in Cheshire', *Special Education*, vol. 4, no. 2, pp. 20–2.

Sheridan, M. (1945), 'The child's acquisition of speech' *British Medical Journal*, vol. 1, p. 707.

Skemp, R. (1982), *The Psychology of Learning Mathematics* (London: Ward Lock).

Smith, C. (ed.) (1985), *New Directions in Remedial Education* (Brighton: Falmer).

Solity, J., and Bull, S. (1987), *Special Needs: Bridging the Curriculum Gap* (Milton Keynes: Open University Press).

Solity, J., and Raybould, E. (1988), *A Teachers' Guide to Special Needs* (Milton Keynes: Open University Press).

Spreen, O. (1965), 'Language functions in mental retardation: a review', *American Journal of Mental Deficiency*, vol. 69, pp. 482–94.

Start, K., and Wells, B. (1972), *The Trend in Reading Standards* (Slough: NFER).

Steed, D. (1985), 'Disruptive pupils, disruptive schools; which is the chicken and which the egg?', *Educational Research*, vol. 27, no. 1., pp. 3–8.

Stevenson, G., (1981), 'Individuals and the social system', in I. Howarth and W. Gillham (eds), *The Structure of Psychology* (London: Allen & Unwin).

Stott, D. (1978), *Helping Children with Learning Difficulties; a Diagnostic Teaching Approach* (London: Ward Lock).

Stott, D. (1982), *Helping the Maladjusted Child* (Milton Keynes: Open University Press).

Stott, D., Marston, N. and O'Neill, S. (1975), *A Taxonomy of Behavioural Disturbance* (London: University of London Press).

Strauss, A., and Lehtinen, L. (1947), *Psychopathology and Education of the Brain Injured Child* (New York: Grune & Stratton).

Sumner, R. (1974), *Looking at School Achievement* (Slough: NFER/Nelson).

Sutherland, E. (1961), *White Collar Crime* (New York: Holt, Rinehart & Winston).

Swann, W. (ed.) (1981), *The Practice of Special Education* (Oxford: Blackwell).

Swann, W. (1983), 'Curriculum principles for integration', in Booth and Potts, op. cit., pp. 100–24.

Tanner, J. (1961), *Education and Physical Growth* (London: University of London Press).

Tansley, A., and Gulliford, R. (1980), *The Education of Slow Learning Children* (London: Routledge & Kegan Paul).

Tattum, D. (1982), *Disruptive Pupils in Schools and Units* (Chichester: Wiley).

Templin, M. (1957), *Certain Language Skills in Children* (Minneapolis, Minn.: University of Minnesota Press).

Tizard, B. (1975), *Early Childhood Education: a Review and Discussion of Research in Britain* (Slough: NFER).

Tizard, J., Schofield, W., and Hewison J. (1982), 'Collaboration between teachers and parents in assisting children's reading', *British Journal of Educational Psychology*, vol. 52, pp. 1–15.

Tomlinson, S. (1982), *A Sociology of Special Education* (London: Routledge & Kegan Paul).

Topping, K. (1983), *Educational Systems for Disruptive Adolescents* (London: Croom Helm).

Topping, K. (1986), *Parents as Educators* (London: Croom Helm).

Topping, K., and McKnight, G. (1984), 'Paired reading and parent power', *Special Education*, vol. 11, no. 3, pp. 12–15.

Tough, J. (1975), *Listening to Children Talking* (London: Ward Lock).

Tough, J. (1978), *Looking into Classrooms* (London: Ward Lock).

Tuckey, L., Parfitt, J., and Tuckey R. (1973), *Handicapped School Leavers – their Further Education and Training* (Slough: NFER).

Tutt, N. (ed.) (1976), *Violence* (London: HMSO).

Tweddle, D. (1982), *DATA-PAC* (Birmingham: School of Education, University of Birmingham).

Tweddle, D. (1987), *Preventive Approaches to Disruption* (London: Macmillan).

Tyerman, M. (1968), *Truancy* (London: University of London Press).

Ulrich, R., Stachnik, T., and Madry, J. (1970), *Control of Human Behaviour* (Dallas, Brighton: Scott Foreman).

Van Riper, C. (1973), *The Treatment of Stuttering* (Englewood Cliffs, NJ: Prentice-Hall).

Weber, K. (1982), *The Teacher is the Key; A Practical Guide for Teaching the Adolescent with Learning Difficulties* (Milton Keynes: Open University Press).

Wedge, P., and Prosser, H. (1973), *Born to Fail* (London: Hutchinson).

Weikart, D. (1972), 'Relationship of curriculum teaching and learning in preschool education', in J. Stanley (ed.), *Preschool Programmes for the Disadvantaged* (Baltimore, Md: Johns Hopkins University Press).

Wells, G. (1979), 'Variations in child language', in P. Fletcher and M. Garmann (eds), *Language Acquisition* (Cambridge: Cambridge University Press).

West, D., and Farrington, D. (1973), *Who Becomes Delinquent?* (London: Heinemann).

Westmacott, E., and Cameron, R. (1981), *Behaviour Can Change* (London: Macmillan).

Wheldall, K. and Merrett, F. (1985), *The Behavioural Approach to Teaching Package* (Birmingham: Positive Products).

Widlake, P., and MacLeod, F. (1984), *Raising Standards – Parental Involvement Programmes* (Coventry: Community Education Development Centre).

Williams, P., and Gruber, E. (1967), *Response to Special Schooling* (London: Longman).

Wilmott, P. (1966), *Adolescent Boys of East London* (Harmondsworth: Penguin).

Wilson, M. (1981), *The Curriculum in Special Schools* (London: Schools Council/Methuen).

Wilson, M., and Franz, M. (1980), *The Education of Disturbed Pupils*, Schools Council Working Paper No. 5 (London: Methuen).

Wing, L. (1976), *Early Childhood Autism: Clinical, Educational and Social Aspects*, 2nd edn (Oxford: Pergamon).

Wolfendale, S. (1983), *Parental Participation in Children's Development and Education* (London: Gordon & Breach).

Wolfensberger, W. (1975), *The Origin and Nature of our Institutional Models* (Syracuse, NY: Human Policy Press).

Wolfensberger, W. (1988a), 'Common assets of mentally retarded people that are commonly not acknowledged', *Mental Retardation*, vol. 26, no. 2, pp. 63–70.

Wolfensberger, W. (1988b), 'Reply to "All people have personal assets"', *Mental Retardation*, vol. 26, no. 2, pp. 75–6.

Wood, H., and Wood, D. (1983), 'Questioning the pre-school child', *Education Review*, vol. 35, no. 2, pp. 149–62.

Wood, S., and Shears, B. (1986), *Teaching Children with Severe Learning Difficulties* (London: Croom Helm).

Wooton, A. (1974), 'Talk in the homes of young children', *Sociology* vol. 8, no. 2, pp. 227–95.

Wright, D. (1971), *The Psychology of Moral Behaviour* (Harmondsworth: Penguin).

Yablonsky, L. (1967), *The Violent Gang* (Harmondsworth: Penguin).

Index

absenteeism (*see school attendance problems*)
accidents 103–4, 109
adjustment difficulties
  concepts and definitions 123–8, 132–5, 152–3
  frequency 128–9, 224–5
  influential factors 135–52
  inservice training 223–4
  provision 129–32, 224–6
  therapeutic approaches 215–23
advice 13
advisors and inspectors 233
amniocentesis 87
Apert's syndrome 88
arthimetic problems (*see mathematics*)
assessment
  of attainments (*see reading*)
  attainment targets (*see national curriculum*)
  criterion-referenced 25, 195, 198
  curriculum-related 24–5, 54, 188
  identification 5–6, 24–6, 243–4
  formal procedures 9–13, 52, 184, 252, 258
  models 5–7
  multiprofessional 13, 26, 63, 242
  normative 25, 34, 252
  prescriptive 25
  teaching through 195–6
  (*see also intelligence, language problems, reading* and *Warnock*)
anoxia 90–1
asphyxia 90–1
asthma 99
ataxia 92
athetosis 92
autism 119–22

behavioural
  approaches and methods 192–201, 218–21

modification 194, 218–19
objectives 188–9, 193
problems (*see adjustment difficulties*)
birth injury 85, 90–1
Black Report 68
blind children (*see visual impairment*)
Bliss symbolics 118, 211
braille 111, 214
brain damage (*see birth injury*)
British Ability Scales 35
Bullock Report 37, 72, 209
bullying 169

categorization 2–3, 4, 23–4, 31–2, 36, 45, 51, 85, 250
cerebral palsy 85, 91–4
child care procedures 238–9
child-rearing practices 69, 138, 158
child sexual abuse 141, 176–80, 241
chromosomal anomalies 60, 76, 86–8
Circulars
  8/81 11
  1/83 11
  1/83 draft revision 16, 183–4, 258
clubfoot 104
clinical medical officers 26, 127, 237
clinical psychologists 237
cognitive deficits 62, 77–9
cognitive styles 80
community health service 234, 235–6, 242
communication problems (*see language difficulties* and *speech difficulties*)
compensatory education 61, 209
conductive
  education 205–6
  hearing loss 106
congenital handicaps (*see genetic disorders*)
counselling 216–18
cretinism 87

criminal offences 154–7, 240–1
criterion-referenced tests (*see assessment*)
cued speech 213
cultural deprivation (*see social disadvantage*)
curriculum
-based assessment (*see assessment*)
behavioural approaches 192–5
'hidden' 74, 146
individualizing 190–1
models 187–9
special needs 182–3, 191–2, 204, 209, 237, 252
terms 147, 148, 185–6, 191
types 186–7
(*see also national curriculum and school*)
cystic fibrosis 98–9

DATAPAC 197, 201, 203
deafness (*see hearing impairment*)
delinquency 145, 154–65
Derbyshire Language Scheme 208
deviance (*see delinquency*)
diabetes 100
diet 80–1, 88, 94, 135
direct instruction 197–8
Disabled Persons Act (1986) 247
disaffected pupils (*see disruptive pupils*)
disapplications 16, 184
dislocation of the hip 104
Distar 197
disturbed behaviour (*see adjustment difficulties*)
disruptive pupils 129–32, 134, 147–52
Down's syndrome 85, 86
drug abuse (*see substance abuse*)
dysarthria 117–18
dyslexia 48–50
dysphasia 116–17, 209

Education Act
(1944) 2, 31–2, 36, 231
(1970) 2, 32
(1976) 5, 231
(1981) 7–11, 52–3, 83–4, 227–8, 231, 242, 243, 248–57
(1988) 16, 184, 231, 257–9
education welfare officers 233
educational psychologists 6, 26, 128, 233, 255, 256
EDY project 200

emotional problems (*see adjustment difficulties*)
encephalitis 90
endocrine disorders 87
epilepsy 86, 100–3, 121
ethnic minority children 14, 53, 66, 71–2, 73, 76, 82, 86

family
adversity factors 138
child rearing practices 69
home and neighbourhood 63, 137, 157
relationships 158
size and birth order 69–70
therapy 22
(*see also parents, poverty, social class and social disadvantage*)
Fish Report 21, 74, 76

general practitioners 234, 235
genetic counselling 87
genetic disorders 60, 87–8
gestational disorders 90
glue ear 106
glue sniffing (*see solvent abuse*)
grand mal 101–2

haemophilia 99
Health Service 230, 234–8
health visitors 235–6
hearing impairment 90, 105–7, 212–14
hemiplegia 92
hydrocephalus 90, 97
hyperactivity 27, 135

identification (*see assessment and Warnock*)
income and poverty 66–8
individualized
learning 190–1
educational programmes (IEPs) 25
(*see also curriculum*)
infant mortality 68
integration 5, 8–9, 11, 14, 18–21, 44, 53, 94, 133, 227–8, 254–5, 259
intelligence
concepts and definitions 32–5, 81–2
intellectual development 85–91
categories of intellectual handicap 32, 36, 45
measurement 32–6, 76

mental age 33–4
(*see also learning difficulties*)
intermediate treatment 163
irradiation 88–9

labelling 24, 28, 30, 250
language difficulties
  alternative communication systems
    211, 212–13
  articulation 115–16, 117
  assessment 206–8
  central difficulties 116–18
  classification of disorders 113–14
  incidence 118
  linguistic differences 61, 70–2
  normal development 112–13,
    210–11
  peripheral difficulties 116
  provision 211–12
  receptive difficulties 114–15
  remediation 208–11
learning difficulties
  assessment 35–6
  concepts and definitions 8, 30–1,
    46–8, 51–3, 59–61
  explanatory theories 61–3
  faulty styles 80
  mild 47, 60, 190, 209
  moderate 47, 51, 208–9
  prevalence 36–8, 51, 85–6
  severe 12, 46–7, 60, 85–6, 188, 191,
    195–6, 200, 208–9
  specific 47–8, 50
  and visual impairment 111–12
  (*see also curriculum, intelligence,*
    schools and *reading*)
lip reading 213
Local Education Authority 7–12, 227,
  231–3

Maketon 213
Manpower Services Commission
  246–7
mathematics 203–4
maturation 76–7
medical model 26–8
meningitis 90
meningocele 94
mental age 33–4
metabolic disorders 87–8
minimal brain dysfunction 49, 50, 62,
  135
mobility problems 91–104, 204–6

modifications 16, 184
mongolism (*see Down's syndrome*)
motivation 70, 79
muscular dystrophy 98
myelomeningocele 95
myopia 111

national curriculum 16, 184, 257–8
neurological deficits 77–8
normalization 18, 21–3, 254
nursery education (*see pre-school*
  provision)

occupational therapists 237
organic factors 59, 76–9, 85–9

Pack Report 142
PAD 223
Paget Gorman 211, 213
paired reading 58, 202
paralysis (*see cerebral palsy, spinal*
  injury and *spina bifida*)
paraplegia 92
parents
  –child relationship 139–42
  in partnership 5, 14, 28–9, 231, 254
  parental involvement in learning
    57–8, 142
parental styles 140–2
partially deaf (*see hearing impairment*)
Peabody Language Development
  Programme 208
pedagogy 147, 148–9
perceptual motor programmes 206
petit mal 102
phenylketonuria 87, 88
physiotherapists 237
Portage project 199–200, 208
post-school provision 17, 244–7
poverty 66, 68, 138
precision teaching 198–9
pre-school provision 7, 243–4, 256–7
psychotherapeutic methods (*see*
  counselling)
psychiatrists 127

radiation 89
reading
  assessment 35, 37, 201
  difficulties 3, 38–40, 78–9
  teaching methods 201–3, 210
  (*see also support teaching*)
remedial education 36–8, 41–4, 51